A WORLD BANK STUDY

Local Content Policies in the Oil and Gas Sector

Silvana Tordo, Michael Warner, Osmel E. Manzano, and Yahya Anouti

THE WORLD BANK
Washington, D.C.

Contents

Figures

Tables

Acknowledgments

Local Content Policies in the Oil and Gas Sector is part of a study aimed at gathering existing knowledge and data on local content policies, with a view to develop guidelines for the design and monitoring of implementation of local content policies. This paper presents the findings of the study. Case studies analyzed in this paper draw from a background paper downloadable from http:// issuu.com/world.bank.publications/docs/local_content_policies_in_the_oil_ and_gas_sector.

The study was undertaken and written by Silvana Tordo (lead energy economist, Sustainable Energy Department, World Bank), with Michael Warner (consultant), Osmel E. Manzano (principal research economist, Inter-American Development Bank), and Yahya Anouti (consultant). Chapters 3 and 4 draw on earlier material contained in Local Content in Procurement by Michael Warner (Greenleaf Publishing 2011).

Key contributors to this paper, on a chapter-by-chapter basis, were as follows:

Executive Summary
Silvana Tordo

Chapter 1
Robert W. Bacon, Silvana Tordo, Yahya Anouti

Chapter 2
Osmel E. Manzano, Jamie Granados, Silvana Tordo

Chapter 3
Michael Warner, Silvana Tordo, Osmel E. Manzano

Chapter 4
Michael Warner, Silvana Tordo

Chapter 5
Silvana Tordo (with comments from Yahya Anouti)

Chapter 6
Silvana Tordo

The comments of peer reviewers Maria Vagliasindi (lead economist, Sustainable Energy Department, World Bank), Graham Davis (professor, Division of Economics and Business, Colorado School of Mines), Fredric Manuel Cegarra Escolano (senior adviser, Sustainable Energy Department, World Bank), and Gary McMahon (senior mining specialist, Sustainable Energy Department, World Bank) are gratefully acknowledged. Helpful comments were also received from Alexander Huurdeman, David Santley, and Kristina Svennson, all from the Sustainable Energy Department, World Bank, and Havard Halland, from the Poverty Reduction and Economic Management Department, World Bank. Special thanks go to Fayre Makeig, who edited the paper.

Abbreviations and Acronyms

ASEAN	Association of Southeast Asian Nations
BLcw	direct backward link (Chenery-Watanabe)
BLr	direct plus indirect backward link (Rasmussen)
CIF	cost, insurance, and freight
EOR	enhanced oil recovery
E&P	exploration and production
FDI	foreign direct investment
FLcw	direct forward link (Chenery-Watanabe)
FLr	direct plus indirect forward link (Rasmussen)
FOB	free on board
FPSO	floating production, storage and off-loading vessels
FTA	free trade agreement
FTE	full-time equivalent
GATS	General Agreement on Trade in Services
GATT	General Agreement on Tariffs and Trade
GDP	gross domestic product
GPA	Agreement on Government Procurement
GTAP8	Global Trade Analysis Project (8th version)
HSE	health, safety, and the environment
IOC	international oil company
ISP	import substitution policy
JVs	joint ventures
KPI	key performance indicator
LCP	local content policy
LCV	local content vehicle
LNG	liquefied natural gas
LPG	liquefied petroleum gas

MDGs	Millennium Development Goals
MNC	multinational company
NAFTA	North American Free Trade Agreement
NBLs	normalized backward links
NFLs	normalized forward links
NGLs	natural gas liquids
NOCs	national oil companies
OECD	Organisation for Economic Co-operation and Development
OFSE	oil field services and equipment
O&G	oil and gas
PDP	productive development policy
PROMINP	Programa de Mobilização da Indústria Nacional de Petróleo e Gás Natural
PSA	production sharing agreement or similar contractual arrangement
R&D	research and development
SAMs	social accounting matrices
SDT	special and differential treatment
SMEs	small- and medium-sized enterprises
TRIMs	Trade-Related Investment Measures
VAT	value added tax
WTO	World Trade Organization

Executive Summary

A number of countries have recently discovered and are developing oil and gas reserves. Policy makers in such countries are anxious to obtain the greatest benefits for their economies from the extraction of these exhaustible resources by designing appropriate policies to achieve desired goals. One important theme of such policies is the so-called local content created by the sector—the extent to which the output of the extractive industry sector generates further benefits to the economy beyond the direct contribution of its value-added, through its links to other sectors.

The use of industrial policy in the petroleum sector to support broad-based economic growth is hardly a new trend in the oil and gas sector. Local content policies (LCPs) were first introduced in the North Sea in the early 1970s and ranged from restrictions on imports to direct state intervention in the oil sector. Over time the aim of LCPs has evolved from creating *backward links* (that is, supplying input to the local economy through transfer of technology, the generation of value-added in domestic supply sectors, the creation of local employment opportunities, and increasing local ownership and control) to creating *forward links* link (that is, processing the sector's output prior to export through, for example, the establishment of refineries, petrochemical industry, and the production of fertilizers).

While LCPs have the potential to stimulate broad-based economic development, which is necessary to alleviate poverty and achieve the United Nation's Millennium Development Goals (MDGs), their application in petroleum-rich countries has achieved mixed results. The use of specialized inputs and the technological complexity of the petroleum sector often limit the possibility of developing backward and forward links into the local economy. An economy that is very limited can hardly be expected to quickly supply services (let alone build forward links). A fast-growing petroleum sector coupled with too ambitious local content targets may exacerbate supply bottlenecks arising from increased aggregate final demand. This would ultimately affect employment and output trends in other sectors of the economy, create distortions and inefficiencies, and in some cases even promote corruption. Furthermore, the size and location of petroleum projects also affect the type of potential links, and the speed at which they can efficiently develop.

The use of LCPs raises a number of questions:

- What exactly is "local content"?
- What is the extent of local content in the oil and gas sectors?
- Why is increasing local content good for development?
- What types of policies can be used to encourage an increase in local content?
- What are the costs and benefits of introducing such policies?
- How can the implementation of such policies be monitored and how can their impacts be measured?
- What are the lessons to be learned from oil- and gas-producing countries that have implemented policies to increase local content?

This study serves to introduce the topic by describing policies and practices meant to foster the development of economic links from the petroleum sector, as adopted by a number of petroleum-producing countries both in and outside the Organisation for Economic Co-operation and Development (OECD). To this end:

- In chapter 1 we define local content and briefly illustrate the links between the petroleum sector and other economic sectors (where policies may be able to increase the economic benefits of the petroleum sector). An attempt is made to measure local content levels in a wide sample of petroleum-producing countries—including net importers and net exporters, and countries at different stages of economic development—to put LCPs in context and to consider if the structure of an economy is a key driver of local content levels.
- In chapter 2 we discuss the arguments that have been used in favor and against the use of productive development policies in general and LCPs in particular.
- In chapter 3 we provide an outline of the tools and types of LCPs that have been used by petroleum-producing countries, and present their strengths and weaknesses.
- In chapter 4 we focus on issues related to the measurement and monitoring of LCPs, and discuss the limitations of alternative metrics.
- In chapter 5 we provide a description of LCP objectives, implementation tools, and reporting metrics used in a selected sample of oil-producing countries—including Angola, Brazil, Kazakhstan, Indonesia, Malaysia, and Trinidad and Tobago—and draw initial lessons that may be relevant to other countries. Detailed case studies are presented in Local Content Policies in the Oil and Gas Sector, http://issuu.com/world.bank.publications/docs/local_content_policies_in_the_oil_and_gas_sector. We also discuss issues to be considered when defining LCP objectives. Country examples—not limited to the six case studies referred to above—are used to document the discussion. This chapter concludes with a discussion of the policy design issues that all study countries have had to address.
- In chapter 6 we highlight aspects of LCP design and implementation that require further analysis.

What This Study Does Not Do

This study does not advocate in favor or against the use of LCPs. We do not attempt to assess the impact of LCPs in any of the countries that we have analyzed. But we report outcomes when these have been measured and are publicly available. We do not compare the relative efficiency of LCPs and other policies, or attempt to develop a tool kit for LCPs and related policy guidelines. We do not analyze the direct or indirect financial links arising from the taxation of the oil and gas sector, or sectors that provide input to the oil and gas sector or utilize the output of the oil and gas sector.

Main Findings

The results of our analysis of economic links generated by the oil and gas sector across 48 countries confirms that financial links (that is, resource rents and returns on capital) are by far larger than productive links for most countries. This is an important consideration that helps to put the economic impact of LCPs in context when comparing to those of other government policies (for example, policies that aim at establishing sustainable macro fiscal management, policies that address the taxation of petroleum activities, and so on).

With the foregoing in mind, our review of countries' experience suggests that LCP design is not solely or principally guided by considerations of economic efficiency and the need to address market failures. On the contrary, it would seem that political imperatives are key drivers, and economic efficiency is often an afterthought. Indeed we were unable to find evidence that countries that had adopted LCPs had assessed the costs and benefits of alternative policy options.

It would seem that countries, particularly new producers, with less developed economies and/or large resource bases, tend to adopt more assertive policies by imposing measures that limit investors' choices with respect to employment, purchasing strategies, localization, and the transfer of knowledge. This often translates into quantitative targets for local content, and the establishment of LCP statements and supporting legal and regulatory frameworks.

Our review of LCPs suggests that governments that wish to introduce LCPs would benefit from taking certain factors into consideration. These are discussed in chapter 5 and include the following:

- *The consistency of LCPs with other economic development policies.* Since LCPs are part of a broader category of policy interventions aiming to strengthen the productive structure of a particular economy, their success largely depends on their interaction and coherence with broader economic development policies and related implementation tools. It is therefore possible that, for example, the success of regulatory interventions to increase local employment in the oil and gas sector may require an improvement in the quality of education, changes in labor mobility, improvement in infrastructure, and so on, while policies leveraging economic diversification through the oil and gas sector may require stable macroeconomic policies that attract foreign investment, provide more leverage in trade agreements, and improve the financial market (or similar but broader policy interventions). Malaysia, for example, has used an integrated approach to the design of productive policies through its Economic Transformation Program and related implementation tools and monitoring arrangements.

- The extent to which LCPs:

  - *Address market inefficiency.* Overall, the oil and gas sector is characterized by high capital investment, specialized input, and technological complexity, which often create barriers to local participation, especially in countries with little existing capacity. Furthermore the sector tends to rely on global supply chains to reduce costs, to increase quality standards, and to ensure the reliability of supplies. These chains are often so well organized that, even when local capability exists, local suppliers may be locked out from the opportunity to tender. There are many reasons why this may be the case. For example, the size of the contract may be too large for local suppliers, the contract itself may call for an integrated package, the tender rule may not encourage association among suppliers, or there may be information asymmetry between local and foreign contractors. Depending on the type of inefficiency, regulatory intervention may be necessary in order to address it. For example, the Kazakhstan regulatory authority created the Registry of Domestic Producers and Foreign Investors to give local suppliers information on current and future tender opportunities. With this information, it is hoped that they can more easily assess potential demand and plan investments to upgrade their processes and plants, in the process becoming become efficient competitors over time. A similar platform was established in Brazil through a multistakeholders initiative, the Program for the Mobilization of the Oil and Gas Industry. The program is managed by the National Organization of the Petroleum Industry, and participation is voluntary. Indeed the level of existing domestic capacity and the convergence of interests at the industry level in Brazil have made it possible to address information asymmetries across suppliers without the need for regulatory intervention.

  - *Promote competition and the emergence of an efficient domestic economy.* The components of the petroleum sector value chain have differing degrees of technological complexity, risk, and rent size, ranging from high to relatively low—starting from exploration and moving to production and then petroleum products distribution. Differences in complexity, in turn, affect the efficiency of local suppliers as well as their ability to benefit from spillovers and outputs. Some countries adopt measures to shelter domestic companies from competition in an attempt to help them focus on developing the necessary competence and economies of scale. Some countries specifically target subsectors with limited technological and investment barriers, focusing on products and services that they are already producing or can produce profitably. Angola offers an example of this strategy. Through the use of reservation policies and related regulatory constraints, the government has supported, among others, the localization of subsea control and flow-lines manufacturing. But careful consideration should be given to the setting, cost, type, extent, and duration of this type of policy. Special privileges afforded to domestic companies tend to become engrained and politically difficult to remove even in cases where their sustainability is in doubt, and may over time become a disincentive to innovation and competitiveness.

- *Foster technology and spillover effects.* Because of the technological complexity of the petroleum sector and its use of specialized input, technology and knowledge spillovers are critical to the successful development of value-adding forward and backward links into the local economy. For this reason, almost all petroleum-producing countries have adopted policies to foster—and in some cases to force—the transfer of technology and knowledge. It is important to note that not all backward and forward links: (1) require the same technological complexity, (2) have the same potential to generate spillover effects, (3) generate the same level of employment, (4) have the same growth potential, or (5) entail the same level of local value addition. Such variety calls for a targeted approach whenever government intervention is considered necessary to correct for market inefficiency or failures. In Brazil the regulator requires oil and gas operators to invest at least 1 percent of their gross revenue in oil- and gas-related research and development (R&D). Up to half of the investment may occur in the operators' facilities in Brazil, while the rest fund research programs carried out by local universities or research institutes accredited by the regulator. Malaysia offers tax incentives for the localization of R&D, and Trinidad and Tobago supports the creation of joint ventures to increase local skills and capacity.

- *Support the development of adequate local skills.* Skill shortages across the industry value chain are pervasive in almost all petroleum-producing countries, although their level and distribution across countries and subsectors varies greatly. In general, common gaps across countries and subsectors appear to exist at highly technical and senior levels, in professional disciplines such as geosciences and various forms of engineering, as well as midlevel technical and managerial positions. Especially in the early stages of its development, a petroleum sector's capacity to meet professional industry requirements is likely to be low, particularly in countries that lack an industrial base. Many factors may contribute to the skills gap, including (1) the quality of the national education system, which may not be adequate to generate a local supply of workers with the necessary knowledge and skills; (2) the size of petroleum reserves, which may not be sufficient to support the development of sustainable backward links; and (3) the pace of exploitation, which may be too fast to permit the development of local skills. This explains why gaps tend to be filled with expatriate workers, especially in technical or management positions. Existing research confirms that a better-educated workforce and the increased supply of skills have a major impact on economic growth by increasing productivity and adaptability to new routines and technological change. It is therefore not surprising that the development of human capital is central to most countries' LCPs. In this respect, countries' approaches vary greatly, from "command and control" types of intervention (as in Angola, Indonesia, and Kazakhstan) to more market-oriented approaches (as in Brazil, Malaysia, and Trinidad and Tobago). The choice of policy and implementation tools is necessarily linked to the nature and level of the gap to be addressed. Indeed, mandatory employment quotas and minimum training obligations are not the correct policy response in all circumstances.

- *Avoid imposing high administrative and compliance costs.* Complex LCPs may make it difficult for policy makers to monitor their implementation, assess their impact, and enforce their application. Target groups may have difficulty in applying LCPs, which may result in misapplication or lack of application, and intended beneficiaries may lack the capacity to take full advantage of implementation. Especially for small businesses, assimilating and complying with complex administrative and technical rules can create an unreasonable burden. Complexity may translate into additional administrative costs for all parties involved—and inefficient or harmful outcomes—and may put small and medium investors at a disadvantage. Furthermore, these costs are normally recoverable when calculating petroleum sharing and/or corporate tax. Therefore, in designing LCPs, regulators should be mindful of introducing measures for which the cost of compliance exceeds the social benefit. As the experience of Kazakhstan shows, the use of standardized definitions of local content and standard reporting templates improves the transparency and the comparability of information provided by different companies. On the other hand, medium- and small-sized companies may face a bigger implementation burden than large companies.

- *Help to develop clusters and regional trade synergies.* Existing research suggests that clusters can contribute to the foundation of knowledge and help stimulate technological innovation through efficient access to public goods, better coordination, the diffusion of best practices, and the ability to share workers among companies. This is an important consideration for the oil and gas industry, which is generally known for the presence of large players, with substantial investment in R&D to reduce costs, improve productivity, and secure technological advantages. In this context collaboration and interaction among oil and gas companies; integrated service providers; national oil companies; and small, specialized (often localized) suppliers and service providers are critical to the sustainable development of a local industrial capacity. Geographical and sectoral clusters have been used by some governments as a means to accelerate the development of local enterprises, as well as to strengthen the national system of innovation. Furthermore, some countries have taken the concept of clusters beyond the domestic market, by supporting the development of regional trade synergies through regional hubs and the integration of LCPs at the regional level, with the objective to help provide the economy of scale necessary to sustain local comparative advantages. In its 2010 Economic Transformation Program, the government of Malaysia laid out a comprehensive package of measures to transform the nation into a regional hub for the oil field services and equipment (OFSE) industry. The regional market for OFSE is fragmented, unlike Europe and the North America, where OFSE operators concentrate their activities in a few centers. This creates an opportunity for Malaysia, which has a competitive domestic workforce, technically challenging domestic reserves that drive a growing local demand for OFSE, and geographical proximity to resource-rich countries in Asia and the Middle East. To capitalize on these advantages, the government has set out a strategy of complementary LCPs to incentivize the rationalization of local fabricators and the establishment of joint ventures with OFSE multinationals in critical value-adding activities.

Once a country has decided to adopt an LCP, there are some key design issues that should be given careful consideration. These have to do with the type of policy (*assertive*, which mandates targets and obliges the preferencing of nationals and local suppliers, or *encouraging*, which incentivizes investors' behavior and proposes targets that are aspirational and not mandated), the definition of what is local (national or domestic content), the role of the national oil company, and whether incentives and penalties should be used to encourage and enforce the application of the policy.

We also find that:

- *The objectives of LCPs should be clearly and realistically defined.* To this end policy makers should consider assessing gaps in skills and capacity to better understand the barriers to local development and set appropriate corrective measures, realistic policy targets, and the metrics to monitor the effects of policy implementation.
- *The costs and benefits of various policies should be estimated before adopting an LCP.* There is no "blueprint" LCP to enhance industrial development and the exploration and extraction of oil and gas. The choice of policy and implementation tools depends on the specific country context. That said, countries' experience with LCPs and industrial policy in general indicates that it is important to understand the trade-offs and pitfalls that the development of such policies may entail. Developing local content without forethought or assessment may lead to the waste of scarce development resources.

- *There should be good coordination among government agencies and clear institutional responsibility for the oversight and monitoring of results.* While duplication and overlap of responsibility among levels of government and government agencies is common to most policy areas, LCPs aimed at promoting economic diversification and growth from the oil and gas sector are inherently cross-cutting, and thus require balancing and careful arbitrage among different, sometimes conflicting, priorities. Lack of coordination among government entities and levels may result in conflicting regulations, increased administrative costs, delays in project execution, and—in some cases—incentives for rent-seeking behaviors and corrupt practices.

Although we have attempted to carry out some quantitative analysis to identify the drivers of LCP design and effectiveness, we do not have sufficient data to provide formal policy advice. The comprehensive data and in-depth analysis needed as background to such advice require future study.

Possible Topics for Follow-Up Research

Our review has highlighted a number of areas where future research could be usefully carried out. There is scope to further our understanding of how trade agreements impact the design of LCPs. Although trade agreements do not appear to have been a principal concern for governments in the design of LCPs, this may change, given that recent trade proposals suggest a renewed interest in promoting the liberalization of energy services, including in the oil and gas sector.

Countries use LCPs to achieve specific economic and social objectives, and choose policy tools that address specific shortcomings (that is, externalities or market failures). For this reason, there is no standard package of LCPs and tools that works for every country in every circumstance. Determining the right level of government intervention is complicated: different activities require different kinds of intervention, and there may be no clear price signals to guide government choices. Certain policy measures may carry unintended consequences; for example they may lead to a fall in government revenue, or limit foreign investment in strategic sectors, or impair strategic interests. Existing research is mainly qualitative, with few attempts to measure the economic impact of LCPs and their sustainability over time. Yet documenting countries' outcomes is a crucial first step toward the development of a reference framework for their design. To this end, further research is necessary to better our understanding of the factors that affect the design and economic impact of LCPs and drive their efficiency.

## CHAPTER 1

Defining Local Content

*Words differently arranged have a different meaning and
meanings differently arranged have a different effect.*
—Blaise Pascal

A number of countries have recently discovered and are developing oil and gas
reserves. Policy makers in such countries are anxious to obtain the greatest benefits for their economies from the extraction of these exhaustible resources by
designing appropriate policies to achieve desired goals. One important theme of
such policies is the so-called local content created by the sector—the extent to
which the output of the extractive industry sector generates further benefits to
the economy beyond the direct contribution of its value-added, as through links
to other sectors. Increasing local content is becoming a policy priority in many
resource-rich developing countries, among both mature and recent entrants to
the industry.

The use of local content policies (LCPs) raises a number of questions:

- What exactly is "local content"?
- What is the extent of local content in the oil and gas sectors?
- Why is increasing local content good for development?
- What types of policies can be used to encourage an increase in local content?
- What are the costs and benefits of introducing such policies?
- How can the implementation of such policies be monitored and how can their
  impacts be measured?
- What are the lessons to be learned from oil- and gas-producing countries that
  have implemented policies to increase local content?

The authors of this paper introduce the topic by addressing a number of issues
and by describing practice in a number of countries. As background to the
analysis of descriptions contained in the main body of the paper, we start the
present chapter with a discussion of the meaning of local content, and then
describe the fundamental notions of economic links—the processes by which
the oil and gas sector is joined to other sectors of the economy and through

which policies may be able to increase the benefits to the economy outside of the oil and gas sector itself. We attempt to measure local content levels in a wide sample of petroleum-producing countries both in and outside the Organisation for Economic Co-operation and Development (OECD). We then describe the various stages in the value chain of the oil and gas industry, pointing out that local content may be very different across the different stages of the industry. Finally, we highlight the importance of local content to the process of economic development.

Links and Local Content

The oil and gas sector purchases inputs (both labor and the outputs of other sectors), which are either supplied domestically or imported. Imported inputs constitute a leakage, while domestic purchases provide further benefits to the economy. For example, local employees will spend much of their wages on domestically produced goods, and thus create more jobs. Similarly, purchasing goods from a local supply company will require that this company buy inputs in order to produce its outputs, and again some of these indirect inputs will be domestically produced. Local content is the share of employment—or of sales to the sector—locally supplied at each stage of this chain. Oil and gas extraction itself also supplies other sectors, such as refineries. Where these are domestically situated, then their supply from domestic oil and gas production helps maintain local employment and local purchases by these sectors from other nonoil sectors.

A number of definitional issues need to be recognized when discussing LCPs:

- LCPs are concerned not only with an immediate increase in local content (for example, increasing the percentage of local employment in the petroleum sector) but with actions that will lead to its longer-term increase (such as the provision of training in appropriate skills to the local labor force). Such a policy does not lead to an automatic increase in local content but, if carried out appropriately, can create and enhance local capabilities that can be transferred to other sectors. This includes the development of skills that are common to all sectors, as well as the creation and support of cluster developments with other industries that have natural synergy with the petroleum sector.
- The concept of "local" is also subject to a range of definitions. The company from which an input is purchased may be locally based and owned, locally based but foreign owned (in total or in part), or even locally owned but located abroad. These distinctions are important for two reasons. Firstly, their direct benefits to the national economy can differ depending on the ownership of the "local" company. For example, foreign investors may be less interested in investing in companies where there is majority local ownership, and may also be reluctant to transfer proprietary technology and other parts of their business if they do not have control (in this way, domestic ownership may even discourage investment). Secondly, any monitoring of local content will need

to consider the nature of ownership. Where local content is defined as sales from domestically owned and located companies, it will be necessary to first establish whether the companies in question qualify as "local" in terms of the policy directive.

- Local content can refer to jobs or value-added that is created anywhere in the domestic economy as a result of the actions of an oil and gas company, or it can more narrowly refer to jobs that are created in the neighborhood of the oil production plant. Although policies mainly refer to local content without specifying its location within the economy, it is common that the communities closest to—and possibly most affected by—oil or gas installations will also exert the most pressure for jobs.

- Local content may even refer to the provision, by the oil company, of infrastructure (schools, medical facilities) that is not an input into its own production but intended for the benefit of the local population (either of the nation generally or the neighborhood of the installations).

- Local content can be considered from different standpoints along the value chain of the oil and gas industry (Tordo 2011), as described in appendix A. For example, the principal backward link of a refinery is oil production, and the principal forward link of oil production would be a refinery (if present). The focus of this study is the oil and gas production sector; both its backward and forward links (including refining) are within the scope of the study.

- Local content, both actual and potential, will vary over the life cycle of the petroleum sector. An individual field will go through phases of exploration, construction, and production; because the inputs used at these various stages can be quite different, the extent and nature of local content can vary over time and across stages. Policies designed to increase local content must take into account the sustainability of the sector. Where the hydrocarbon potential is unknown, the rationale for developing a local supply chain will be weak at best. For example, if few fields are producing and the geological potential is unknown, local companies are unlikely to risk investing, since sale volumes may not be sustainable.

Sector Links

Our analysis of local content centers on the concept of sector links. The study of industrial structure (Hirschman 1958) specifies three types of links: backward links relate to the demand of one industry for the outputs of other industries (to be used as its inputs); forward links relate to the output of one industry as supplied to other industries (as input for their output); and financial links relate to the taxes paid by the industry to the government (which can then be spent on other goods and services or saved). Hence an increase in the output of a given industry affects other industries by, for example, (1) increasing demand for their products; or (2) increasing its output, which then is available to them as input; or (3) increasing government revenue, which can in turn be used to support economic development objectives. Employment links are also key, in the form of both direct and indirect links. Direct employment refers to the numbers actually employed within the oil and gas sector; indirect employment refers to those jobs created by sales to the oil and gas sector, or by sales of the oil and gas sector to other sectors.[1]

The measurement of backward and forward links was formalized by Rasmussen (1956) and Chenery and Watanabe (1958), based on the use of input-output tables (see appendix B). An important distinction is made between direct and indirect links. Chenery and Watanabe concentrate on the immediate inputs into a sector (the direct backward links), while Rasmussen focuses on inputs into the sector, the inputs into these inputs, and so on (or, in other words, the indirect links). LCPs are most often concerned with the direct links (those sectors supplying the oil and gas sector) and more rarely with how supply sectors affect yet other sectors.

Measuring local content levels across countries is a nontrivial effort. As has been pointed out earlier in this chapter, the definition of local content has many dimensions and is likely to vary between economies. This in turn implies that it is difficult to compare the extent of local content across economies. A limited amount of indirect evidence is available from the analysis of links from input-output tables. Although such analysis is not directly aimed at calculating local content, whether direct or indirect, it is closely linked to possible measures of local content. To measure local content in intermediate goods and services, in addition to sectoral backward and forward links, we use social accounting matrices (SAMs) extracted from the eighth version of the Global Trade Analysis Project (GTAP8).[2] The Chenery and Watanabe (1958) and the Rasmussen (1956) backward and forward links are then calculated and normalized using the domestic input-output matrix of each country (see appendix B for equations). The results of our analysis are shown in appendix D, which ranks the oil and gas sector across types of links—a rank of 1 indicates that the sector has the lowest value of that link across all sectors, while the maximum rank that can be attained (equal to the number of sectors) indicates that the oil and gas sector has the highest value for that particular link.

Measures based on Chenery and Watanabe (1958) take into account only direct links between key sectors—that is, the amount of output that is purchased by the sector (backward) or supplied to another sector (forward). Measures based on Rasmussen (1956) take into account both direct and indirect links (inputs required to supply inputs to the key sector, and so on). The measures related to forward links gauge the key sector's demand if all sectors in the economy using the key sector's output as an input grew by one unit (rather than weighting by the relative importance of the purchasing sectors). Hence forward links do not specifically highlight individual sectors that depend on oil production as an input—instead they present the average use of oil as an input at the margin. "Normalized links" are the ratio of the oil and gas sector link to the average (unweighted) link over all sectors; a value greater than unity implies that the key sector has a greater link than the average across other sectors in the economy.

While any comparison of input-output data across countries is inexact, the exercise can help provide a general picture of conditions. In most countries the oil and gas sector gives rise to fewer backward links (both direct and indirect) than other economic sectors. On the other hand, as shown in figure 1.1, forward links are numerous in most countries analyzed in our sample. These findings seem to be robust; they apply both to developing countries (where the petroleum industry is still in its infancy and the degree of industrialization and tertiarization is low) and developed countries (where both petroleum and the secondary and tertiary sectors are well advanced). Figure 1.2 proposes a categorization of countries based on the relevance of direct and indirect forward and backward links. In particular, sectors within each economy are grouped into four categories:

• Key sectors in the economy: both normalized backward links (NBLs) and normalized forward links (NFLs) are greater than unity
• Sectors exhibiting strong forward links and weak backward links: NBL<1 and NFL>1
• Sectors exhibiting weak links: both NBL and NFL are smaller than unity
• Sectors exhibiting strong backward links and weak forward links: NBL>1 and NFL<1.

Figure 1.1 Chenery-Watanabe (left) and Rasmussen (right) Links from the Oil and Gas Sector

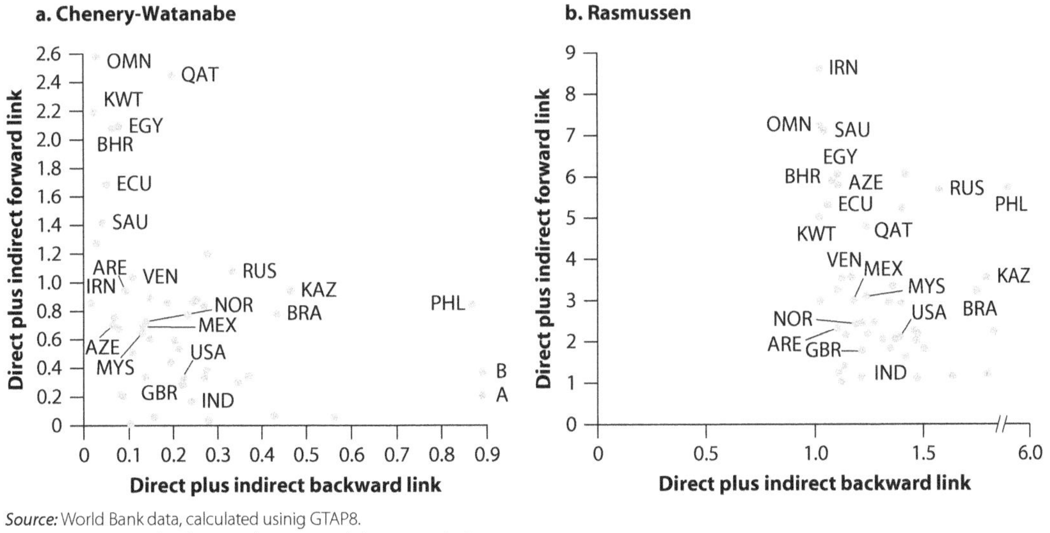

a. Chenery-Watanabe

b. Rasmussen

Source: World Bank data, calculated usinig GTAP8.

Note: Acronyms used in these graphs are provided in appendix D.

Figure 1.2 Normalized Chenery-Watanabe (left) and Rasmussen (right) Links from the Oil and Gas Sector

a. Chenery-Watanabe

b. Rasmussen

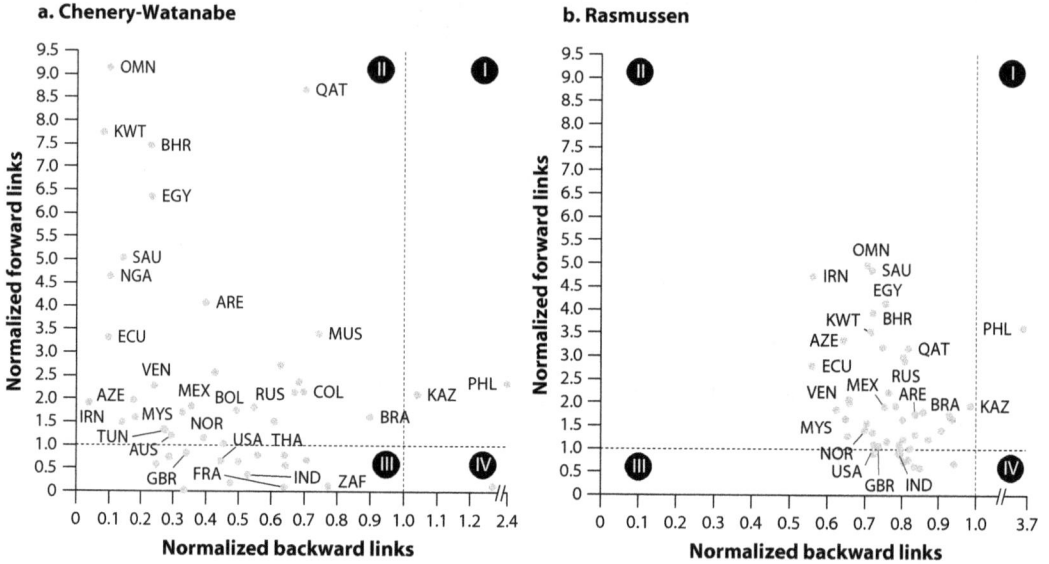

As should be expected, figure 1.3 shows that for most countries, the R (direct plus indirect) normalized backward link of the oil and gas sector is substantially larger than the CW (direct).

Figure 1.3 Chenery-Watanabe versus Rasmussen Links

a. Rasmussen

b. Chenery-Watanabe

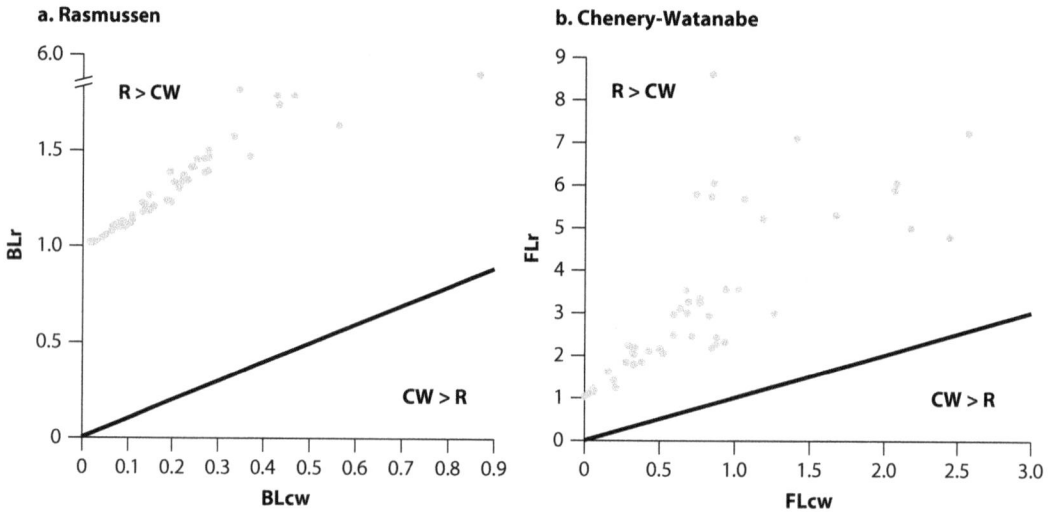

Our analysis allows some broad inferences to be drawn:

- The direct Chenery-Watanabe backward link (BLcw) of the oil and gas industry is low compared to that of other sectors. Few, if any, industries have a lower direct backward link.
- The direct Chenery-Watanabe forward link (FLcw) is substantially larger than the average for other sectors in 33 of the 48 countries in sample. In these 33 countries the forward link was among the highest across sectors. An overall expansion of output across the board increases average demand for the output of the oil and gas sector. In every case the FLcw is greater than the BLcw.
- The direct plus indirect backward link (BLr) of the oil and gas sector is substantially larger than the BLcw but still less than unity for most countries. Allowing for the indirect effects of oil sector purchases, the sector's pull on the rest of the economy is lower than the average for other sectors. Across sectors, oil and gas has among the lowest values of indirect backward links.
- The direct plus indirect forward link (FLr) is greater than unity in most countries, often reaching high values. Across sectors, oil and gas has among the highest values of forward links.

These high-level results for sector links have substantial relevance to the issue of local content. It is clear that the direct backward link is typically much smaller than for other industries, and is usually among the lowest value for any sector. The low values typically observed may explain in part why governments are so interested in policies that could increase local content in supplying industries. With such low values governments may feel that the scope for increased inputs from local firms is substantial if a successful policy can be designed to improve the backward link and the local content of the sector. The direct forward link in 33 countries was substantial and among the highest across all sectors. For Australia, Argentina, Azerbaijan, Bolivia, Brazil, Canada, Ecuador, the Arab Republic of Egypt, Indonesia, Kuwait, Mexico, Malaysia, Nigeria, Oman, the Russian Federation, Qatar, Saudi Arabia, and the United Arab Emirates the direct plus indirect forward links were almost the highest of any sector. This suggests that where the sectors downstream of the oil sector are well established, the demand for output from the oil sector is high. This in turn may indicate why governments may be interested in establishing such sectors at home—they can then draw heavily on the domestic oil sector and use this to create value-added, all the while avoiding the costs of international transportation.

The mere fact that backward links are typically low and forward links can be high should not by itself lead to support for policies that aim to increase local content upstream and downstream of the oil sector. Policies need to be evaluated by their effectiveness and costs to the economy, as explained in the following chapters.

The links discussed above relate the portion of a sector's gross output that is supplied by—or to—other sectors. If the backward link is low, say, this implies that local suppliers' sales to the oil sector are relatively low. It is important to

Figure 1.4 A Breakdown of the Oil and Gas Sector's Total Output Value, 2007
$ billions

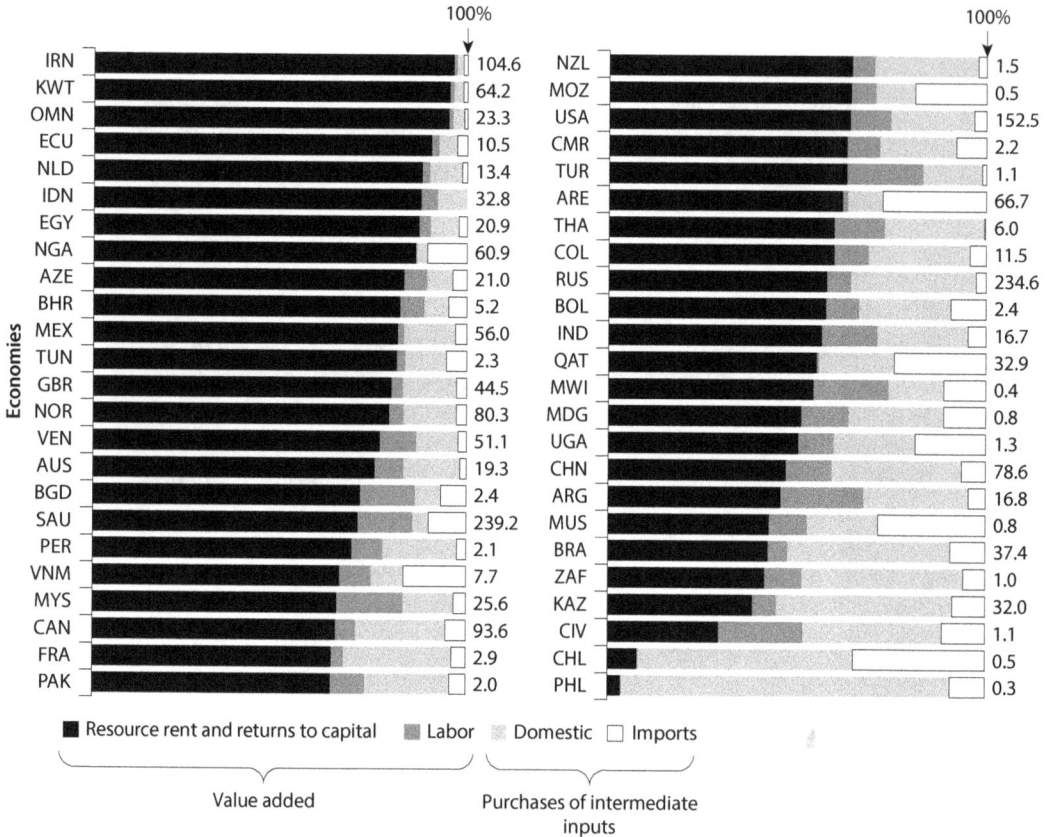

| | Resource rent and returns to capital | Labor | Domestic | Imports |

Value added | Purchases of intermediate inputs

Source: World Bank data.
Note: Acronyms used in these graphs are provided in appendix D.

note that this does not necessarily mean that the value-added by the supplying industries is low, or that employment created by these supplying industries is low. Indeed the total output of the oil and gas industry can be broken into two components: purchase of intermediate goods and services and value-added. The second appears to be dominant among the countries analyzed in our sample (see figure 1.4).

Using the values of sectoral intermediate import and domestic purchases reported in appendix D, we measure local content levels as the ratio of domestic purchases of intermediate goods and services to total purchases of intermediate goods and services. The results are shown in figure 1.5, and suggest that local content levels are considerable in at least 50 percent of the countries in our sample.[3]

In designing LCPs policy makers should therefore give due consideration to the fact that value-added can be relatively high even when gross sales are relatively low (depending on relative profit margins), and employment can also be

Figure 1.5 Oil and Gas Sector: Local Content Level of Intermediate Purchases

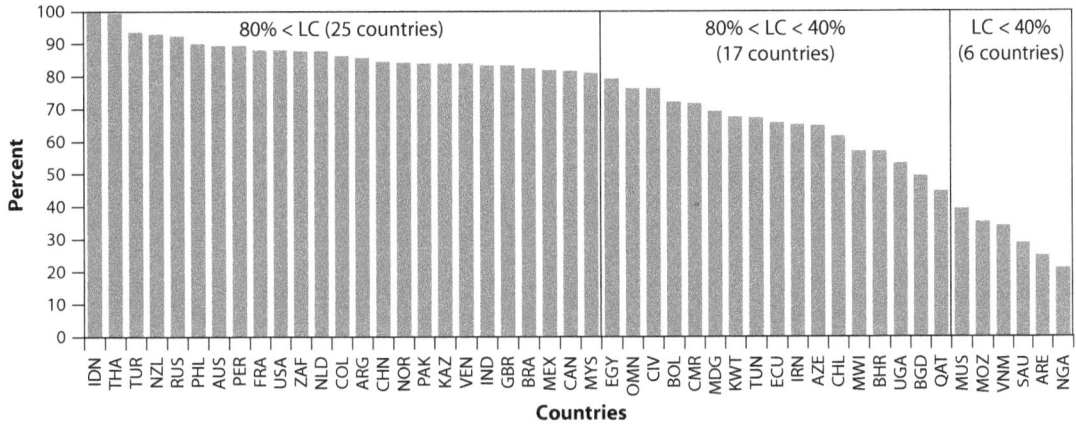

Source: World Bank data.
Note: Acronyms used in these graphs are provided in appendix D. LC = local content.

relatively high when gross sales are relatively low. Moreover a distinction must be made between wages and employment created by links. Where total wages may be relatively low, employment might be less so (since wage rates were probably particularly low in the domestic supply sector). Hence it follows that a policy to create substantial extra local sales will not necessarily create substantial skilled- and managerial-level local employment.

The apparent low value of the backward links may be due to a number of factors:

• The oil and gas industry tends to experience very high value-added relative to gross output because of the large element of rent. Inputs into the sector will therefore tend to be low relative to output.

• Extraction of oil and gas tends to be highly capital intensive, not only leading to a low direct labor content, but also a small share of such inputs coming from domestic suppliers, whose ability to supply large quantities of specialized capital goods is limited.

• Where the discovery of oil and gas is a recent phenomenon it initially tends to produce an extremely unbalanced set of sector outputs:

  - For some inputs to the oil sector there are distinct economies of scale in production; small domestic suppliers cannot initially compete with international suppliers. Only with the passage of time (and possibly boosted by policies to encourage domestic production) will domestic firms expand sufficiently to be able to lower production costs and compete.

  - In some countries the prospects of further finds, following initial discovery and development, may be low. Accordingly, the requirement for inputs into the production of oil and gas may appear to be concentrated in a few years of peak construction. In such a case attempting to increase local content from domestic suppliers may be a short-sighted policy given the likely fall-off in demand as the field matures and then declines without further discoveries to keep demand for inputs at a fairly constant level.

- Significant discoveries are typically exploited commercially on a large scale. Meanwhile, most sectors in an economy develop slowly, by small increments starting from a low base. Supply sectors are at first unable to adjust to a new oil sector's high demand for specialized inputs, meaning that the local content of inputs is extremely low.

It is outside the scope of this paper to analyze the factors that explain differences across countries in the level and extent of links from the oil and gas sector. But identifying these factors is the first step toward the design of effective LCPs. Indeed, LCPs are in essence a trade-off between short-term efficiency and long-term economic development. Yet policy makers often have few quantitative tools to estimate the effects of alternative policies, and to gauge the optimum levels of local content. Certain policy measures may carry unintended consequences; for example they may lead to a fall in government revenue, or limit foreign investment in strategic sectors, or impair strategic interests. The development of specific quantitative models would allow policy makers to determine which regulations will have what degree of impact, on whose strategic interests. This requires further research.

Local Content and the Value Chain

The oil and gas sector is spread along a value chain of recognizably different stages, some of which may even act as separate subsectors. At each stage of the value chain different technologies and inputs are utilized, so that the potential for local content enhancement is likely to be different along the value chain. Over time, as the oil industry develops from its initial stages, the nature and extent of local content is likely to vary; some stages lend themselves more to the use of local inputs while others tend to rely more on imported inputs. The ability of the local economy to supply these various inputs also depends on its level of development and industrialization. Appendix A shows the typical goods and services utilized at the various stages of the production chain. The following description of the stages of the value chain is adapted from Tordo (2011).

- *Exploration.* Suitable sedimentary basins for oil and/or gas exploration are usually identified using relatively simple means such as aerial and satellite photography, as well as magnetic surveys. More detailed information about specific locations is then obtained through seismic surveys, which are considerably more expensive. Through complex computer analysis, the data are interpreted to create images of geological formations and possible deposits of hydrocarbons. Exploratory drilling using rigs suitable for the specific environment (that is, land, shallow water, or deep water) is the next step. Much ancillary equipment, products, and services are associated with drilling, and many petroleum companies typically contract an outside services company for these purposes. This stage of the value chain is very highly specialized, and areas where oil has been newly discovered will find that there is little domestic capacity to supply the inputs. Although there will be some demand for relatively unskilled services and for basic construction, these will be small in scale since exploration is in itself a relatively constrained activity.

- *Development*. If hydrocarbons have been found in sufficient quantity, the development process begins with the drilling of appraisal wells in order to better assess the size and commercial viability of the discovery. The development phase also is relatively small in scale and specialized, so that again local content is likely to be very limited. Moreover, as with the exploration phase, the search for oil can prove financially unviable, leading to the cessation of activity. Any local content created would then be short lived. This in turn suggests that local firms will be cautious about investing in exploration and development activities—unless and until the results suggest that economically viable amounts of oil can be recovered.

- *Production*. The development phase is followed by drilling for full-scale production, and the building of infrastructure to connect the wells to local processing facilities or evacuation routes. Onshore infrastructure tends to be less complex and much cheaper than offshore infrastructure. The speed at which the pressure in the reservoir forces the petroleum upward is known as the flow rate; it depends, for example, on the properties of the reservoir rock and, in the case of crude oil, on the viscosity—in short, on the reservoir's characteristics. Natural (primary) pressure typically recovers much less than 50 percent of oil and 75 percent of gas. In order to boost flow rates and overall recovery factors in the face of inevitable natural decline rates, various methods can be used. Secondary recovery methods include the injection of water or gas into the reservoir, and the installation of surface-mounted or submersible pumps. Tertiary recovery methods (or enhanced oil recovery, EOR) involve the use of sophisticated techniques that alter the original properties of the oil.

Even in a standard upstream project it is not unusual for five years to pass between the initial exploration stages and full-scale commercial operations. For projects with challenging access, geological, or infrastructure requirements, the lead times can be longer still. These time horizons, coupled with the fact that sudden changes in well-flow management can damage underlying reservoirs, result in structural rigidities in petroleum supply.

As an oil project moves into the production phase, the scale of operations increases and the duration for which inputs are required lengthens substantially. The inputs required may also, on average, be less specialized than during the exploration and development phases, providing better opportunities for local firms to gear up to take part in supplying some components of goods required, and some of the less-specialized skills. The scale of the activity may suggest opportunities to increase local content but, once the initial investment has been carried out, the level of inputs required is small relative to the value of the output produced. Indeed, once the major production structures are in place, the actual requirements for continuing inputs declines sharply, apart from crucial utility inputs such as electricity and water. These will often be supplied by local companies, but in certain cases the oil company has to provide its own sources for such inputs.

- *Oil and gas treatment and liquefied natural gas.* Natural-gas-processing plants purify raw natural gas produced from underground gas fields or extracted at the surface from fluids produced by oil wells. A fully operational plant delivers pipeline-quality natural gas that can be used as fuel by residential, commercial, and industrial consumers. In the plant, contaminants are removed and heavier hydrocarbons are captured for other commercial uses. If gas is to be transported in the form of liquefied natural gas (LNG) then a liquefaction plant is needed prior to transportation. The relation to local content possibilities is similar to that for oil production itself.
- *Transport and storage.* From a production site, crude oil and gas need to be transported to the appropriate processing facility; from there they are distributed or marketed. Petroleum can also be stored at various points along the value chain for reasons that include securing supply and price hedging/speculation.

  Crude oil is stored in large-diameter holding tanks and is transported by pipeline, truck, railroad, and/or tanker to refineries for processing. Ocean tankers are the most common medium of intercontinental transport. Refineries, which usually are located near major import hubs to limit additional transport charges, purchase crude oil on the open market or directly from producers.

  Having completed the refining process, oil products can be distributed by the same means as crude oil. Road transport is most common, but extensive networks of product pipelines can be found around the world.

  Natural gas may be stored underground in a variety of methods, most commonly in depleted reservoirs, aquifers, or salt caverns. The transport options for gas depend on its physical state. Natural gas liquids (NGLs) can be transported either by pipeline or by tanker truck, but dry gas (methane) can only be transported by pipeline, and even then not across the seabed of deep oceans. An option for long-distance gas exports is LNG.

  Piped gas has to be transported all the way from the production site to the final destination (a power station, industry, or domestic consumer, for example) using multiple types of pipelines and pipeline networks along the way. By adjusting the degree of pipeline compression, such networks can also be used as additional storage facilities.

  The construction of pipelines and storage facilities can generate large demands for construction workers, although these are only temporary. Moreover, in the case of pipelines, the location of the construction demand moves across country, spreading these temporary jobs among a larger number of people. The use of road transport requires a permanent staff of drivers and other facilitators—jobs that will most often be filled by local labor.

- *Refining.* Crude oil almost always needs to be refined into oil products prior to consumption, with the main product categories being fuel oil, gas oil, jet/kerosene, gasoline, naphtha, and liquefied petroleum gas (LPG). The three main energy-related uses for oil are transport, power generation, and heating. There are also nonenergy or process uses, such as feedstock for the petrochemicals industry, that require a further conversion of the input in order to produce a product for the final market.

  Oil refining is the process of separating the hydrocarbon molecules present in crude oil and converting them into more valuable, finished petroleum products. Refineries can consist of a number of different process units that undertake the separation, conversion, and treatment of oil. The initial stage of a refinery run involves the heating and separation of crude into its constituent parts in a distillation column. Then the different fractionations are directed to conversion units to be chemically altered through the introduction of heat, pressure, catalysts, or hydrogen. The output of these conversion units is then treated or blended.

  Refining is another stage with very specialized capital inputs, and low levels of employment. Moreover once the refinery is constructed, the demand for inputs apart from crude oil and utilities will be very low.

- *Primary distribution.* Marketing refers to the distribution and sale of refined products, whether through wholesale or retail. Road transportation fuels are primarily distributed at retail stations; heating oil is usually delivered to residential and industrial customers; kerosene is purchased directly by individual airlines and airports or is distributed to households through retail outlets; and residual fuels are also sold directly to shipping companies, utilities, and industrial plants.

  The distribution of piped gas to the end consumer is usually done by utility companies, but petroleum firms are involved in longer-distance transmission and in direct deliveries to industrial users, power plants, and so on. NGLs are also sold to industrial, wholesale, and retail clients (in the latter case usually through stations).

  Primary distribution requires less specialized capital, and many of the associated jobs are not highly skilled, so that the local content tends to be larger.

Why Do Governments Wish to Increase Local Content?

There are a number of apparent reasons that governments may wish to increase the local content of sectors linked to the oil and gas production sector (or to industries upstream or downstream of it). The desire to increase domestic valued-added by substituting domestically produced goods for imported goods, and to create more local employment by substituting domestic labor for imported or foreign-based labor are among the most frequently cited objectives of LCPs. These two objectives are linked—domestic production equals increased jobs, many of which may use local labor. These goals are reinforced by the typically low level of local content observed in many countries. Governments feel that there must be economic benefits to be captured by policies that increase the local content with respect to value-added and employment.

As chapter 2 explains, however, there are a number of questions that must be answered before a government should embark on policies to increase local content:

- Why is the market itself not providing higher local content? Are there market failures that require government action, or does the present situation provide the most efficient use of domestic resources?
- What are the costs (including opportunity costs) of implementing LCPs? Is there a potential net benefit to the economy of implementing these policies?
- Are there obstacles to the successful implementation of such policies, including legal obligations under international treaties?
- Are the policies designed to have an immediate impact, or to produce benefits in the medium to long term?

The presence of the very large financial links typical of oil and gas production, with its large element of rent resulting in large financial flows to the government, does not automatically lead to the creation of higher levels of local value-added and employment in the economy. The use of oil and gas taxation revenues presents a substantial macroeconomic and intertemporal challenge. Taxes may be partly saved, as in a petroleum or sovereign wealth fund, to provide benefits for future generations that could at that time include employment and the creation of value-added. Taxes can also be used to reduce public debt, smooth the effect of petroleum revenue volatility, or they can be spent on various objectives of the government. The pattern of spending itself may be directed toward sectors with high local content and job creating potential, but other objectives may prevail and such spending may not improve local content seen from a national standpoint. Further, inefficiencies in government spending resulting from poor procurement or project design, may also work against the hope of creating more local employment and welfare through the use of the financial links of the oil and gas sector.

In addition to purely economic considerations for increasing local content, if this can be done in a fashion with overall benefit to the economy, there are reasons of political economy that have led governments to adopt the use of such policies. Despite the very large financial flows to the government that are widely recognized even if not accurately known, individuals may not perceive what they may think of as commensurate benefits. This can lead to pressure from the population to increase the more tangible benefits—increased jobs and sales from local companies would seem to answer such concerns.

In a more narrowly focused context, communities near to the oil and gas facilities, especially when it is located onshore, may suffer various adverse effects from its operation:

- Oil and gas activities may create environmental damage and interfere with local production.
- The labor hiring that is done by the operator forces up local wages and costs, thus adversely affecting those not employed in the operation.
- The location of the facilities may be viewed by local communities as taking place on their traditional land, while the taxation agreements with the government do not ensure adequate local compensation for their loss of resource.

Although these problems could be addressed by specific policies designed to take into account the exact grievance, it may also be that governments see LCPs as a way of bringing jobs and income to an area where there is considerable dissatisfaction for the presence of the oil and gas operations.

Notes

1. Employment created by the oil and gas sector also has induced effects (Bacon and Kojima 2011). Induced employment is the extra employment made possible by outputs—produced by all sectors—to meet the extra demand of workers directly and indirectly employed by the oil and gas sector. This paper will not consider induced employment or output for the purposes of LCP analysis.

2. GTAP8 is a representation of the world economy, reporting intermediate demand and bilateral trade flows for the years 2004 and 2007. The database, which can be accessed through www.gtap.org, is built using national input-output tables, trade flows, and macroeconomic data. GTAP8 covers 129 regions, 57 sectors, and 5 factors of production. In our analysis, we focus on 2007 and consider 48 countries where oil and gas production is reported, 49 sectors with an aggregated upstream oil and gas sector, and 3 factors of production. The building blocks of the general equilibrium model are presented in appendix C.

3. These values appear at odds with the levels reported in existing literature and presented later in this paper. For instance, local content levels from domestic sourcing of goods and services in the Indonesian oil and gas industry was believed to be between 10 percent and 20 percent in the early part of 2000s. These discrepancies may be caused by the fact that input-output tables used in GTAP8 have various sources, base years, and sectoral details.

References

Bacon, R., and M. Kojima. 2011. *Issues in Estimating the Employment Generated by Energy Sector Activities.* Washington, DC: World Bank, Sustainable Energy Department. http://siteresources.worldbank.org/INTOGMC/Resources/Measuring_the_employment_impact_of_energy_sector1.pdf.

Chenery, H., and T. Watanabe. 1958. "International Comparisons of the Structure of Production." *Econometrica* 46: 73–84.

Hirschman, A. 1958. *The Strategy of Economic Development*. New Haven, CT: Yale University Press.

Rasmussen, P. 1956. *Studies in Intersectorial Relations*. Amsterdam: Holland.

Scottish Government. 2011. "Input Output Introduction." http://www.scotland.gov.uk/Topics/Statistics/Browse/Economy/Input-Output.

Temurshoev, U. 2004. "Key Sectors in the Krygyzstan Economy." Discussion Paper 2004–135, CERGE-EI, Czech Republic.

Tordo, S., B. Tracy, and N. Arfaa. 2011. "National Oil Companies and Value Creation." World Bank Working Paper 218, World Bank, Washington, DC. http://siteresources.worldbank.org/INTOGMC/Resources/336099-1300396479288/NOC_Vol_II.pdf.

## CHAPTER 2

The Case for (and against) Local Content Policies in the Petroleum Sector

Failure is success if we learn from it.

—Malcolm Forbes

As suggested in chapter 1, governments may feel that economic benefits could be captured by policies that increase the local content with respect to value-added and employment. In practice, it is not clear that there are net economic benefits. The fundamental question is whether or not there is a need for government intervention and, if so, what kind of intervention. This question goes beyond the issue of local content policies (LCPs) and is part of a wider debate on the role of the state in productive development policies.

After World War II, the developing world established a heavy and complex set of productive development policies that was generally referred to as import substitution policies (ISPs). But these policies were felt as mostly inefficient and burdensome to competitiveness and, in many cases, fiscal accounts. Though market failures were recognized, the main concern was "government failures" and their costs. Along with the reforms connected to the Washington Consensus, there was a general shift toward dismantling these policies. Nonetheless, many of these policies survived and new ones were introduced. Most recently, a new debate has started on the role of the state in productive sector development. LCPs are part of this debate.

This chapter reviews the reasons for and against the use of LCPs. The authors first provide a brief historical review of the use of LCPs. We then present a conceptual framework that summarizes the theory behind policy intervention in productive sector development, and apply it to LCPs. No attempt is made to advocate for or against the use of LCPs.

Productive Development Policies and the Role of Local Content Policies: A Brief History

As highlighted in chapter 1, there are a number of definitional issues that need to be recognized when discussing LCPs. In broad terms, LCPs are government interventions that look to increase, in the long term, the share of employment or of sales to a sector that are locally supplied at each stage of the value chain. They are part of a broader category of policy interventions called productive development policies (PDPs).

PDPs (or industrial policies) can be broadly defined as initiatives that aim to strengthen the productive structure of a particular national economy. This broad definition includes any measure, policy, or program aimed at improving the growth and competitiveness of large sectors of the economy (manufacturing, agriculture), specific sectors (textiles, automobile industry, software production, and so on), or key activities (research and development, exports, fixed capital formation, human capital formation). The final objective is to "raise growth and improve the competitiveness of the overall economy while maintaining a rising trend in living standards" (Melo and Rodríguez-Clare 2006).

After World War II, countries tried to diversify their productive sector through various policies. The reasons behind this trend were diverse. In Latin America, for example, many were concerned that the region had specialized in natural resources. In 1950 Raul Prebisch argued that resource-based Latin American countries should diversify their economies, lest they develop at a slow pace due to the decrease in relative commodity prices over time. In the case of Asian countries, the argument was slightly different: the idea was that they had the comparative advantage to develop labor-intensive sectors that also had a relatively high level of education.

This period witnessed a raise in protectionism and the use of a very complex system of policies—including LCPs—aimed at fostering the development of the productive sector. For example, the licensing of technology by foreign firms to local suppliers was critical to the development of Asian countries' productive sectors. In 1944 *República Bolivariana de Venezuela* passed a hydrocarbons law that forced oil companies to refine oil in *República Bolivariana de Venezuela* . In Brazil in 1953 President Vargas proclaimed that Petrobras, the national oil company, should use only Brazilian capital, workers, and know-how. Developed economies were not immune to LCPs. For example, Nordas, Vatne, and Heum (2003) argue that even if "Norway did not have specific requirements as to the share of local content ... the oil companies never doubted that the Norwegian government and politicians appreciate the choice of local firms to supply the oil and gas activities with goods and services, and were pretty sure that this would be honored in negotiations for future licenses. Thus, during the late 1970s and early 1980s local firms probably were chosen even if they were not the most cost effective."

Existing literature suggests that differences in policy instruments and objectives could help to explain differences in countries' performances. In general terms, it seems that countries that: (1) focused on exports and productivity; (2) had a stable macroeconomic environment; (3) were more concerned about activities than sectors; and (4) clearly, explicitly, and publicly disclosed the government objectives, were more likely to develop sizeable and complex productive sectors. Countries that lacked these characteristics tended to develop noncompetitive productive sectors that (over time) generated sizeable economic costs.

In the 1980s governments that had made use of PDPs started to reverse their course. The shift was reinforced by a push for more trade liberalization, with the Uruguay Round and the creation of the World Trade Organization (WTO), and by the need to implement market reforms in developing countries that were facing a debt crisis. New priorities included securing property rights, ensuring fiscal discipline and sectorally neutral taxation, strengthening expenditure policies, liberalizing the financial sector, introducing unified and competitive exchange rates, opening to foreign trade and investment, privatizing, and deregulating. This set of policies became known as the Washington Consensus. This approach did not deny the existence of market failures and externalities. But the risks associated with "government failures" in attempting to correct for market failures were considered so high that it was better to abstain from intervention. As a result many countries started to undo their PDPs.

As time passed, disappointing results in many developing countries and the Asian financial crisis of the late 1990s contributed to a crisis of faith in the Washington Consensus, which triggered a renewed interested in targeted policy interventions. Indeed, Asian economies are often looked to as models: they have derived great benefits from increasing integration with the international economy—and without surrendering national autonomy in economic and cultural spheres—by pursuing decidedly nonneutral policies with respect to the promotion of specific industrial activities.

For natural resource producers, including oil and gas exporters, the development of a nonresource productive sector has been more pressing. Recent trade trends point to the commoditization of world trade. Commodities account for between 25 percent and 74 percent of total exports of different developing countries. South-South trade has become particularly dynamic due to higher growth rates in developing countries, where the per capita consumption of commodities has been rapidly increasing (UNCTAC 2008). Over the period 2000–06, the share of developing countries' imports of commodities from other developing countries in total merchandise trade increased from 60 percent to 70 percent, fueling concerns over these countries' vulnerability and interest in policies aimed at diversifying exports.

China's PDPs are regarded as a successful case of economic diversification. As argued in Rodrik (2006), the Chinese government's targeted policy interventions have helped nurture domestic capabilities in consumer electronics and other technologically advanced sectors that would most likely not have developed in their absence. To this end, foreign investors were required to form joint ventures with local companies, to transfer technology, and to source their inputs locally. New evidence on the effect of the promotion of foreign direct investment (FDI) suggests that, when combined with policies aimed to foster the transfer of technology, FDI is likely to drive faster and more sustainable productivity gains for local producers (Harrison and Rodriguez-Clare 2010).

As mentioned above, although most of the heavy and complex PDPs that were commonplace in developing countries were dismantled at the beginning of the 1980s, some PDPs survived, and new ones were introduced in the 1980s and 1990s (see Melo and Rodríguez-Clare 2006). Import substitution policies are largely gone, but most countries still maintain fiscal incentives for exports and FDI, tax breaks for certain sectors (for example, hotels and forestry), public development banks, and fiscal incentives for research and development (R&D). More recently, governments have introduced export promotion programs, technology funds, cluster promotion, and strategies in support of information and communication technologies.

The Role of the State in Productive Development Policies: A Conceptual Framework

Historically, the argument for PDPs (or industrial policies) is based on the idea that some sectors or industries exhibit Marshallian externalities—that is, local externalities that increase with the size of the industry. These externalities can arise through various channels, including localized industry-level knowledge spillovers (Harrison and Rodriguez-Clare 2010). Marshallian externalities give rise to the geographic agglomeration of industries, as emphasized in the literature on economic geography. To encourage the emergence of these industries, the classic policy intervention was infant-industry protection through the imposition of tariffs. Over time, arguments in support of this policy response have evolved even in the face of evidence in favor of Marshallian externalities (Rosenthal and Strange 2004). Furthermore, as discussed later in this chapter, other market failures may exist that would lead to a different response.

PDPs result from a variety of factors. In some cases they are the result of lobbying by rent-seeking organizations, or simply bad policies. But often they are introduced as a genuine response to perceived market failures or needs, or in pursuit of specific public goods. For example, existing literature on market failures suggests that spillovers associated with exports and FDI may explain the prevalence of subsidies or tax breaks to these activities. Information spillovers associated with innovation may explain fiscal incentives to R&D and programs to encourage innovation (Hausmann and Rodrik 2003). Coordination failures at the level of sectors or clusters may explain the introduction of a host of programs under the umbrella of competitiveness strategies in the mid-1990s (Rodríguez-Clare 2005; Rodrik 2007). Other researchers have looked at the pros and cons of sector selections, and proposed methodologies to guide the choice. Basically, according to this line of thoughts, not all public goods and policies benefit the whole economy. There are interventions that benefit certain sectors. For example, rural roads will mostly benefit agricultural production. Additionally, governments face budget constraints, and are not able to provide public goods to all sectors. As a consequence, paraphrasing Hausmann and Rodrik (2006), governments are "doomed to choose."

Although these lines of thought are not mutually exclusive, policy instruments that address general market failures are different from those used to promote specific sectors. While a government interested in developing externalities would usually support *activities* such as R&D or training, a government interested in certain goods and services would support *specific sectors* (for example, microelectronics). These considerations also apply to the design of PDPs in general, and LCPs for the oil and gas sector in particular.

The distinction between policy interventions for sectors and for activities is fundamental because of their distinctive economic rationale and institutional requirements. Policy interventions for sectors or clusters entail choosing favorites, or as some would say, "picking winners." Most economists would agree that these policies have the potential to solve specific bottlenecks in a focused way, but are more prone to capture by lobbies. In other words, government may easily fail. Policy intervention for activities, on the other hand, appears less subject to political economy pressures and government failure. For these reasons, "horizontal" policies of this kind have been generally preferred by economists provided that a market failure exists to justify the intervention.

Instrument and Objectives of Productive Development Policies

Researchers at the Inter-American Development Bank have recently proposed a framework to analyze alternative options for the design of PDPs (IDB 2009). PDPs are categorized on the basis of whether they target a sector (vertical) or they apply to all sectors (horizontal), and the degree to which policy intervention takes the form of a public input that is complementary to the market (for example, infrastructure)—either directly provided or outsourced—or it uses the power of the state to affect market incentives and alter market outcomes (for example, subsidy or regulation). We apply this framework to the analysis of LCPs.

Either the provision of a public input or the use of incentives and regulations may be viable solutions, irrespective of the degree of policy horizontality. The choice depends in part on the flexibility and resourcefulness of existing markets to achieve the desired outcome. For example, if a cluster requires a road to be developed, the solution is a public action that leads to the building of the road, unless the private sector is sufficiently developed to react to the use of specific subsidies or incentives. Sometimes, the public good is simply a

Table 2.1 A Classification of Productive Development Policies

		Transversality	
		Horizontal (H)	Vertical (V)
Channel of intervention	**Public input (P)**	• Business climate • Educated labor force • Basic infrastructure	• Roads for certain areas • Full, fair, and reasonable access to procurement opportunities for domestic suppliers
	Market intervention (M)	• R&D subsidies • Higher tariffs	• Import quotas • Sector-specific subsides • Disaggregated minimum local content targets
		• Requirement to purchase local goods • Minimum training obligations for nationals • Minimum participation of domestic subcontractors/suppliers	

regulation, for example, in the case of LCPs, the passage of a law or regulation to ensure full, fair, and reasonable access to procurement opportunities for domestic suppliers.

Table 2.1 identifies and organizes PDPs along two metrics—the span of the policy (or its *transversality*) and the public/market channel of intervention (or its *horizontality*). Examples of policies that could fall under each quadrant, including some wLCPs, are also provided.

The horizontal-public (HP) quadrant is the core of traditional macroeconomic studies on competitiveness, and the preferred domain of policies inspired by the Washington Consensus (such as a good business climate, appropriate basic infrastructure, and so on). PDPs for activities, or horizontal policies, would be confined to the horizontal-market (HM) quadrant. PDPs for sectors or clusters—or vertical policies—can be classified into either the VP quadrant or the VM quadrant (perhaps the most common).

In theory, governments implement PDPs when government intervention is necessary to overcome market failures. In the case of externalities, the best theoretical solution would be a "Pigouvian" tax or subsidy to achieve the optimal provision of the good. Therefore, if an externality is believed to exist, policy makers should: (1) confirm its existence and (2) ensure that the chosen policy corrects the externality as efficiently as the optimal theoretical solution would. For example, when a firm invests in R&D it generates knowledge that can be used by other firms. Consequently, it cannot fully appropriate the benefits from its investment due to the presence of externalities. It can be argued that without any government intervention investment in R&D will be less than the socially desirable amount. On the other hand, imposing higher tariffs on imported goods to protect local producers and stimulate local R&D in general would not address the cause of the market failure. As a consequence, this type of government intervention may not be appropriate.

At least in theory PDPs targeted to sectors take into consideration each sector's latent competitive advantage. For example, if a country has the natural endowment to develop tourism, but there is a coordination failure between the establishment of hotels and the development of air transport infrastructure, the government might intervene by either developing the necessary infrastructure or by granting tax incentives to the private sector to so do. Similarly, if a country has the endowment of the natural resource as well as a good geography to establish a petrochemical park, but there is coordination failure between the establishment of different plans and the development of the infrastructure to supply the industrial park, the government could intervene in developing infrastructure or providing incentives for the private sector to do so.

On the other hand, providing subsidies to the textile sector in a country that has lost its advantages to compete with textiles imported from other countries would normally be considered unnecessary and costly, at least from a strictly economic standpoint. In the oil and gas sector, a similar case could be made of back-office operations. Providing subsidies to back-office operations of the oil and gas sector in a country that has lost its advantage in competing with services provided from other countries could become unnecessary and costly. It is therefore evident that the first nontrivial issue for policy makers is how to decide which sectors should receive government support.

Another important issue relates to the type of interventions when targeting a sector. Should governments use public goods (VP) or market interventions (VM)? Countries' experience with ISPs suggests that VM policies might not be the best option. It is in fact hard to argue that externalities and/or market failures of this type are product specific. Furthermore, once subsidies are provided it is normally difficult for the government to discontinue them.

It is important to note that, given the bias introduced by the specificity of the demand from the oil and gas sector, LCPs are unlikely to be sector neutral. Hence, policies such as the general requirement to source local goods, minimum training obligations for nationals, or minimum participation of domestic suppliers and subcontractors would fall in the middle of the HM/VM quadrants. Furthermore, some LCPs impose sector-specific disaggregated minimum targets. Therefore, besides some type of public goods—such as a law or regulation for full, fair, and reasonable access to procurement opportunities for domestic suppliers—most LCPs would be VM.

Arguments for the Use of Local Content Policies

As mentioned earlier, there are a number of apparent reasons for which governments may wish to increase the local content of the oil and gas production sector (or of industries upstream or downstream of it). This section contains a brief overview of the arguments used to promote LCPs. These are grouped into three broad categories: increasing value-added, market failures/externalities, and social objectives.

To Increase Value-Added

Most developing countries that produce oil and gas have relatively small industrial sectors. Hence, their governments may feel economic benefits could be captured by policies that increase the local content with respect to value-added. The following arguments could support this claim:

- *Diversification.* This argument revolves around the debate on the so-called resource curse. Recent literature suggests that in an economy with any market imperfection/failure, the volatility of commodity prices could lead to an inefficient specialization in nontradable goods. In these cases gains could be derived from an explicit diversification policy. This argument goes beyond the framework presented before, though one might think about it as a negative externality that the resource sector has on the nonresource sector. The critical question is whether LCPs are indeed the right instrument to tackle this problem.
- *Discovery.* The process of discovery of a new product entails externalities. When an entrepreneur "discovers" that in a certain setting she can produce and export a product that was previously not produced in that setting, she will be quickly imitated. As a result the risks involved in the process of "discovering" the new product, including trial and error, will not be entirely remunerated. This implies that at market equilibrium there will be fewer discoveries than socially optimal. This argues in favor of policies that support new product development, similar to those used to address market failure in the presence of externalities (see next subsection).

To Correct for Market Failure

The correction of market failure is often used to justify LCPs. The following reasons could be considered:

- *Learning.* When a country is "relatively new" to the oil and gas sector, it tends to lack the specialized labor required by the sector. To overcome this deficiency oil companies might (and usually do) bring in foreign workers with the relevant skills and knowledge. But this could lead to a situation in which local workers do not get jobs because they do not have the expertise, but they cannot get the expertise because they do not get jobs. In such cases, government intervention aimed to support the development of specific skills and capacities of the local labor force could be justified. A similar argument could be used to support the development of the local productive sector. Imagine the case of a country with a mature and competitive ship-building sector that discovers large quantities of oil and/or gas. The ship-building sector could well be displaced by the oil sector because it lacks the specific experience and knowledge required to work for the oil sector. A government policy that leads to the development of capacities of the local ship-building sector could be justified. Using the analytical framework described in section "The Role of the State in Productive Development Policies: A Conceptual Framework", the most suitable policy tools to be used in this case would lie in the HM quadrant. Finally, labor mobility in the oil and gas sector could generate learning externalities. Companies might offer less training than the socially optimal level if labor mobility is high, as workers may leave to work in other companies. In this case there is a positive externality. This is likely to occur with respect to public officials employed by the sector ministry or even the national oil company; many move to the private sector since it usually offers salaries and benefits that are beyond the government remuneration scale.

- *Productive externalities*. Policy makers and academics often argue that FDI can be a source of valuable productivity externalities for developing countries. Prominent among the mechanisms often highlighted for these externalities are knowledge spillovers and "links" from multinational companies (MNCs) to local firms in host countries. When local firms start interacting with MNCs, productivity gains occur through the transfer of technology from MNCs and the decision by local firms to invest in technology upgrades.

  A recent paper by Alfaro and Rodriguez-Clare (2004) presents evidence of negative horizontal externalities (in the same sector) arising from MNCs' activity while confirming the existence of positive externalities from MNCs to local firms in upstream industries (vertical externalities). This suggests that MNCs' activities have positive spillovers over suppliers. Alfaro and Rodriguez-Clare's research on the effect of FDI in Latin American countries suggests that MNCs have a higher link coefficient than domestic firms in Brazil, *República Bolivariana de Venezuela* , and Chile. This should lead to a positive backward link effect. The authors also found a positive externality from MNCs to suppliers. This externality, rather than being evidence for backward links, could point to the existence of positive knowledge spillovers, which would in turn lead to higher total factor productivity among suppliers. This is an important consideration for the design of LCPs. Consider, for example, the case of a country with a competitive metal-mechanic sector. The sector might be competitive at producing valves and tubes. But requirement for the oil sector could be sector specific, and once the sector starts meeting those requirements it gets a productive upgrade. Applying the concepts described in table 2.1 the solution would lie in the HM quadrant, though VM policies could be used in some cases.

- *Market failures*. The superior market power of large corporations is often used to corroborate market failures. Usually companies that supply the oil and gas sector are big MNCs that have enough market power to displace small local firms from the value chain of the sector. Furthermore, they tend to have well-established and long-term relationships with oil and gas companies. This may create a bias against the use of local suppliers similar to the distortions generated by the practice of *dumping* in international trade.[1] Similarly, regulation aimed at other policy objectives may also foster existing market failures. For example, safety and environmental standards imposed on oil and gas companies by petroleum or environmental laws and regulations may create a barrier to the development of the local supply industry, in favor of established large corporations with market power. In this case a careful review of the regulatory systems may be necessary and would constitute a public good. Applying the concepts described in table 2.1, the solution would lie in the VP quadrant.

To Support Employment and Other Social Objectives

Finally, there are some social arguments for the setting of LCPs. These can be grouped into two broad areas:

- *Employment.* The oil and gas sector is capital intensive. Therefore its contribution to national employment levels tends to be very limited. LCPs aimed to affect the level of local employment in the oil and gas sector respond to social pressure to increase the participation of nationals as part of the "license to operate."
- *Compensation for the adverse socioeconomic impacts of oil and gas activities on local communities and vulnerable groups.* It is generally accepted that communities close to infrastructure projects need to be compensated for a temporary or permanent loss of economic livelihoods. The international standards for environmental and social impact set principles for compensating individuals for the loss of the potential to earn an income. In practice, this could involve project proponents directly tendering opportunities to suppliers who source labor or materials from affected communities, or it could mean obliging their major contractors to meet targets for the employment of displaced and affected persons.

Arguments against the Use of Local Content Policies

Both history and the conceptual framework presented in table 2.1 help emphasize some of the dangers of policy intervention in productive sectors. These can be broadly grouped into four categories: misallocation of resources and/or inefficiencies, misalignment between instruments and policy objectives, international regulation, and institutional frameworks.

First-Best versus Second-Best Interventions: Misalignment between Policy Objectives and Instruments

The principal challenge to the use of LCPs rests on the misalignment between objectives and instruments. If a policy maker thinks that there is an externality, she should ensure that (1) there is indeed an externality and (2) the instrument chosen corrects the externality. For example, if the labor force is not adequately trained to satisfy the requirements of the oil sector, the policy maker should first establish whether training would be sufficient or if the situation demands structural changes to the country's educational system. If training would overcome the shortfall, imposing minimum local employment targets on oil companies may not provide the optimal outcome. Policies to support the training of nationals would be more closely related to the externality in question. Furthermore, as argued by Weitzman (1974), when there is uncertainty about costs and benefits, price interventions tend to produce results closer to the optimal result than quantity regulations. In our example, incentives and/or subsidies for training may produce better results than mandatory requirements.

A similar case can be made about market failures. Consider MNCs' superior market power. The imposition of minimum local content targets may not produce the optimal outcome. The problem may be a lack of adequate competition regulation and/or market supervision. Therefore, regulations that try to ensure full, fair, and reasonable access to procurement opportunities for domestic suppliers might generate outcomes that are closer to the optimal solution.

In respect to each argument for LCPs previously outlined, we could argue whether or not LCPs are the first-best policy intervention. In some cases, however, the first-best option may not be feasible. If alternative interventions are made, it is important to consider how far they fall from the first-best option.

Misallocation of Resources and/or Inefficiencies

The second argument against any type of industrial policy measure is whether or not it improves welfare. Much literature supports industrial policy. As reviewed in Harrison and Rodriguez-Clare (2010) industrial policy improves welfare in the presence of Marshallian externalities. But the application of such policy should pass both the Mill and Bastable tests. The Mill test requires the protected sector to eventually survive international competition without protection; the Bastable test is more stringent and calls for the present value of future benefits arising from the policy to compensate the present costs of protection. To be viable, LCPs in the oil and gas sector would need to pass both tests.

In this context, and looking at past experience, Maloney (2002) compares the development strategy of resource-rich countries in Latin America to the cases of Australia, the Scandinavian countries, and the United States. The author argues that Latin American countries followed the standard import substitution policy while the other countries diversified around the comparative advantage of their resource sector. Quoting Blomström and Meller (1991), "Latin American countries filled all the numbers [of the input-output tables] at the same time." This diversification strategy, together with other factors, led to more competitive nonresource sectors in Australia, Scandinavia, and the United States. These findings would support the use of policies aimed to develop sectors connected to the resource sector where countries have a comparative advantage.

Harrison and Rodriguez-Clare show that even in the absence of a latent comparative advantage in a sector, PDPs could be justified when the losses from going against the comparative advantage are dominated by gains associated with the economywide externalities generated by the policy. Nevertheless, they conclude that, in practice, a latent comparative advantage is necessary for infant-industry protection and useful to guide policy discussions. Two reasons are provided to underpin this conclusion. First, in all cases in which infant-industry protection has supposedly been successful, the nascent sector eventually generated significant exports. Second, if there are resource constraints that prevent the sector from becoming large, then it is likely that the benefits of PDPs would be small while the associated costs and risk would be relatively large. These findings are relevant to the design of LCPs for the oil and gas sector since the sector tends to be relatively large with respect to the nonoil economy of many developing countries. Consequently, it is possible for the nonoil sector to face resource constraints once it begins to supply the oil sector.

In addition, the empirical evidence reviewed in Alfaro and Rodriguez-Clare (2004) suggests that policies aimed to support FDI are most successful when they are associated with increasing exposure to trade. Therefore interventions that increase exposure to trade (such as export promotion) are likely to leverage the result of other types of interventions (such as tariffs or LCPs).

International Regulations

A nontrivial issue connected to LCPs is their compliance with international regulation. Both multilateral and regional negotiated agreements regulate trade between nations. The World Trade Organization (WTO) oversees compliance with these rules. The most relevant agreements among WTO members with implications for LCPs include the General Agreement on Tariffs and Trade (GATT), the agreement on Trade-Related Investment Measures (TRIMs), the General Agreement on Trade in Services (GATS), and the agreement on Government Procurement (GPA).

The agreement on TRIMs is based on the "national treatment" principle of Article III of the GATT, and pertains to trade in goods. TRIMs apply to all WTO members, and prohibit local content requirements that mandate particular levels of local purchases by an enterprise. The rules also prohibit trade-balancing requirements that restrict the volume or value of imports that an enterprise can purchase to an amount related to the level of products it exports. In essence, the rules require a host country to extend to foreign investors a treatment that is at least as favorable—insofar as the purchase of products is concerned—as the treatment it accords to national investors in like circumstances. The TRIMs agreement allows for transitional arrangements to maintain certain (protectionist) measures for a limited time following a country's entry into the WTO. The grace period is two years in the case of developed countries, five years for developing countries, and seven years for least-developed countries. In this regard, with the exception of Vietnam, all developing countries that produce oil and/or gas acceded to the WTO prior to 2006, which would suggest that their eligibility for transitional arrangements under GATT has expired. The foregoing may impose restrictions on the design of LCPs. For example, the imposition of minimum targets for the participation of domestic subcontractors/suppliers may be contrary to a country's WTO undertakings.

Part III of the GATS contains provisions on access to WTO members' markets by foreign suppliers, and the treatment of national suppliers. In the case of market access, all WTO members should accord services and service providers from other WTO member countries and show them treatment no less favorable than that provided for under the common terms, limitations, and conditions mutually agreed among WTO members. Furthermore, Article XIII of GATS extends to government procurement.

As with TRIMs, GATS has provisions for the "special and differential treatment" (SDT) of developing countries, which allow for certain exceptions from the general rule. In addition, there are provisions that allow flexibility to encourage foreign suppliers to assist in technology transfers and training through offsets (of particularly relevance to the design of LCPs). Offset transactions are contractual conditions that require the seller (usually a foreign supplier) to transfer additional economic benefits to the buyer (usually a host government or domestic company) as a condition for the sale of a base good or service. Offsets include preferential hiring and training of nationals, preferences for local sourcing, encouragement of inward investment, support to domestic suppliers to develop future competitiveness, and support of the development of operational infrastructure to be made available for public use (for example, roads, power, water supply, and so on). Therefore, LCPs that encourage offset activities in countries that benefit from SDT would not be in breach of such countries' WTO commitments.

GATT and GATS are based on what it is known in the international trade law as positive lists. In other words, countries that wish to join the WTO are asked to put forward a list of sectors and commitments for the liberalization of trade in services, access to technology, and training. Therefore, they only apply to those commitments put forward by each country. The actual list of sectors depends on the outcome of the negotiations between the country and WTO.

The GPA entered into force on January 1, 1996, and regulates government procurement among WTO members that are party to this agreement (the European Union members and thirteen other countries, including Norway, the United States, South Korea, and Chinese Taipei). The GPA rules are intended to counter internal political pressure to favor domestic suppliers of goods and services over foreign competitors, and thereby open up government-transacted business to international competition. A large part of the rules concerns tendering procedures for contracts above specified financial thresholds. An important cornerstone principle in this regard is nondiscrimination: parties to the GPA are required to accord to the products, services, and suppliers of any other party to the GPA a treatment that is "no less favorable" than that given to their domestic products, services, and suppliers. GPA utilizes a negative list—that is, rules apply to all sectors except those that the country chooses not to include in the agreement. The use of offsets is explicitly excluded under the GPA. But exceptions are made for developing countries that negotiate the conditions for their use at the time of accession, provided that offsets are used exclusively for the qualification of interested bidders to participate in the procurement process and not as criteria for the award of contracts. The GPA also requires participating countries to adopt procedures that ensure the transparency of laws, regulations, procedures, and practices regarding government procurement. Although currently no developing country has signed the GPA, the restrictions imposed by this agreement may pose a challenge to countries that use LCPs and would like to sign it. It is important to note that some GPA members are extending its application to non-GPA members through bilateral free trade agreements (FTAs) with developing countries. Therefore, depending on how exceptions to offsets were negotiated on those FTAs, the GPA may impact the use of offsets in developing countries.[2]

It is worth noting that oil and gas have not been negotiated as a separate sector under GATS. But energy is considered a prerequisite for social and economic development since it underpins virtually every human activity, and ensuring the supply of reliable and affordable energy is one of the basic responsibilities of governments (WTO 2010). As a consequence oil and gas activities are currently included in other service sectors, such as transport, distribution, construction, consulting, and engineering. But drawing a line between trade in goods and trade in services remains difficult in the energy sector, in particular with respect to activities surrounding the production and transformation of the resource (such as exploration, drilling, oil refining, gas liquefaction, and regasification). The foregoing, coupled with the exclusion of government procurement from the scope of GATS, affects the scope and depth of governments' intervention in the energy sector. Indeed governments at local and central levels are often directly involved in the provision and purchase of energy services, and in many petroleum-producing countries the national oil company plays a dominant role. Thus, depending on the status and purpose of the entity purchasing energy services, a transaction may be qualified as government procurement and fall outside the scope of specific commitments.

The number of GATS commitments in the sectors of services incidental to mining, services incidental to energy distribution, and pipeline transportation of fuels is modest. Sectoral limitations exist, and market access and national treatment commitments are liberal overall. The number of commitments in other energy-related services varies greatly depending on the sector concerned. For example, 79 countries made commitments in engineering services, 50 in the maintenance and repair of equipment, and 70 in general construction work for civil engineering. Often specific references to activities related to the energy sector appear under various sectors. In most cases, these references aim at excluding energy-related activities from a sector, though there are a few cases that explicitly include them. In some schedules, limitations on market access or national treatment specifically targeting energy-related activities have been listed.

Owing to the limited coverage of WTO rules for the oil and gas sectors, some WTO members have identified the need to negotiate commitments in the oil and gas sector, for example, for exploration services, services incidental to mining, technical testing and analysis, and toll refining services. Some countries have presented position papers (Unites States; WTO 1998), others tabled proposals (Canada's proposal, WTO 2001; Chile, the European Community and its member states, Japan, and the United States submitted the Proposed Guide for Scheduling Commitments on Energy Services in the WTO ([OB(03)/89, May 12, 2003]); Indonesia proposed a list of activities in its Proposal on Classification of Energy Services (Revision, S/CSC/W/42/Rev.2, 28 April 2006), and a background note was made by the Secretariat (WTO 2010).

To summarize, although the scope of LCPs and the use of certain policy tools may be limited by international trade agreements, there is at present still scope for government intervention in this area. The extent of such scope depends on the specific agreements a country has entered into and the exceptions it has negotiated. Table 2.2 provides an outline of current WTO commitments for a selected group of countries.

Institutional Framework

As mentioned earlier in this chapter, PDPs for sectors appear more prone to capture by lobbies, more so if they are market interventions. Beneficiary sectors have no incentive to become more productive and will lobby government to maintain the benefits indefinitely. Furthermore, most LCPs are not associated with an explicit fiscal cost (that is, in most cases the government foregoes revenue but does not incur an explicit expenditure), and are therefore easily disguised.

Nonetheless, there are successful cases where countries (for example, emerging Asian economies) have used specific market intervention (Rodrik 2007). In these cases the critical elements of policy success have been (1) government commitment to achieving competition in protected sectors; (2) clear performance and enforcement criteria (in terms of productivity and/or exports); (3) clear sunset clauses; and (4) a set of clear complementary interventions (like infrastructure, regulation, education). In addition, anecdotal evidence and new research suggests that FDI has been particularly important in cases where governments were actively engaged in strategies of technological upgrading in certain sectors, and involved foreign companies as part of those strategies (Alfaro and Rodriguez-Clare 2004). Typically, these efforts were part of a set of complementary policies that included increasing the supply of skilled workers in a targeted industry, improving regulation and infrastructure, promoting new activities and innovation, and increasing exports.

This literature suggests that for LCPs to increase welfare they have to occur in an institutional setting where:

- The government also provides public goods (for example regulation and infrastructure) required by the sector.
- Clear performance indicators are used to measure competitiveness of the beneficiary sector (for example the level of exports).
- Transparent, clear rules, including sunset clauses, are established.

Table 2.2 International Agreements between Selected Countries

Agreement	Angola	Brazil
General Agreement on Trade in Services (GATS)	Angola's GATS schedule contains specific commitments in three areas: banking and money lending; hotel and restaurant; and recreational and sporting services. Angola maintains MFN exemptions in the areas of coastal and long-distance shipping	Brazil's specific commitments under the GATS cover only 38 of the 160 services subsectors or 7 of the 12 broad areas defined in the Services Sectoral Classification List 104: business services, communication services, construction and related engineering services, distribution services, financial services, tourism and travel-related services, and transport services
Relevant bilateral agreements		
With the United States	Trade and Investment Framework Agreement (TIFA)	Agreement on Trade and Economic Cooperation
With the European Union	"Joint Way Forward Angola-European Union" (July 2012)	
Other		Mercado Común del Sur (MERCOSUR): Flexibility in the use of LCPs

Source: World Bank data.

Agreement	Indonesia	Malaysia	Trinidad and Tobago
General Agreement on Trade in Services (GATS)	Professional and business services; telecommunications; construction and engineering services; educational services; financial services; health services; tourism; and maritime cargo handling	Professional services, communications services, construction and related services, financial services, health-related social services, tourism and travel-related services, and transport services. Malaysia did not make any commitments in distribution, education, environmental services, or in recreational, cultural, and sporting services	Business services; communications services; construction services; distribution services; educational services; services related to the environment; financial services
Relevant bilateral agreements			
With the United States	Trade and Investment Framework Agreement (TIFA)	Trade and Investment Framework Agreement (TIFA)—No negotiations for the FTA since July 2008	
With the European Union			Economic Partnership Agreement between the Caribbean Forum (CARIFORUM) States and the European Community: "The State reserves the right to adopt or maintain measures on investment in this sector [manufacture of refined petroleum]."
Other		Malaysia-Australia Free Trade Agreement (MAFTA): - Engineering services: Commercial presence can be established only through a representative office, regional office, or locally incorporated with Malaysian individuals or Malaysian-controlled corporations or both for the purpose of services contracts awarded in Malaysia. The aggregate foreign shareholding in the joint-venture corporation shall not exceed 30% - Research and development services: Permitted with no restriction, except for those involving Malaysia's natural resources	CARICOM: Extend local content policies to other members of the agreement

Conclusion

LCPs are part of a broader category of policy interventions known as PDPs—that is, policies that aim to strengthen the productive structure of a particular economy. The fundamental question behind PDPs and LCPs is whether or not there is a need for government intervention, and if so, what type of intervention should be considered.

PDPs have been used for a long time with various degrees of success. Existing literature suggests that countries that (1) focused on exports and productivity; (2) had a stable macroeconomic environment; (3) were more concerned about activities as opposed to sectors; and (4) clearly, explicitly, and publicly disclosed the government's objectives, were more likely to develop sizeable and complex productive sectors. Countries that lacked these characteristics tended to develop noncompetitive productive sectors that overtime generated sizeable economic costs.

The historical argument for government intervention or industrial policy is based on the idea that some sectors or industries exhibit Marshallian externalities, which are local externalities that increase with the size of the industry. More recent literature highlights that most governments implement PDPs to address market failures, and successful PDPs appear to be those that target sectors that have a latent competitive advantage. The use of PDPs could therefore be justified in order to: (1) promote economic diversification, (2) correct market failures, and (3) promote employment and other social objectives.

There are, however, potential down sides to the use of PDPs: (1) resources could be misallocated to noncompetitive sectors, which would yield a net welfare loss; (2) the policy and its implementation tools could be misaligned with the market failure or problem that they aim to correct; (3) there could be restrictions on or conflicts between the policy tools and international agreements; and (4) policies could lack coherence with the broader institutional framework, which would render them ineffective even when they are theoretically justified, properly designed, and compliant with international agreements.

These pros and cons need to be taken into consideration in the design of PDPs in general, and LCPs in particular, and the choice of their implementation tools.

Notes

1. Dumping is bringing a product onto the market of another country at a price less than the normal value of that product in the home market of the producer. The practice is condemned but not prohibited by WTO law.

2. In recent trade agreements with the United States, like CAFTA-DR, countries committed to open up government procurement and to put forward and negotiate list of sectors that will be excluded from liberalization. Similar commitments have also been made under South-South free trade agreements, like the case of the Caribbean countries and their commitments in the Caribbean Community (CARICOM).

References

Alfaro, L., and A. Rodríguez-Clare. 2004. "Multinationals and Links: An Empirical Investigation." *Economia (Journal of LACEA)* 4 (2): 157–63.

Blomström, M., and P. Meller. 1991. *Diverging Paths: Comparing a Century of Scandinavian and Latin American Economic Development.* Washington, DC: Inter-American Development Bank.

———. 2010. "Trade, Foreign Investment, and Industrial Policy." In *Handbook of Development Economics*, edited by D. Rodrik and M. Rosenzweig, vol. 5. Amsterdam: Elsevier.

Hausmann, R., and D. Rodrik. 2003. "Economic Development as Self-Discovery." *Journal of Development Economics* 72 (2): 603–33.

IDB (Inter-American Development Bank). 2009. "Industrial Policies in Latin America." Working Papers from the Research Network, Inter-American Development Bank, Washington, DC. http://www.iadb.org/research/projects_detail.cfm?lang=es&id=3776.

Maloney, W. 2002. "Missed Opportunities: Innovation and Resource-Based Growth in Latin America." *Economia* 3 (1): 111–51.

Melo, A., and A. Rodriguez-Clare. 2006. "Productive Development Policies and Supporting Institutions in Latin America and the Caribbean." RES Working Papers 1005, Inter-American Development Bank, Research Department, Washington, DC.

Nordas, H., E. Vatne, and P. Heum. 2003. "The Upstream Petroleum Industry and Local Industrial Development: A Comparative Study." SNF Report 08/03, Institute for Research in Economics and Business Administration, Norway.

Prebisch, R. 1950. "The Economic Development of Latin America and its Principal Problems." *Economic Bulletin for Latin America* 7 (1): 1–22, Reprinted in the (1962).

———. 2005. "Coordination Failure, Clusters, and Microeconomic Interventions." *Journal of Latin American and Caribbean Economic Association (LACEA), Economia* 6 (1): 1–42.

Rodrik, D. 2006. "What's So Special about China's Exports?" *China and World Economy* 14: 1–19. http://www.un.org/esa/sustdev/publications/industrial_development/1_1.pdf.

———. 2007. "Industrial Development: Stylized Facts and Policies." In *Industrial Development for the 21st Century.* New York: United Nations.

Rosenthal, S. S., and W. C. Strange. 2004. "Evidence on the Nature and Sources of Agglomeration Economies." In *Handbook of Regional and Urban Economics*, edited by J. V. Henderson and J. -F. Thisse, vol. 4. Netherlands: Elsevier.

UNCTAC (United Nations Conference on Trade and Development). 2008. *Globalization for Development: The International Trade Perspective.* New York and Geneva: United Nations.

Weitzman, M. L. 1974. "Prices vs. Quantities." *Review of Economic Studies* 41 (4): 477–91.

WTO (World Trade Organization). 1998. S/C/W/58 20 October 1998 (98–4051), Council for Trade in Services, Communication from the United States Energy Services.

———. 2010. S/C/W/311 12 January 2010 (10–0109), Council for Trade in Services, Energy Services Background Note by the Secretariat.

## CHAPTER 3

Types of Local Content Policies

Laws too gentle are seldom obeyed; too severe,
seldom executed.

—Benjamin Franklin

Local content policies (LCPs) in the oil and gas sector generally aim to encourage the participation and development of national labor, goods and services, technology, and capital. The objectives and guiding principles of these policies are sometimes outlined in overall or specific policy statements and/or economic plans. Often principles and objectives are further detailed in primary or secondary legislation, as well as in negotiated contracts, licensing agreements, or concession agreements. We call these "channels of policy implementation." Implementation itself may rely on a variety of policy tools, including petroleum rights allocation systems, taxes, tariffs, incentives, penalties, procurement rules, and training arrangements. In this chapter, we briefly describe the policy statements, channels, and tools used by petroleum-producing countries in connection with the design and implementation of LCPs. Reporting and monitoring arrangements are also discussed.

We focus on policies associated with the exploration, development, and production of oil and gas aimed at strengthening local employment and the development of a local supply sector. In particular, we discuss the intended scope of LCPs within supply chains, and the extent to which they grant margins of domestic preference to national citizens in employment or to national suppliers in procurement. Differences in LCPs at different stages of maturity in the petroleum sector are also discussed, and a typology of LCPs is proposed. Examples are provided for a number of petroleum-producing countries (these are summarized in appendix E).

Policy Statements, Channels, Tools of Implementation, and Reporting Arrangements

The objectives and guiding principles of LCPs in the oil and gas sector may be outlined in overall or specific policy statements and/or economic plans. Principles and objectives may then be detailed in primary or secondary legislation, and more often than not, in negotiated contracts, licensing agreements, or concession agreements.

Policy Statements, Strategies, and Plans

Policy objectives and principles are sometimes summarized in broad statements of government policy on local content that may or may not be specific to the oil and gas sector, and/or in national or departmental strategic plans at the central government level or at regional or provincial authorities' levels such as national or regional economic development plans, poverty reduction strategy papers, and medium-term fiscal or expenditure frameworks. Local content may relate to job creation, training, industrial development, the creation of backward and forward links from existing economic sectors, attracting inward investment and improving the investment climate, or some combination of the foregoing.

In addition, some governments have issued freestanding LCPs. These documents vary widely, from academic reports with concluding policy recommendations, such as the 2011 report on Enhancing National Participation in the Oil and Gas Industry in Uganda, to statements of broad principles, such as those contained in the 2010 policy framework on Local Content and Local Participation in Petroleum Activities in Ghana or the 2004 Local Content and Local Participation Policy Framework for Trinidad and Tobago.[1]

Primary Legislation

The manner in which an LCP is codified under law varies considerably. Local content provisions may be embedded within the wider primary legislation governing petroleum exploration and development, or they may be the object of a separate law on local content, as shown in box 3.1.

Box 3.1

Examples of Local Content in Primary Legislation

Article 50 of the Law on Sub Soil and Subsoil Users in Kazakhstan mandates that bids for new subsurface mineral rights include commitments to minimum levels of local content in goods, works and services, and the training of Kazakh personnel. Article 1 of the same law establishes a minimum requirement for 95 percent of employees to be Kazakhstani citizens, and Article 78 requires that, for the purpose of contractor selection, procuring entities reduce the price of bids from Kazakhstani producers by 20 percent.[2]

The 2010 **Nigerian** Oil & Gas Content Industry Development Act provides for, among other items:

- Nigerian content targets, including 80 percent for detailed engineering for floating production, storage and off-loading vessels (FPSO) measured by man-hours, 50 percent local content by tonnage in the fabrication of topsides, and 100 percent local content by tonnage in the procurement of steel plates
- A local content monitoring regime integrated with the process of contracting suppliers and service providers

(box continues on next page)

Box 3.1 Examples of Local Content in Primary Legislation *(continued)*

- Penalties for noncompliance with the local content legislation
- Ministerial waivers for certain requirements of the legislation for a temporary period, including where targets established by law cannot be complied with due to limited local market capabilities
- The establishment of a Nigerian content development fund to support the development of national suppliers.[3]

Secondary Legislation

LCPs may also be the object of special regulation as in Angola and Kazakhstan, or be embedded in broader regulation for the petroleum industry, as in Mozambique (see box 3.2).

Box 3.2

Examples of Local Content in Secondary Legislation

In **Mozambique** local content requirements form part of Decree No. 24/2004 on Petroleum Operations Regulations, which mandate that contracts for the procurement of goods and services be awarded on an internationally competitive basis. Specifically, Article 38 mandates that the operator is to "give preferential treatment to the purchase of local goods and services when such goods and services are internationally comparable in terms of quality, availability, and quantity required and are offered at prices inclusive of taxes not higher than ten percent of the available imported goods."[4]

In **Angola** the dominant secondary legislation for local content in procurement in the petroleum sector is the Ministerial Order No. 127/03 on the Contracting of Services and Goods from Angolan Companies by Petroleum Industry Companies.[5] The regulation (1) reserves certain categories of procurement expenditure to Angolan companies, including logistics, catering, pressure tests for storage tanks and pipelines; (2) identifies spending categories that fall under a "semicompetitive regime," where bidding by foreign suppliers and service providers is predicated on these companies first forming joint ventures with Angolan companies (expenditure categories under this regime include geophysical sciences, drilling controls and fluid analysis, and the operations and maintenance of production facilities); (3) establishes a "competitive regime," which places all other categories of expenditure into international competitive tender, yet provides for "Angolan State companies and/or private companies the right of first refusal, provided that the value of the relevant bid is no more than 10 percent higher than those of other companies."

In **Kazakhstan**, Decree No. 965/2012 stipulates that operators must formulate and submit to the government their procurement plans.[6] The aim of this regulation is inform Kazakhstani suppliers of the short- and long-term procurement plans of different oil and gas companies operating in the region, such that they may better appreciate the risks and opportunities for investing in building their capabilities and capacities.

Secondary legislation on local content is not always underpinned by associated primary legislation. For example, during the three years prior to the passing of the 2010 Nigerian Oil & Gas Content Industry Development Act 2010, various ministerial directives were issued stating local content minimum targets. It is worth noting that where primary legislation exists, contracts may shelter investors from its application if stability clauses have been negotiated to protect the project from changes in legislation.

Petroleum Agreements

Petroleum agreements—including concessions, leases, licenses, production sharing contracts, and service agreements—commonly contain legally binding requirements on local content, and have traditionally been the dominant vehicle for mandating local content. Whereas primary and secondary legislation on local content contains overall principles and general requirements, some petroleum agreements may be quite specific as to the operators' obligations in connection with specific projects.

The 2008 model production sharing agreement (PSA) adopted in Tanzania to support negotiations for new exploration blocks illustrates the types of obligations on local content that may be contained in such documents. Two articles of the model agreement oblige the contracting parties, including the Tanzanian Petroleum Development Company, to implement the government LCP.[7] The 2006 model PSA for Uganda includes similar requirements with respect to the employment and training of nationals in the workforce. The relevant clauses are summarized in box 3.3.

Petroleum Rights Allocation Systems

Some countries pursue local development objectives through the procedures for the licensing of petroleum rights, for example, by promoting local ownership through restrictions on local companies' ability to transfer their rights to foreign companies, or by mandating minimum levels of local content in bids for oil and gas exploration and production (Tordo 2009).

Among the criteria for award announced in the 2000, 2005, and 2006 licensing rounds in Nigeria was that bidders commit to the development of Nigerian expertise and know-how as part of their intended operations. In addition, training and local employment obligations were included in petroleum contracts. The local content requirements became more stringent in the 2005 marginal fields licensing round: bidders were required to associate their bids with local content vehicles (LCVs) in the form of Nigerian companies (that is, locally incorporated companies with a majority—usually 60 percent—of Nigerian shareholders). The Nigerian company would provide local goods and services, while the international company would be the technical partner. But the market's low uptake indicates that the restrictions were too ambitious, given local capacity levels (Tordo 2009).

In Brazil the emphasis on local content has changed over time. In licensing rounds 1 to 4 from 1999 to 2002, weightings in the evaluation of local content

Box 3.3

Tanzania and Uganda: Local Content Provisions in Model Petroleum-Sharing Agreements

Tanzania:
Article 18—Tanzanian Resources

- Maximize the use of local goods and services, where available on a competitive basis
- Pass-through local content considerations to subcontractors
- Scope subcontracts to match local capabilities
- Provide a list of goods and services to be procured locally
- Weight tender evaluation for local value-added
- Implement tender procedures to deliver the above.

Article 19—Employment, Training, and Transfer of Technology

- Maximize employment of qualified Tanzanian citizens
- Establish programs to train, employ, and promote Tanzanian citizens
- Provide grants to support training in petroleum sector within the Tanzania Petroleum Development Corporation and the government.

In addition, Article 11 on the Recovery of Costs and Expenses (and its associated Annex D and Schedules) specifies whether the costs involved in training nationals and sourcing from domestic suppliers would be recoverable against expenditures.

Uganda:
Article 20—Purchases in Uganda

- Maximize use of local goods and services, where available on a competitive basis
- Implement tender procedures that give adequate opportunity for local suppliers to compete
- Report achievements in utilizing Ugandan goods and services.

Article 21—Training and Employment

- Train and employ suitably qualified Ugandan citizens following commencement of production
- Undertake the schooling and training of Ugandan citizens for staff positions, including administrative and executive management positions.

Provide grants to support the training of government officials on matters related to the management and oversight of the petroleum sector.

Figure 3.1   Average Local Content Offered for Various Bidding Rounds: Brazil, 1999–2007

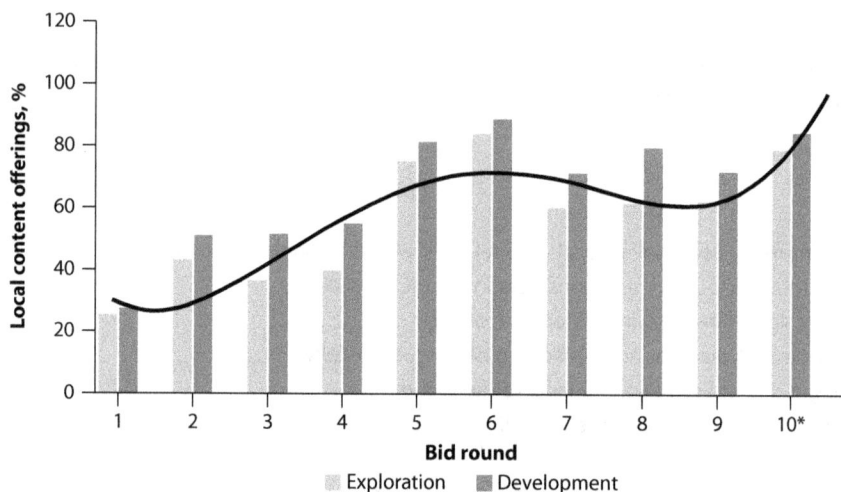

* Only on-shore blocks

Source: Local Content Regulations for Concession Agreements. Agência Nacional do Petróleo, http://www.braziltexas
.org/attachments/files/401/ANP-Marcelo.pdf.

in concession award were at 20 percent. The weighting rose to 40 percent for
rounds 5 and 6, with an increase in political attention to this topic; then fell
again to 20 percent in rounds 7 to 10, as concerns grew over the impact of local
content objectives on investment costs and field exploration and development
schedules (Gholzani 2010). In broad terms, these weightings had the effect of
changing the level of local content commitments in concession agreements, as
shown in figure 3.1.

Petroleum contracts typically require operators to submit exploration and
development plans as a condition for the grant of, respectively, an exploration
and a production license or authorization. To varying degrees these plans may
contain specific local content commitments, for example, the precise numbers
of nationals to be employed in the workforce or the estimated expenditure for
training and sourcing of local goods and services.

Taxes and Tariffs

Taxes on import and customs duties may be imposed by a country to affect the
import of specific goods in support of LCPs aimed at protecting noncompetitive local producers. Aside from welfare and economic efficiency considerations, these mechanisms have similar effects to the imposition of nontariff
barriers such as price preferencing for local companies, and directly create
revenue for the government. For example, imposing higher tariffs on finished
products than on components may incentivize local assembly in an effort to
stimulate employment.

In the oil and gas sector it is common practice to allow contractors or subcontractors under a petroleum contract or host government agreement to

import and reexport (free of tax) machinery, equipment, fixed assets, goods, works, and services for use in petroleum operations. This may require a customs duty exemption certificate from the customs authority or other relevant authority, or a positive or negative list of equipment, goods, and services—often issued by the ministry of finance and/or the ministry of petroleum. These exemptions are affected by the government's LCPs. For example, since January 2003 there are no customs tariffs on financial transactions or trade in locally manufactured goods between member states where the local shareholding is 51 percent (Bahrain, Kuwait, Oman, Qatar, Saudi Arabia, and the United Arab Emirates)—if products have at least 40 percent local value-added content (Ernst and Young 2012).

There are many ways in which the fiscal regime may be used as a tool to implement LCPs. Corporate income tax may be used to incentivize local ownership. For example, in India domestic companies are subject to tax at a rate of 30 percent, while foreign companies bear a 40 percent rate. It is worth noting that through the fiscal regime and the mechanism of production sharing a part of the additional costs arising from the imposition of special taxes and tariff may end up being borne by the host government (Tordo 2007).

Market Regulation

Market regulation may be used to support the development of local service and industrial capacity. This may include health, safety, environmental, and security aspects of petroleum activities and related manufacturing operations, as well as internal and external financial, corporate governance, competition, pricing, market participation, and so on. For example a new concept for developing local content was introduced in the 2005 licensing round in Nigeria. Locally incorporated companies with a majority of Nigerian shareholders (LCVs) were to be involved in all new licenses as full-paying partners with a minimum 10 percent participating interest. Operators were to train and develop LCVs into capable indigenous oil companies, while LCVs had a special responsibility for securing local goods and services. (See below for more on the regulation of procurement by oil and gas companies.)

Employment Regulation

Employment regulation is one of the most commonly used tools in LCPs. Such regulation may be accomplished through the imposition of minimum local employment obligations, minimum salaries, and training requirements; the reservation of certain jobs or levels for citizens; the restriction of certain jobs/levels to citizens; and the oversight of work visas. For example, in Azerbaijan export-oriented oil and gas operations that are expected to last for more than six months require the company to employ at least 80 percent Azerbaijani citizens at all staff levels. The regulation applies to all contractors and subcontractors. Exemption may be granted on a case-by-case basis by the relevant state authority. (See below for an overview of LCP objectives and tools related to the regulation of employment.)

Tender Procedures

The rules, principles, and processes by which goods and services are to be procured by the holders of oil and gas exploration and production rights (usually the operator on behalf of the rights holders) are normally contained in tender procedures. These are usually agreed between the operator and the sector ministry or the national oil company, as the case may be, and may simply reflect the principles and processes adopted by the operator across its global business or specific procedures applicable to the license in question. The setting of these procedures may be influenced by a combination of the operator, its partners, the national oil company, and relevant government entities and regulatory agencies.

Tender procedures are important documents since they invariably state the basis upon which contracts are to be awarded. They also mandate whether the process of bidding and the evaluation of bids are on an internationally competitive basis or give preference to domestic suppliers and subcontractors. The procedure may further detail the weight that shall be given to local content in the process of evaluating bids—a 10 percent to 20 percent weight is not uncommon—and whether a bidder's score for local content is to form part of the overall award of the contract, or simply be a hurdle to cross before accepting the lowest-priced bid.

Tender procedures that are negotiated with or imposed by governments through regulation may be influenced by prevailing local rules for public procurement, although it should be noted that these rules rarely apply directly to procurement expenditure of private oil and gas companies. Box 3.4 compares

---

Box 3.4

Comparison of Extracts from Public Procurement Regulations and Local Content Regulations: Mozambique

Public Procurement Regulation	Petroleum Operations Regulation
Decree no. 54/2005—Regulations for Public Works Contracts and Supply of Goods and Services to the State, including 100 percent state-owned companies	Decree 24/2004—Petroleum Operations Regulations—Article 38 Procurement:
Definition of Mozambican bidder: more than 50 percent national capital. Options for domestic preferencing within regulations include domestic margins of price preference on tender award: • 10 percent works • 15 percent goods and services • Minimum targets for the percentage of goods of domestic origin (for example, 30 percent of factory door price) • Finance minister allowed to adjust preferences and targets.	The operator shall give preferential treatment to the purchase of local goods and services when such goods and services are internationally comparable in terms of quality, availability, and quantity required and are offered at prices inclusive of taxes not higher than 10 percent of the available imported goods.
Tender evaluation criteria: Presumption in favor of "lowest price" Combined criteria—technical and price—also allowed	The National Petroleum Institute may request the operator to reconsider its awarding decision.

extracts of public procurement regulations with the regulations for local content in Mozambique, where recent discoveries of giant natural gas fields have been made (Spinola 2010).

Box 3.5 outlines what might constitute a typical set of tender procedures to promote local content.[8]

Incentives and Penalties

A number of governments have sought to positively incentivize the behavior of oil and gas companies toward local content. Notable are an array of fiscal incentives. These include allowing investments in the training of nationals to be recoverable against capital and operational costs. An example of this type of

---

Box 3.5

Overview of Typical Tender Procedures to Promote Local Content

- Definitions of local content, including of national citizen, national producer, and goods or services of domestic origin
- The extent to which local content is to be considered in the formulation of procurement and contracting strategies
- The types and eligibility of different contract award procedures, for example, open competition, negotiated contract, exclusive tendering, single sourcing
- Principles for formulating criteria for sourcing local goods and services, including criteria that ensure national suppliers full, fair, and reasonable access to procurement opportunities
- Guidance on what questions should be asked of bidders on local content in invitations to tender, and whether these questions should solicit quantitative information on nationals in the workforce and expenditure on locally produced goods in contract execution, and/or more open, qualitative information on local content activities that better differentiate bids
- The principles for formulating tender evaluation criteria and awarding contracts, specifically the relative weighting of different aspects of local content within the scoring of bids, whether margins of domestic preference will be factored into contractor selection, and the overall way in which the final score on local content is to be integrated across the technical and commercial parts of a bid
- Identification of who is authorized to evaluate bids, who can take the final decision on a contract award, and whether rights of veto are to be afforded to the government or the national oil company
- Formulae for the reporting of contractors' performance on delivering local content
- The tender procedures that shall apply further down the supply chain to the procurement of goods and services by the winners of major contracts.

incentive can be found in Article 61 of the PSA for the Shakh Deniz project in Azerbaijan, which requires the contractor to "provide training for citizens of the Azerbaijan Republic," and stipulates that related "expenditures in excess of two hundred thousand (200,000) Dollars in any year [are] Cost Recoverable."

Other types of incentive include the following:

- Offers by national and provincial authorities to share infrastructure investment costs with oil and gas companies in cases where operational infrastructure concurrently supports local business (for example, port developments, road construction, telecommunications, and water supply).
- The granting of waivers on tariffs for equipment used in petroleum operations, in return for playing a part in delivering the LCP. An example is Australia, where tariff relief on certain equipment is granted in return for demonstrating the provision of full, fair, and reasonable opportunity to Australian suppliers, with particular reference to small- and medium-sized enterprises (SMEs).[9] Brazil has a special custom regime for bonded warehouse for oil and gas platforms. The regime applies to bonded areas located in oil and gas platforms contracted by companies located abroad for research and drilling purposes. The special bonded warehouse may be used in construction or conversion platforms, shipyards, or other manufacturing establishments located by the sea and destined for the construction of marine structures, oil platforms, and modules for such platforms. This measure, which grants full suspension of federal taxes otherwise due on imports, is meant to encourage local assembly, testing, and construction of platforms (Ernst and Young 2012).

Furthermore, some countries, such as Oman, Angola, Kazakhstan, Indonesia, and Saudi Arabia, link the attainment of quotas for employment of national citizens to the right of the operator or foreign suppliers to acquire expatriate visas. This practice creates an incentive to further local content for companies that need highly skilled expatriate staff in critical positions in order to operate efficiently.

Some countries, including Brazil, Kazakhstan, and Indonesia, impose penalties for lack of compliance with LCPs. These range from fines to exclusion from tenders to even the withdrawal of permits and licenses.

Local Content Passed Through to Suppliers and Subcontractors

Contracts for the procurement of goods and services may stipulate minimum levels of local content to be achieved, either in adherence to agreed tender procedures, or as part of an oil or gas company's own interpretation of LCPs (and, in some cases, as a means to deliver a company's corporate social responsibility program). Local content minimum levels may be set by the procuring entity and included in the scope of work or terms of purchase, or they may be proposed by the supplier or contractor as part of a bid and subsequently incorporated into the contract as proposed or in a revised form.

The terms of delivery of an agreed scope of work in a service contract, or the terms and conditions of purchase agreements for the supply of equipment and materials, are binding under contract law. Therefore applicable contract law offers another tool for enforcing LCPs.

Reporting and Monitoring Regulation

A number of countries do not have mandatory reporting requirements for local content, and leave it to individual companies to report as they deem fit. Chapter 4 discusses some of the issues that arise from this approach. Where requirements to report local content performance do exist these may be specified in petroleum sector laws and regulations, or petroleum agreements, or may be detailed in local content laws or regulations, such as in Indonesia, Nigeria, and Brazil. For example, in Indonesia, official procurement guideline PTK 007/ Revision 2, issued by the Upstream Oil and Gas Executive Agency (BPMIGAS), sets out the formulae operators are to use to calculate local content in the procurement of goods.

In some countries rules for local content reporting are mandated through freestanding regulations, dedicated wholly to local content reporting. This is the case in Kazakhstan, where Decree No. 367/2009 provides for a unified methodology to calculate local content in goods, works, and services, and Decree No. 965/2012 sets for the criteria to be used in calculating and reporting local content in the workforce.[10]

The Recruitment, Training, and Promotion of Nationals

Petroleum-producing counties use a variety of policies to improve the quantity and quality of local employment. This section contains a brief outline of such policies and discusses the extent to which they may apply to contractors and subcontractors along the supply chain.

Types of Policy

Local content policies in support of the recruitment and development of national human capital can be grouped into three broad categories:

- *Policies designed to increase the absolute and/or relative number of nationals employed in an organization or workforce.* For example in Angola, Decree No. 5/95 mandates that national and foreign companies can only employ nonresident foreigner workers if at least 70 percent of the workforce is formed by Angolan nationals and the company employs more than five workers.[11]
- *Policies that promote the development of higher technical and managerial skills for national employees.* For example, in Angola, Decree Law 17/09 requires companies who are engaged in petroleum-processing activities to submit, annually, a human resources plan and enter into a contract with the government to

implement this plan. In Azerbaijan this type of arrangement is negotiated in PSAs where the parties agree on the percentage of national citizens that will progress in different job categories over time. Article 6 of the PSA for the Shah Deniz Prospective Area in the Azerbaijan sector of the Caspian between the state oil company, BP, and partners contains the following targets for the employment of national employees:
- Prior to the commencement of development, 30–50 percent professionals and 70 percent nonprofessionals
- Upon the commencement of production, 70 percent professionals and 85 percent nonprofessionals
- Five years after the commencement of petroleum production, 90 percent professionals and 95 percent nonprofessionals.

• Policies designed to restrict the number of foreign workers and the duration of their employment. These policies aim to promote local workforce recruitment and progression. For example, in Angola, Decree 6/01 establishes policy for the recruitment of expatriate workers only if "obtaining confirmation that no Angolan personnel duly qualified to perform the job required is available in the local market." The same decree limits the length of a foreign nonresident contract to 36 months, and allows temporary work by such individuals below 90 days only on the explicit authorization of the Labor Ministry Inspection Department.[12]

Quantitative Targets

The use of targets and quotas in policies for national recruitment, training, and progress appears to be somewhat linked to the maturity of the exploration and production (E&P) sector in that country. For example, Nigeria, Kazakhstan, and Angola, with their mature E&P sectors, all meet quantified expectations for national content in recruitment. Table 3.1 summarizes these targets.

In contrast, based on available information, in the frontier E&P markets of Mozambique, Uganda, and Liberia, no such quantifications are yet apparent.

Table 3.1 Minimum Targets for Local Content in the Workforce: Three Countries Compared

Country	Minimum Target (%)	Metric	Regulation
Nigeria	95	Nigerian national in management position by head count	Local Content Act 2010
	100	Nigeria nationals in junior and intermediate position by head count	
Kazakhstan	70	Kazakh nationals in high level management positions by head count	Decree 45/12
	90	Kazakh technicians, specialists, and workers by head count	
Angola	70	Angolan citizens in the workforce by head count	Decree 5/95

Source: World Bank data.

These countries policies on national recruitment are expressed in general stipulations under petroleum law and production agreements, for example the requirement in Uganda—under Article 123 of the 2012 Petroleum Exploration, Development and Production Bill—that: "The Licensee shall, within twelve months after the grant of a Licence, and on each subsequent anniversary of that grant, submit to the Authority for approval, a detailed programme for recruitment and training of Ugandans … [and that] … The programme shall provide for the training of Ugandans in all phases of petroleum operations."[13]

Article 5.4 of the 2010 Policy Framework for Local Content and Local Participation in Ghana emulates policy in more mature E&P markets—perhaps motivated by expectations arising from the production of the Jubilee field—with the setting targets as follows:

- "at least fifty percent (50%) of the management staff are Ghanaians from the start of petroleum activities of the licensee and the percentage shall increase to at least eighty
- percent (80%) within five (5) years after the start of the petroleum activities;
- core technical staff, at least thirty percent (30%) of the technical staff are Ghanaians from the start of petroleum activities of the licensee and the percentage shall increase to at least eighty percent (80%) within five (5) years after the start of petroleum activities and ninety percent (90%) within ten (10) years; and
- other staff are one hundred percent (100%) Ghanaians"[14]

It is important to note that quantitative local employment targets are not necessarily linked to the maturity of the petroleum sector. Social pressures may also lead regulators to adopt similar policies to those applied in neighboring countries.

Extent of Policy Pass-Through
A key variance in the scope of different local content recruitment policies is the extent to which the associated regulations drive these policies down supply chains. For example, the training and recruitment provisions set forth in Uganda's Petroleum Exploration, Development and Production Bill No. 1/2012 do not explicitly direct the licensee to ensure that its contractors and suppliers abide by the provisions on training and employment of Ugandan nationals set forth in Articles 123 and 124. In contrast, in Liberia, the legal framework for E&P explicitly requires that "the holder of a petroleum contract, as well as his subcontractors, shall give preference to Liberians in the hiring of qualified personnel." Likewise, Article 18 of the 2004 Mozambique Petroleum Operations Regulations (Decree 24/2004) requires that the "Concessionaire shall endeavor to utilize citizens of the Republic of Mozambique having appropriate qualifications to the maximum extent possible at all levels of its organization, as Sub-Contractors or employed by Sub-Contractors."[15]

Domestic Preference

Inherent in some of the legal and regulatory requirements for local recruitment, training, and promotion of nationals is the intent to preference nationals over foreign workers. The setting of mandatory targets carries the possibility that lower-skilled or less-experienced nationals may be preferred over more-skilled or more-experienced foreign workers. To reduce this risk, some local labor policies clarify when such a preference is to be granted. For example, the quoted 2002 Petroleum Law of Liberia preferences Liberians in the hiring of personnel "provided the Liberians meet the need and requirements of the operations." Other local recruitment policies are more flexible, promoting what might be described as best endeavors. For example, in Tanzania, the 2008 model PSA requires the contractor to "employ Tanzanian citizens having appropriate qualifications to the maximum extent possible."

In Nigeria targets and preferences for national recruitment, training, and promotion are mandated by a combination of primary legislation and intervention by the regulator. Article 35 of the 2010 Nigerian Content Development Act requires that only Nigerians be employed "in junior and intermediate cadre [positions]." It is then left to the regulator—the Nigerian Content Development Monitoring Board—to agree with oil and gas companies on the minimum percentage of Nigerian labor in different job grades. This is mandated under Article 24 of the Nigerian Content Development Act, which requires a "Labor Clause" to be inserted in project agreements (or similar contracts) mandating the use of a minimum percentage of Nigerian labor in specified job levels.

Sourcing of Goods and Services

Given the relatively low level of direct employment in the E&P of oil and gas compared to other sectors, the development of domestic suppliers of goods and services is one of the possible benefits of petroleum exploitation. This section provides an overview of policies commonly utilized in petroleum-producing countries to strengthen or develop the local supply industry. A typology is proposed based on the degree to which a policy may depart from free market principles.

Competitiveness of Contract Award

Most petroleum codes and contracts require that the holders of petroleum E&P rights afford some measure of preference for domestic goods and services. The domestic content provision may be quite limited, or may contain elaborate criteria to compare and select from among competing suppliers. Examples of local preference provisions are shown in box 3.6.

Indeed, policies for the sourcing of local goods and services can be classified on the basis of their compliance with competitive market principles. In general terms, the further a policy is from the principle of competitiveness, the higher

Box 3.6

Examples of Local Preference Provisions from Three Countries

In **Chad** the local preference provision requires the licensee to "give priority to those goods and services available in Chad insofar as their prices, qualities, quantities, delivery terms and sales conditions compare to goods and services available aboard and do not require the licensee to bear any kind of extra economic burden."

A similar principle is set forth in **Timor-Leste's** model petroleum contract, where the contractor is required to "give preference to the acquisition of goods and services from persons based in Timor-Leste, provided they are offered on competitive terms and conditions." Equatorial **Guinea's** model petroleum sharing contract requires that "The Contractor and its subcontractors undertake to give preference to Equatoguinean services, materials, equipment, consumables and other goods whose quality and time of delivery are comparable to those available internationally, provided that the cost in Equatorial Guinea is no more than ten percent (10 percent) above the cost of similar services, materials, equipment, consumables and other goods available internationally."

the costs and sustainability risks associated with its implementation. This approach is followed in table 3.2, which groups local sourcing policies and regulations into three categories:

- Policies that involve the setting of local content targets
- Policies built around a margin of preference to domestic suppliers
- Policies that use the process of contractor selection to grant unfair advantage to local suppliers.

Table 3.2 Local Sourcing Policies and Competitive Contract Awards: Principles

Types of Local Content Policies	Awards Contracts on an Internationally Competitive Basis? (Yes/No)
Minimum targets	
Blanket minimum local content targets—intentionally exceeds price competitiveness of domestic supplier industry in order to drive inward investment	**Possibly** (In some subcategories of expenditure local suppliers will be competitive, in others not)
Disaggregated minimum local content targets—in each case exceeding price competitiveness of domestic suppliers in order to drive inward investment	**Possibly** (Until and unless inward investment is forthcoming and successful in driving domestic competitiveness)
Disaggregated minimum local content targets for expenditure—within domestic limits of international price competitiveness	**Yes**
Local supplier preferences	
Domestic-only tender lists—benchmarked against capability, but not internationally competitive on price, quality, and delivery	**No**

(table continues on next page)

Table 3.2 Local Sourcing Policies and Competitive Contract Awards: Principles *(continued)*

Types of Local Content Policies	Awards Contracts on an Internationally Competitive Basis? (Yes/No)
Domestic-only tender lists—benchmarked against international competitiveness	**Yes**
Full, fair, and reasonable access to procurement opportunities for domestic suppliers	**Yes**
Mandated foreign/domestic consortia or subcontractor alliances	**Possibly** (If foreign suppliers assure the overall competitiveness of the bid—for example, through additional supervision, training, or up-front investment)
Minimum participation of domestic subcontractors/ suppliers in contracts awarded to foreign suppliers (by $ value)	**No** (If this leads to uncompetitive pricing)
Minimum national ownership of suppliers awarded contracts	**No** (If this leads to uncompetitive pricing)
Preference to domestic suppliers so long as performance, quality, and time of delivery are competitive with international performance and prices	**Yes**
Nominal price advantage to domestic suppliers compared to import price, including transport and duties	**No**
Process of Contract Award and Execution	
Reduced prequalification criteria for domestic suppliers	**Possibly** (Does not necessarily imply contract award on an uncompetitive basis
Bid evaluation—all things being equal, preference local suppliers or highest levels of local content	**Yes**
Economically advantageous basis for contract award, that is, the application of weightings or coefficients that reward a bidder's proposal on local content alongside other technical attributes such as health, safety, environment, and management quality, as well as against the bid price[a]	**No** (If award is contracted on the basis of higher levels of local sourcing)
Contract award veto for government authorities on tender board on basis of insufficient local content or inadequate local content plan	**No** (If veto is exercised without due regard to the principle of contract award on an internationally competitive basis)
Advance payments to domestic suppliers, for example 30 percent	**Not necessarily** (Need for advance payment is indicator of supplier having insufficient access to credit)
Minimum training obligations for nationals, such as first consideration to nationals for training, targets by cost, or training hours	**Yes** (If applied equally to all bidders)
Minimum obligations for growing competitiveness of domestic suppliers, for example, minimum investment requirements, minimum training obligations beyond that needed for contract execution	**Yes** (If applied equally to all bidders)
Obligations to report on local content performance	**Yes** (If not tied to mandatory minimum targets that breach domestic competitiveness)

Source: Adapted from Warner 2011.
Note:
a. This can be achieved in various manners. For example, (1) the contract award may go to the bidder who receives the highest score on local content as a share of the total available score for all technical plus commercial proposals; (2) more complex coefficients may impose a penalty on the bid price (that is, increase the bid price) of those bidders whose proposals on local content are at variance with the score of the highest scoring proposal; or (3) the contract may be awarded on the basis of the lowest technically acceptable price.

Local Sourcing Policies Involving Targets

Policies that involve the setting of targets for local sourcing are not inherently protectionist. This depends on where the target is set in relation to the capability, capacity, and competitiveness of the local supply industry.

In Brazil local content targets in procurement associated with the criteria for the award of petroleum exploration and production rights have changed over the years. The first licensing rounds set global minimum targets for local procurement that operators and their partners—including the national oil company, Petrobras—were obligated meet. The targets were global—that is, they referred to the total aggregation of local content across all categories of spending in either the exploration phase or development phase.

Later licensing rounds set both global targets and subtargets for each subcategory of expenditure. For example, round 7 in 2007 established a global minimum of 37 percent local content for all expenditure during exploration, and targets for individual segments of spending, including 40 percent for the interpretation of geological survey data, 10 percent for logistical support to drilling and completion services, and 95 percent for detailed engineering for field production systems (Guimaraes 2011).

We may question whether these targets represent the capabilities, quality, delivery, and price competitiveness of the Brazilian upstream petroleum supplier market. If so, then arguably supplier and subcontractor contracts would have been awarded on an internationally competitive basis. If not, then:

- Price premiums would have been paid to provide for additional management, quality control supervision, critical investments, and training
- Local and international suppliers would have been expected to invest capital to improve in-country capabilities and competitiveness
- No premiums would be paid, but standards of quality, delivery, and reliability would have been allowed to fall below international standards.

Table 3.3 lists which subcategory targets in the Brazilian upstream petroleum industry might have been set at above or below the threshold of international competitiveness (Fried 2011). In this example, which has not been independently validated, valves produced in Brazil were found to be 10–30 percent more expensive than those of international suppliers, but delivery times were faster than sourcing internationally; heat pressure vessels were found to be 30–50 percent more expensive, with faster delivery times. The study did not take into account the effect of faster delivery times, and did not specify whether the contract price included service and maintenance arrangements for which faster delivery would command a premium.

Local Sourcing Policies Involving Margins of Preference

Rules and criteria aimed to afford special preference to domestic firms are very common in petroleum contracts, regulations, and associated tender procedures. A typical clause might read as follows: *The Operator shall give preferential*

Table 3.3 Relative Pricing of Brazilian-Produced Equipment

Product Families	Price (Brazilian Market)	Delivery Time (Brazilian Market)
Pumps	Similar	Better
Valves	10–30% more expensive	Better
Pipes	20–40% more expensive	Similar
Pipes accessories	30–50% more expensive	Better
Pressure vessels	30–50% more expensive	Good
Heat exchanger	30–40% more expensive	Good
Instrumentation	20% more expensive	Good
Electrical		
- Panels	- Similar	- Better
- Cables	- 10–15% more expensive	- Good

Source: Adapted from Fried 2011.

*treatment to the purchase of local goods and services when such goods and services
are internationally comparable in terms of quality, availability, quantity required,
and are offered at prices inclusive of taxes not higher than ten percent [10 percent]
of the available imported goods.*

A more stringent form of domestic preference places restrictions on operators
such that only national firms are eligible to tender for certain categories of goods
and services. This policy does not necessarily imply that contracts are awarded
on an uncompetitive basis. It is possible that goods and services on the restricted
list are available in-country at prices and quality that are competitive with international suppliers. But these rules contravene the principle of open international
competition, and can sometimes affect companies' decisions and strategies with
respect to the incorporation of local subsidiaries. For example in Angola,
Ministerial Order 127/03 establishes an exclusive procurement regime whereby
categories of expenditure are reserved for Angolan-owned companies (see
box 3.7). The list comprises activities "not requiring heavy capital investment
and with a basic, medium or higher level of nonspecialized know-how, where
foreign companies shall only take part on the initiative of Angolan companies."

The 2010 Nigerian Oil and Gas Industry Content Development Act goes
further, stipulating not only local sourcing targets for a wide range of goods and
services but also, under Article 41(b), requiring that international companies
operating as Nigerian-registered companies "shall demonstrate that a minimum
of 50 percent of the equipment deployed in the execution of work be owned
by Nigerian subsidiaries." This means that international companies that wish to
be eligible to tender for work in Nigeria have to place into Nigerian ownership
(that is, local companies with greater than 51 percent Nigerian equity) at least
50 percent of their equipment and technologies to be used in the contract.[16]

The advantage of this particular policy for technology transfer to the Nigerian
economy is clear. But the policy is also not without challenges. These obligations
may challenge the ability of equipment producers and service suppliers to protect propriety technologies. Meanwhile, not finding solutions to this challenge
may prevent these companies from accessing local markets.

Box 3.7

Overview of Typical Tender Procedures to Promote Local Content: Angola

The following list draws from Article 2, Order No. 127/03 on General Regulatory Framework on the Contracting of Services and Goods from Angolan Companies by Petroleum Industry Companies:

- Pressure tests for storage tanks and oil and/or gas pipelines
- Transport of equipment, materials, and foodstuffs, or drilling and production platforms
- Supply of industrial and drinking water
- Catering
- Supply of technical materials
- General cleaning and gardening
- General maintenance of equipment and vehicles
- Supply postoperators and managers (airports, ports, and service stations)
- Quality inspection of products distributed and marketed (oil products and derivatives)
- Retail sales of kerosene, gas, and lubricants
- Transport of products from terminals to supply posts.

Local Sourcing Policies Using Contract Award

The process of contractor selection is central to a number of policies and regulations pertaining to local content. The two most influential components of this process, vendor prequalification and tender evaluation, are discussed below.

Vendor Prequalification

Prequalification is the process of sieving potential vendors—suppliers of equipment and materials or service providers—to determine if they might be suited to participate in a competitive tender process. There is often considerable debate within the procurement departments of both national and international oil and gas companies, as to whether the criteria adopted to prequalify vendors should be relaxed to avoid excluding local suppliers and contractors from an opportunity to participate in tenders. On the one hand, the procuring entity is concerned by the possibility that substandard vendors may be allowed to bid—particularly on contracts that require minimum levels of health and safety, quality and management experience—as this could affect project implementation leading to delays, cost overruns, and/or accidents. Vendors' prequalification criteria most commonly used in the petroleum E&P sector are adaptations of criteria applied in mature petroleum sectors—specifically the North Sea and the Gulf of Mexico. As such, these criteria may not be appropriate to many emerging economies and frontier countries. To accommodate both local content and procuring entities' objectives, it may be necessary to allow some flexibility in prequalification criteria, taking into account the level of risk that their relaxation may entail. For example, the requirement that all local suppliers submit certified accounts for the previous three years may exclude the participation of newly formed suppliers that are well financed, well stocked, staffed with employees with considerable experience in the product in question, have signed long-term agreements with original equipment manufacturers, and have tooled up for installation and maintenance.

On the other hand, a rigorous prequalification process may help local vendors to understand and address their weaknesses. Local vendors that successfully obtain prequalification may become more attractive to international partners. Often an alliance with an international partner allows a local vendor to fast track the learning curve with regard to good industry practices in quality assurance and health, safety and the environment (HSE), and provides management and supervisory oversight during contract execution. In summary, because of both the risks involved and the benefits for increasing local content and building local industrial capabilities, introducing some flexibility in prequalification criteria is an important policy consideration.

Tender Evaluation

The tender evaluation criteria and weightings in contract awards are important tools to support and drive LCPs. Depending on the legal framework, policy makers may be able to require procuring entities to introduce tender evaluation criteria that support government LCP objectives. For example, thresholds can be introduced: vendors may become ineligible for contract awards should they not meet minimum targets for local content, such as for the recruitment of nationals or sourcing of local goods and services. Alternatively, criteria can be set that reward vendors for higher levels of local content or more investment in developing local skills and supplier capabilities.

Furthermore, the relative weight assigned to each criterion, as well as the absolute weight that local content carries among overall criteria (which will usually include technical capability and commercial terms) need to be given careful consideration. For example, should policy makers wish to emphasize the training of nationals and their progression into management positions, the relevant scores can be given a higher weight compared to that assigned to the score related to, say, the proportion of equipment sourced from locally based suppliers. Also the relative weight of the aggregate score for all tender parameters related to local content, may range from 3 percent to 40 percent of the overall technical score, or may be blended into a combined final score for technical plus commercial.

In practice, it is more likely that local content will command a lower weight in contract award in cases where the opportunities to use local labor or materials is weak. This might include contracts for drilling services, proprietary equipment, or specialist engineering design services. In contrast, one might expect local content within logistics and accommodation contracts to command higher weighting.

Pass-Through Obligations

The scope of application of LCPs in procurement—that is, how far down the supply chains they are designed to penetrate—largely depends on the maturity of the local petroleum industry. In frontier countries, with a few exceptions, the setting of targets for sourcing local goods and services and the use of margins of domestic preference are aimed primarily at transactions between the operating company and their direct suppliers and contractors. In more mature petroleum settings, local content targets, and margins of preference are cascaded to lower tiers of suppliers. The recently mandated formulae for reporting local content in Kazakhstan illustrates a policy of driving local content regulations down through supply chains. The Republic of Kazakhstan Decree 964/2010 mandates a unified method for calculating local content in the procurement of goods, works, and services.[17] The formula explicitly requires the measurement of the proportion of Kazakh labor and goods in both first- and lower-tier subcontracts and suppliers. In brief, the method involves tracking both the level of local content delivered by the primary contract holder through its direct suppliers and contractors, as well as the local content delivered by the first-tier contractors and suppliers in fulfillment of the contract. For each of these first- and lower-tier tranches of the original contract, the foreign component of labor or goods is deducted. The local content figure is then the total of the residual local value of each tranche, presented as a proportion of the original contract sum. A similar approach is taken to driving LCP in supply chains in Brazil.[18]

The choice of metric has a strong bearing on the implementation outcomes of a policy on local sourcing.[19] For example, if the metric for setting targets for local content in the purchase of equipment is based on whether the supplier is owned by national citizens, the policy will drive national ownership, and the outcome will be wealth creation for (some) national citizens. The black economic empowerment rules in South Africa were originally conceived along these lines after the end of apartheid. On the other hand, if the metric is defined as a combination of different economic empowerment indicators, including (1) the number of nationals employed by the supplier, (2) the number of nationals in management positions, (3) the value-added to the product in-country, and (4) ownership, then achieving higher levels of local content (assuming the weightings of these different indicators in any tender evaluation are evenly balanced) would have a broader economic impact. This is indeed how the South African regulations evolved, with a shift toward broad-based black economic empowerment, founded on a weighted scorecard of different local sourcing metrics.[20]

Local Content versus Local Content Development

In the upstream E&P sector most countries continue to rely on setting ambitious targets for local content combined with margins of domestic preference as primary mechanisms for developing national industrial capabilities. Few policy makers seem to have considered how to regulate for local content development in the sector, as opposed to local content level—in other words, how to drive the development of competitive, capable, and sustainable local skills and supply industries, rather than simply driving an increased share of local content in total expenditure, regardless of its competitiveness and long-term sustainability.

Indeed, if not carefully designed, LCPs run the risk of entrenching unproductive practices, higher costs, and lower quality for lack of competition. This risk is probably greatest in emerging countries with mature or large-scale upstream petroleum sectors. In Brazil, Mexico, Nigeria, Indonesia, the Russian Federation, and Kazakhstan, the sheer scale and potential profitability of existing and future business opportunities in the E&P sector, afford these governments considerable power to set stringent local content regulations. Box 3.8 provides examples of alternative policy design.

Box 3.8

Sustainable Local Content Policies: Brazil, Indonesia, and Australia

In **Brazil** the strong local content policy (LCP) framework and regulations have driven an increasing share of local employment, goods and services, and are contributing to reestablish Brazil as a shipbuilding nation. Brazilian regulations mandate targets for goods and services of domestic origin. In this sense, they encourage the emergence of a competitive local supply industry by incentivizing inward investment by international suppliers and service contractors that strive to meet these targets. If set too high compared to existing and short-term local supply capability, policy targets might reward less than competitive suppliers. Some industry observers have voiced concerns over the extent to which the industrial base that is being constructed through the current mandatory local content targets is competitive and sustainable, when compared to similar industries in China, South Korea, Singapore, and Norway.[21]

Local content regulations in **Indonesia** are also based on targets, but oil and gas companies (and their lead suppliers and service contractors) can achieve higher scores (that is, reach the targets more efficiently) if they execute work in ways that actively develop local industry. The effective local content of a company in executing work can be nominally increased by up to 15 percent if the company demonstrates success in one or more of four areas of local capacity development:

- Empowering domestic suppliers to partner and cooperate in small enterprises (weighted 30 percent of the maximum achievable 15 percent elevation)
- Achieving certification OHSAS 18,000 or SMK/ISO 14,000 (weighted 20 percent)
- Contributing to community development/corporate social responsibility (weighted 30 percent)
- Providing an after-sales service facility based in Indonesia (weighted 20 percent).

Australia's LCP is designed to promote the development of a sustainable local industry, while abiding closely to international obligations on trade and competition law. Thus, incentives, rather than mandated obligations, are the crucial policy tool. One of the most notable

(box continues on next page)

Box 3.8 Sustainable Local Content Policies: Brazil, Indonesia, and Australia *(continued)*

incentives is the exemption from import tariff on equipment related to petroleum operations—where such equipment is proven not to be available in Australia—granted to oil companies and service companies in exchange for the formulation and execution of an Australian Industry Participation (AIP) plan. The criteria adopted by the federal government to assess AIP plans include the anticipated impact of the investments on employment of nationals and participation of Australian suppliers, and take into account whether the project will:

- Introduce new or enhanced skills into the Australian workforce
- Encourage efforts to develop strategic alliances with Australian suppliers
- Promote regional development
- Support Australian research and development activities
- Create innovative products and/or processes
- Integrate Australian industry into global supply chains.[22]

Furthermore, companies bidding for large Commonwealth procurement contracts (over $20 million) may be required to prepare and implement an AIP plan. The process provides a mechanism for potential suppliers to familiarize themselves with the capabilities of small- and medium-sized enterprises and to identify qualified suppliers.

Classification of LCPs by Channel of Intervention and Transversality

As discussed in chapter 2, LCPs in the oil and gas sector would generally fall under the category of vertical market interventions (VM quadrant; see table 2.1) since these policies affect the market of certain goods. Using the terminology of Harrison and Rodriguez-Clare (2010), these interventions support activities in specific sectors. But this is not always the case. Some forms of local sourcing regulations could very well be classified as a sector-specific public good (VP). The distinction between regulations that are VP and VM will depend on their objective, design, and implementation. For example, regulation aimed at solving issues of market power—such as a law or regulation on fair access of local suppliers—would in principle provide a public good. A similar case could be argued with respect to some forms of recruitment policies. In this case, too, the key issue is where the target is set in relation to local capabilities. Regulations that call for local employment, but only where local skills meet the need and requirements of the specific operation, aim to address certain market inefficiencies and tend to generate less distortion. This type of intervention could also be classified as VP.

Training targets set by regulation are another interesting case, in that they may be classified as VM depending on their objectives, design, and implementation. As discussed earlier in this chapter, the market equilibrium for training could be less than optimal. This is an argument for intervention to encourage training trough general incentives policies (HM). But if training obligations are imposed only on the oil and gas sector, the policy would then fall under VM.

The extent of the regulatory requirement could also affect the classification of the policy. Broad requirements, such as blanked requirements for the sector or for employment, are closer to HM policies than disaggregated targets by sector or by job category. Given the specific requirements of the oil and gas sector, it is hard to classify blanket requirements as "pure" HM policies, but they are clearly less "vertical" than disaggregated targets. Similarly, regulation that establishes pass-through local content obligations also makes the policy more VM.

Keeping in mind that policy objectives, design, and implementation determine the classification of a policy, figure 3.2 proposes an a priori classification of some of the policy tools discussed in this chapter, and depicts a continuum along the two axes as opposed to the clear demarcation of quadrants (as shown in chapter 2, table 2.1) so as to represent cases in which the channel of intervention is neither a pure public input or a full market intervention, and the transversality of the intervention is neither fully horizontal nor fully vertical.

Figure 3.2 shows that the more a policy intervention disregards competitiveness and simply imposes minimum shares of local goods and services instead of focusing on activity outcomes, the more such an intervention moves to the right-hand side of the matrix. It is worth stressing that design and implementation will

Figure 3.2 Classification of Local Content Policies by Channel of Intervention and Transversality

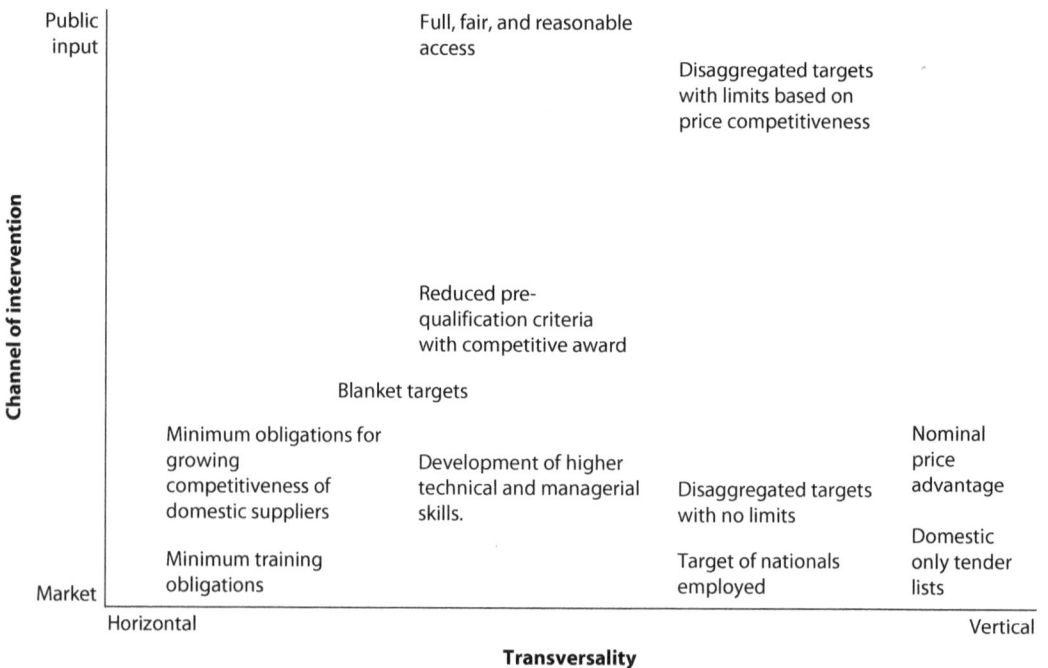

drive the outcome and classification of the intervention. But in general terms policies that are either more horizontal or done through public inputs would be less prone to capture by local interests.

Conclusion

Local content is a complex and fast-evolving area. Until quite recently most international oil and gas companies viewed local content as part of their corporate social responsibility agenda. But a plethora of new government policies and regulations has shifted local content into a compliance regime. Indeed, many oil companies have recently introduced new positions at headquarters and individual operations dedicated to ensuring compliance with regulations on the recruitment of nationals, expenditure on local suppliers, and reporting of local content performance. Likewise, legal, finance, procurement, and human resource functions within these companies have modified their internal procedures to assure compliance with local content requirements. In addition, most companies in countries with local content regulations now have their own stated policies and strategies on local and national content, designed in part to align closely with the regulatory requirements.

At present, policies and regulations on local content differ widely among countries. In some countries, governments would rather "encourage" local content, with incentives for training, and targets that are aspirational but not mandated. Other countries, primarily those with more mature upstream petroleum industries, impose "assertive" regulations that mandate targets and oblige preferencing of nationals and local suppliers. Other countries—like Tanzania and Uganda for the time being—can be considered "neutral" on local content, providing some indication that local recruitment and local sourcing is preferable, but with few incentives or obligations to drive the policy.

Most LCPs rely on setting ambitious targets for local participation combined with mechanisms—regulations, incentives, tariffs, and so on—that afford a preference for domestic labor and suppliers. Few countries appear to have devised local content implementation strategies predicated on the development of competitive, capable, and sustainable local labor and supply industries.

Notes

1. The reader is referred to: Enhancing National Participation in the Oil and Gas Industry in Uganda, Ministry of Energy and Mineral Development (http://wildugandablog.com/wp-content/uploads/2010/06/national-oil-and-gas-policy-for-uganda.pdf); Local Content and Local Participation in Petroleum Activities, Ministry of Energy, Republic of Ghana. (http://ghanaoilwatch.org/images/laws/local_content_policy.pdf); and Local Content and Local Participation Policy Framework for the Republic of Trinidad and Tobago, Ministry of Energy and Energy Industries (http://energy.gov.tt/content/Local_Content_&_Local_Participation_Framework.pdf).

2. Law on Subsoil and Subsoil Users in Kazakhstan, No. 291-IV, June 2010, Republic of Kazakhstan. http://www.eisourcebook.org/cms/Kazakhstan%20Law%20of%20 Subsoil%20and%20Subsoil%20Use%202010.pdf, and Resolution of the Republic of Kazakhstan (dated November 28, 2007) 1139 on ratification of Regulations for Acquisition of Goods, Works and Services While Performing Operations on Subsurface Use (with changes as of January 4, 2010)—http://camng.kz/en/3-e/ 3-22-e/3-2-e/337-5.html.

3. The bill is downloadable from http://www.nogicjqs.com/NOGICD_Act_2010.pdf.

4. The full text of the regulations is available at http://www.inp.gov.mz/content/download/180/742/file/Petroleum%20Operations%20(Revised%20English%20 Translation).pdf.

5. The full text of the regulations is available at http://www.global-edgeconsulting.com/ wp-content/uploads/2011/11/ANGOLA-DECREE-127-03.pdf.

6. The reader is referred to, Decree No. 965/2012 on the Approval of the Forms and Rules for Preparation and Submission of the Annual, Medium-Term and Long-Term Programs of Procurement of Goods, Work and Services, Subsoil Users' Reports on Acquired Goods, Work and Services and on the Fulfillment of Obligations on Local Content in Personnel, Government of the Republic of Kazakhstan.

7. The reader is referred to articles 18 on Tanzania Resources and 19 on Employment, Training, and Transfer of Technology. The full text of the model agreement is available at http://www.tpdc-tz.com/MPSA%20_2008.pdf.

8. It is worth noting that specific tender procedures are normally confidential documents. The information contained in box 3.5 draws from the authors' experience with tender procedures in several countries, and is provided for illustration purposes only.

9. See Australian Industry Participation Plan Guide for the Enhanced Project By-Laws Scheme, Version 1.1 April 2010: http://www.ausindustry.gov.au/programs/importexport/epbs/Documents/EPBS-AIPPlanGuide.pdf.

10. See Decree No. 367/2009 on Single Methodology to Calculate Kazakhstani Content Pertaining to Purchased Goods, Works and Services, and Decree No. 965/2012 on Approval of the Forms and Rules for Preparation and Submission of the Annual, Medium-Term and Long-Term Programs of Procurement of Goods, Work and Services, Subsoil Users' Reports on Acquired Goods, Work and Services and on the Fulfillment of Obligations on Local Content in Personnel.

11. Decree No 5/95 on the Employment of Foreign Citizens Non-Resident is downloadable from http://www.sme.ao/attachments/article/209/Decree%20No.%205-95%20 of%20April%207%20-%20Employment%20of%20Foreign%20Citizens%20 Non-resident.pdf.

12. Decree 6/01 governing the Exercise of Professional Activity of the Non-resident Foreign Worker, can be downloaded from http://www.sme.ao/attachments/ article/219/Decree%20No.%206-01%20of%20January%2019%20-%20 Regulation%20on%20the%20Exercise%20of%20Professional%20Activity%20of%20 the%20Non-resident%20Foreign%20Worker.pdf.

13. Petroleum Exploration, Development and Production Bill, NO.1/2012, Ministry of Energy and Mineral Development, Republic of Uganda—http://www.acode-u.org/ documents/oildocs/Petroleum_(EDP)_Bill_2012.pdf.

14. Policy Framework for Local Content and Local Participation, Ministry of Energy, Republic of Ghana (February 2010)—http://ghanaoilwatch.org/images/laws/local_content_policy.pdf.

15. See Decree 24/2004 governing Petroleum Operations Regulations in Mozambique http://www.inp.gov.mz/content/download/180/742/file/Petroleum%20 Operations%20(Revised%20English%20Translation).pdf.

16. Local content targets specified in the Act include the following 100 percent of steel plates by tonnage, 45 percent of high voltage cables by length, 80 percent of well-completion services by spending, and 50 percent of engineering on liquid natural gas (LNG) projects by man-hours, and 100 percent of all fabrication and welding services.

17. Unified Methodology of Calculation by Organizations of Kazakhstan (Local) Content in Case of Procurement of Goods, Work and Services, Decree No. 964 of September 2010 (http://www.kca.kz/files/files/PPRK_ob_utverg.Edinoi_metodiki_ras.ks_TRU.html).

18. For a detailed discussion of local content measurement in Kazakhstan and Brazil the reader is referred to Local Content in Oil and Gas: Case Studies, downloadable from http://issuu.com/world.bank.publications/docs/local_content_policies_in_the_oil_and_gas_sector.

19. This is further discussed in chapter 4.

20. See for example, subsection Code Series 500 on the Measurement of the Preferential Procurement Element of Broad-Based Black Economic Empowerment, in the Broad-Based Black Economic Empowerment Act (53/2003): Codes of Good Practice on Black Economic Empowerment, gazette in February 2007.

21. See for example, "Brazil oilfield reveals local sourcing problem", Financial Times, June 30, 2011 (http://www.ft.com/cms/s/0/fbaba8a2-a341-11e0-8d6d-00144feabdc0.html#axzz209yHb9DY).

22. Enhanced Project By-law Scheme, Developing and Implementing Australian Industry Participation Plans, Department for Innovation, Industry, Science and Research (DIISR), Federal Government of Australia. http://www.innovation.gov.au/INDUSTRY/AUSTRALIANINDUSTRYPARTICIPATION/Pages/EnhancedProject By-lawScheme.aspx.

References

Ernst and Young. 2012. "Global Oil and Gas Tax Guide." http://www.ey.com/Publication/vwLUAssets/2012-global-oil-and-gas-tax-guide/$FILE/EY_Oil_Gas_Tax_Guide_2012.pdf.

Fried, A. 2011. *Supply Chain Opportunities with Petrobras*. San Diego, CA: Universal Consensus. http://www.scribd.com/doc/90945336/19/Local-Content-Requirement-Prominp.

Gholzani, K. 2010. "Clients Metrics for Measuring Local Content: Brazil Experience," 14th African Oil, Gas and Minerals, Trade and Finance Conference and Exhibition, São Tomé and Príncipe, November 24.

Guimaraes, A. 2011. "Opportunities and Challenges to Maximise Local Content in Brazil: A View from the Brazilian Petroleum Institute." Presentation at IPQC Local Content Summit, The Bloomsbury Hotel, London, United Kingdom, September 27–28.

Harrison, A., and A. Rodriguez-Clare. 2010. "Trade, Foreign Investment, and Industrial Policy." In *Handbook of Development Economics*, edited by D. Rodrik, and M. Rosenzweig, vol. 5. Amsterdam: Elsevier.

Spinola, M. 2010. "Public Procurement in Mozambique." MGA&PLMJ Avogados. http://www.legal500.com/assets/images/stories/firmdevs/public_procurement.pdf.

Tordo, S. 2007. "Fiscal Systems for Hydrocarbons: Design Issues." World Bank Working Paper 123/07, World Bank, Washington, DC.

Tordo, S., with D. Johnston and D. Johnston. 2009. "Petroleum Exploration and Production Rights: Allocation Strategies and Design Issues." World Bank Working Paper 179/09, World Bank, Washington, DC.

Warner, M. 2011. *Local Content in Procurement: Creating Local Jobs and Competitive Domestic Supply Chains*. London: Greenleaf Publishing.

## CHAPTER 4

Policy Metrics

*When you run the marathon, you run against the distance,
not against the other runners and not against the time.*
—Haile Gebrselassie

Performance metrics, indicators, and formulae form a central part of petroleum companies' local content strategy and governments' local content regulations. The importance of the choice of metric to measure local content cannot be overemphasized; often, metrics ultimately drive company and regulator behavior.

To illustrate this point, if an oil field service company is required by the regulator to meet 35 percent local content as a minimum prerequisite to tender for work, then it matters whether this metric is defined as 35 percent by head count of nationals in the workforce, or 35 percent by share of total gross salaries paid to nationals (as is the case for certain service contracts in Indonesia).[1] In the former case, the service provider may be able to satisfy the requirement simply by ensuring that all semiskilled and administrative positions in the workforce are nationals, while in the latter the service provider may be compelled to establish a comprehensive workforce succession program that ensures that nationals are trained or recruited to assume higher-paying skilled and management positions to achieve the target 35 percent share over time. The Nigerian Oil and Gas Industry Content Development Act (2010) identifies minimum Nigerian content targets for the procurement of local materials and services. This includes the requirement for 70 percent by tonnage of work in the fabrication of accommodations to be carried out in Nigeria. What if instead of tonnage the metric had been man-hours of national labor, or the value added to the domestic economy? Would these alternative metrics drive different behavior by the contractor executing the fabrication work? Would the contractor become less productive over time? Would more or less jobs be created? In short, in managing local content, metrics matter.

This chapter gives an overview of metrics commonly applied to measure and report performance in local content in the oil and gas sector. The advantages and disadvantages of selected metrics are discussed, and a comprehensive inventory of metrics is provided.

Categories of Metrics

The metrics adopted in the oil and gas sector fall into two broad categories, as shown in figure 4.1. These include metrics that measure:

• The extent to which national citizens or domestic suppliers are able to capture expenditure by oil and gas companies on labor and on goods and services, for example through the number of nationals by head count within a workforce or expenditure with locally based or locally owned suppliers engaged in contract execution

• The efforts of a company, government, or supplier to grow its share of local content over time, for example by building skills in the national workforce through training and education, or investing in developing the capabilities and competitiveness of domestic supply chains.

Tables 4.1 and 4.2 contain an inventory of the metrics most commonly used to measure local content and local content development. Table 4.1 indicate where the data are likely to be sourced from, the level of confidence in the reported local content, and the administrative simplicity of the collection and data reporting process. For metrics that are designed to measure expenditure on local suppliers, an indication is given of how far into the supply chains the metric penetrates, and at what stage of the procurement process data need to be captured. Table 4.2 contains measures of inputs, such as the cost of training

Figure 4.1 Categories of Local Content Metrics in the Oil and Gas Sector

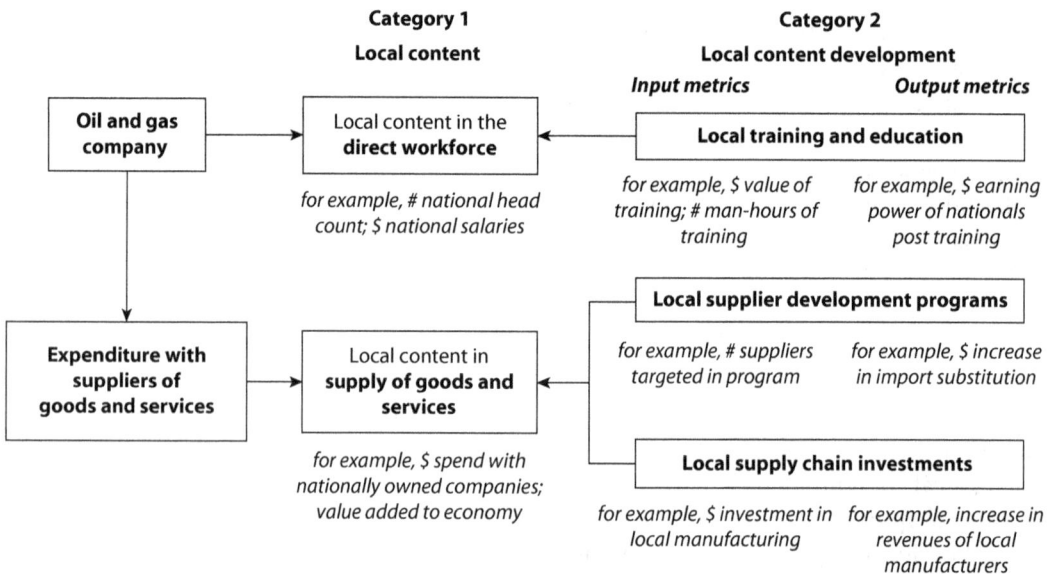

Source: World Bank data.

Table 4.1 Metrics for Measuring Local Content

Workforce

Metric	Key Feature	Information Source	Supply Chain Penetration	Stage of Procurement	Expenditure Category	Confidence in Data	Simplicity to Administer
# FTE national citizens employed as % of total	**Head count**	Human Resources data	n.a.	n.a.	OPEX	Good	Simple
# FTE national citizens in Senior, Supervisory and Skilled positions (or other job or grade disaggregation)	**Head count by job type**	Human Resources data	n.a.	n.a.	OPEX	Moderate	Simple
# man-hours of national labour per year	**Man-hours**	Human Resources data	n.a.	n.a.	OPEX	Good	Simple
$ value of wages, benefits and social taxes paid to FTE national citizens employed as % of total	**Wages**		n.a.	n.a.	OPEX	Good	Moderate
$ value of wages, benefits and social taxes paid to FTE national citizens in Senior, Supervisory and Skilled positions (or other job or grade disaggregation), as % of total	**Wages by job type**	Human Resources data	n.a.	n.a.	OPEX	Moderate	Moderate
$ value of wages, benefits and social taxes paid to FTE national citizens employed and $ value of social taxes and expenses paid to expats, as % of total	**National wages and Expat expenses/taxes**	Human Resources data	n.a.	n.a.	OPEX	Good	Moderate

Services and goods

Metric	Key Feature	Information Source	Supply Chain Penetration	Stage of Procurement	Expenditure Category	Confidence in Data	Simplicity to Administer
# nationally registered vendors on company vendor register	**Vendor register**	Company vendor register	1st Tier	Vendor registration	CAPEX or OPEX	Good	Simple
# community-based vendors on company vendor register	**Vendor register - community**	Company vendor register	1st Tier	Vendor registration	CAPEX or OPEX	Moderate	Moderate
# contracts awarded to nationally registered vendors	**Tax registered**	Contracts Plan	1st Tier	Commitments (contract award)	CAPEX or OPEX	Good	Simple
# contracts awarded to nationally owned vendor (>50% equity), as % of total	**National equity**	National Company Register/ Company Vendor Register/ Contracts Plan	1st Tier	Contract award	CAPEX or OPEX	Poor/ Moderate	Complex/ Moderate
$ value of contracts awarded to vendors with office address (PO or Invoice) within the country, as % of total	**Office address - national**	Contracts Plan/ Company Vendor Register	1st Tier	Commitments (award) or Actuals (invoice)	CAPEX or OPEX	Good	Simple

(table continues on next page)

Table 4.1 Metrics for Measuring Local Content *(continued)*

Metric	Key Feature	Information Source	Supply Chain Penetration	Stage of Procurement	Expenditure Category	Confidence in Data	Simplicity to Administer
$ value of contracts awarded to vendors with office address (PO or Invoice) within local/ affected community or region, as % of total	**Office address - regional/ community**	Contracts Plan/ Company Vendor Register	1st Tier	Commitments (award) or Actuals (invoice)	CAPEX or OPEX	Good	Simple
$ value of contracts awarded to nationally registered vendors	**Tax registered**	Contracts Plan/ Company Vendor Register	1st Tier	Commitments (award) or Actuals (invoice)	CAPEX or OPEX	Good	Simple
$ value of contracts awarded to community-based vendors	**Community-based**	Contracts Plan/ Company Vendor Register	1st Tier	Commitments (award) or Actuals (invoice)	CAPEX or OPEX	Moderate	Simple
$ value of contracts awarded to nationally owned vendor (>50% equity), as % of total	**National equity**	Contracts Plan/ National Company Register	1st Tier	Commitments (award) or Actuals (invoice)	CAPEX or OPEX	Poor	Complex
Services-specific							
# national FTE employees employed by service provider, as % of total	**Total head count of Supplier**	Information submitted by vendor, eg upon contract award and/ or with invoice	1st Tier	Commitments (award) or Actuals (invoice)	CAPEX or OPEX	Good	Simple
# FTE national employees employed under contract, as% of total employees under contract	**Head count under contract**	Information submitted by vendor, eg upon contract award and/or with invoice	1st Tier	Commitments (award) or Actuals (invoice)	CAPEX or OPEX	Moderate	Moderate
# FTE national employees in Senior, Supervisory and Skilled positions (or other job or grade disaggregation) employed under contract, as % of employees under contract	**Head count by job type**	Information submitted by vendor, eg upon contract award and/or with invoice	1st Tier	Commitments (award) or Actuals (invoice)	CAPEX or OPEX	Moderate	Moderate
# man-hours of FTE national employees under contract	**Man-hours**	Information submitted by vendor, eg upon contract award and/or with invoice	1st and lower tiers	Commitments (award) or Actuals (invoice)	CAPEX or OPEX	Moderate	Moderate
$ value spent on with FTE national employees under contract as part of services contracted directly or indirectly (subcontracts), as % of total contract value	**Wages**	Information submitted by vendor, eg upon contract award and/or with invoice	1st and lower tiers	Commitments (award) or Actuals (invoice)	CAPEX or OPEX	Moderate	Moderate

(table continues on next page)

Table 4.1 Metrics for Measuring Local Content *(continued)*

Metric	Key Feature	Information Source	Supply Chain Penetration	Stage of Procurement	Expenditure Category	Confidence in Data	Simplicity to Administer
$ value of contracts on wages, social taxes and benefits to FTE national employees under contract, as % of total contract value	**Build-up (Stakeholder) method**	Information submitted by vendor, eg at time of invoice	1st and lower tiers	Commitments (award) or Actuals (invoice)	CAPEX or OPEX	Poor	Complex
As above, but for the set of largest contracts by value (eg top 10)	**Largest contracts**	Contracts Plan/ Information submitted by vendor	1st and lower tiers	Commitments (award) or Actuals (invoice)	CAPEX or OPEX	Moderate	Moderate
$ value of contracts less proportion of contract value on salaries and bonuses (but not social taxes or expenses) of FTE foreign employees under contract, as % of contract value	**Build-down method**	Information submitted by vendor, eg at time of invoice	1st and lower tiers	Commitments (award) or Actuals (invoice)	CAPEX or OPEX	Moderate	Moderate
As above, but for the set of largest contracts by value (eg top 10)	**Largest contracts**	Contracts Plan/ Information submitted by vendor	1st and lower tiers	Commitments (award) or Actuals (invoice)	CAPEX or OPEX	Good	Moderate
Goods-specific							
For suppliers and sub-suppliers certified as supplying goods of Domestic Origin, $ value of contracts for goods, as % of total expenditure	**Step 1 -Domestic Origin companies only. Step 2 -all of contract value**	Information submitted by vendor, eg upon contract award and/or with invoice	1st and lower tiers	Commitments (award) or Actuals (invoice)	CAPEX or OPEX	Poor/Good (depends on quality of certification)	Complex
For suppliers and sub-suppliers certified as supplying goods of Domestic Origin, proportion of $ value of contracts for goods retained in the domestic economy, as % of total expenditure	**Step 1 -Domestic Origin companies only. Step 2 portion of contract value retained in national economy**	Information submitted by vendor, eg upon contract award and/or with invoice	1st and lower tiers	Commitments (award) or Actuals (invoice)	CAPEX or OPEX	Poor/Good (depends on quality of certification)	Complex
$ value of contracts less proportion of imported components of purchased goods, eg Cost-Insurance-Freight	**Build-down method**	Information submitted by vendor, eg upon contract award and/or with invoice	1st and lower tiers	Commitments (award) or Actuals (invoice)	CAPEX or OPEX	Moderate	Moderate
As above, but for the set of largest contracts by value (eg top 10)	**Largest contracts**	Contracts Plan/ Information submitted by vendor	1st and lower tiers	Commitments (award) or Actuals (invoice)	CAPEX or OPEX	Good	Moderate

Source: Adapted from Warner 2010.

Note: FTE = full-time equivalent; PO = purchase order; n.a. = not applicable.

Table 4.2 Metrics for Measuring the Development of Local Content

Metric	Key Feature	Information Source	Supply Chain Penetration	Stage of procurement	Expenditure Category	Confidence in data	Simplicity to administer
Input Metrics							
Workforce development							
# manhours training for nationals, as % of total national manhours	**Training by manhours**	Human Resources	n.a.	n.a.	OPEX	Good	Simple
# manhour straining for national son-the-job and in-the-classroom, as % of total national manhours	**Training by manhours and by type**	Human Resources	n.a.	n.a.	OPEX	Good	Simple
$value of training for nationals	**Training by $**	Human Resources	n.a.	n.a.	OPEX	Good	Simple
$value of training for nationals on-the-job and in-the-classroom	**Training by $ and by training type**	Human Resources	n.a.	n.a.	OPEX	Good	Simple
$value of Community Contribtions-vendor development and support programmes	**Community vendor programmes**	Information submitted by vendor, eg upon contract award and/or with invoice	n.a.	n.a.	CAPEX or OPEX	Good	Simple
$value of Community Contributions-public infrastructure	**Community infrastructure**	Information submitted by vendor, eg upon contract award and/or with invoice	n.a.	n.a.	CAPEX or OPEX	Good	Simple
Local Supplier development							
# manhours on-the-job training for nationals under contract (including sub-contractors), as % of total national manhours under contract	**Training by manhours**	Information submitted by vendor, eg upon contract award and/or with invoice	1st Tier	Commitments (award) or Actuals (invoice)	CAPEX or OPEX	Moderate	Complex
# manhours on-the-job training for nationals under contract (including sub-contracts) on-the-job and in-the-classroom, as % of total national manhours under contract	**Training by manhours and by type**	Information submitted by vendor, eg upon contract award and/or with invoice	1st Tier	Commitments (award) or Actuals (invoice)	CAPEX or OPEX	Poor	Complex
$value of training for nationals under contract (including subcontractors)	**Training by $ value**	Information submitted by vendor, eg upon contract award and/or with invoice	1st Tier	Commitments (award) or Actuals (invoice)	CAPEX or OPEX	Poor	Complex

(table continues on next page)

Table 4.2 Metrics for Measuring the Development of Local Content (*continued*)

Metric	Key Feature	Information Source	Supply Chain Penetration	Stage of procurement	Expenditure Category	Confidence in data	Simplicity to administer
$value of training for nationals under contract (including subcontracts) on-the-job and in-the-classroom	**Training by $ value and by type**	Information submitted by vendor, eg upon contract award and/or with invoice	1st Tier	Commitments (award) or Actuals (invoice)	CAPEX or OPEX	Poor	Complex
$ value of on-the-job management supervision and QA/ QCto support nationally registered suppliers under contract (including sub-contractors)	**Management supervision and QA/ QC**	Information submitted by vendor, eg upon contract award and/or with invoice	1st Tier	Commitments (award) or Actuals (invoice)	CAPEX or OPEX	Poor	Complex
$of contract value as capital investments in enhancing the capabilities of nationally registered suppliers charged to parent company, as% of contract value	**Capital investments to develop local suppliers - charged**	Information submitted by vendor, eg upon contract award and/or with invoice	1st Tier	Commitments (award) or Actuals (invoice)	CAPEX or OPEX	Moderate	Moderate
$ capital investments in enhancing the capabilities of nationally registered suppliers not charged to parent company, as % of contract value	**Capital investments to develop local suppliers - leveraged**	Information submitted by vendor, eg upon contract award and/or with invoice	1st Tier	Commitments (award) or Actuals (invoice)	CAPEX or OPEX	Moderate	Complex
%of contract value as capital investments in Dual Purpose infrastructure charged to parent company, as % of contract value	**Dual purpose infrastructure**	Information submitted by vendor, eg upon contract award and/or with invoice	1st Tier	Commitments (award) or Actuals (invoice)	CAPEX or OPEX	Moderate	Moderate
Output Metrics							
Contractor management performance (CPM) of nationally registered firms	**CPM score cards for local suppliers/ contractors**	Company CPM Reports/ Company vendor register	1st Tier and lower tiers	Contractor Performance Management	CAPEX or OPEX	Moderate	Moderate
% of tender lists comprising nationally registered suppliers(by different procurement categories)	**Successful Pre-Qual/ Tender lists**	Company tender tracking system, eg PROCON	1st Tier	Commitments (award) or Actuals (invoice)	CAPEX or OPEX	Good	Simple
# contracts awarded to nationally registered vendors on an internationally competitive basis	**Competitive contract award**	Contracts Plan/ Company vendor register	1st Tier	Commitments (contract award)	CAPEX or OPEX	Good	Simple
$value of contracts awarded to nationally registered vendors on an internationally competitive basis	**Competitive contract award**	Contracts Plan/ Company vendor register	1st Tier	Commitments (contract award)	CAPEX or OPEX	Good	Simple

(table continues on next page)

Table 4.2 Metrics for Measuring the Development of Local Content (continued)

Metric	Key Feature	Information Source	Supply Chain Penetration	Stage of procurement	Expenditure Category	Confidence in data	Simplicity to administer
# contracts awarded "consequential" of supplier support from parent company	**Contract award growth**	Market Survey	1st and 2nd Tier	n.a.	CAPEX or OPEX	Moderate	Moderate
$ of contracts awarded "consequential" of supplier support from parent company	**Revenue growth**	Market Survey	1st and 2nd Tier	n.a.	CAPEX or OPEX	Poor	Moderate
Reduction in price variance of labour rates or product prices between nationally registered suppliers and internationlly competitive pricing	**Price competitiveness improvements**	Market Survey	1st Tier and lower tiers	Contractor Performance Management	CAPEX or OPEX	Good/ Poor (depends on quality of survey)	Complex
Reduction in labour productivity variance between nationally registered suppliers and internationally competitive productivity	**Labour productivity improvements**	Market Survey	1st Tier and lower tiers	Contractor Performance Management	CAPEX or OPEX	Good/ Poor (depends on quality of survey)	Complex
Reduction in defects rates variance between nationally registered suppliers and internationally competitive rates	**Defect rates improvements**	Market Survey	1st Tier and lower tiers	Contractor Performance Management	CAPEX or OPEX	Good/ Poor (depends on quality of survey)	Complex
Improvement in HSE performance variance between nationally registered suppliers and internationally competitive HSE performance, eg Loss Time Injuries, Total Recordable Incident Frequency, First Aid Cases	**Hse performance improvements**	Market Survey	1st Tier and lower tiers	Contractor Performance Management	CAPEX or OPEX	Good/ Poor (depends on quality of survey)	Complex
Improvement in volume/capacity variance between nationally registered suppliers and internationally competitive suppliers, eg maximum crane tonnage lift, maximum fabrication yard area, maximum piping storage volume	**Volume/ capacity improvements**	Market Survey	1st Tier and lower tiers	Contractor Performance Management	CAPEX or OPEX	Good/ Poor (depends on quality of survey)	Complex

Source: Adapted from Warner 2010.

Note: HSE = health, safety, and the environment; n.a. = not applicable.

programs or levels of capital investments in new plant and equipment in local suppliers, and measures of outputs, such as the impact of training programs on earning potential or the increase in supplier competitiveness. These metrics and their application are further discussed later in this chapter.

Metrics for Measuring Local Content in the Workforce

Nationals in the Workforce by Head Count

The most popular measure of local content within the direct workforce of an oil and gas company appears to be the number of nationals employed as a proportion of total full-time equivalent (FTE) employees. This metric is often used in laws, regulations, and petroleum contracts. For example, Decree 5/95 in Angola prevents companies from employing nonresident foreigner workers unless at least 70 percent of the workforce is formed by Angolan nationals.[2]

This metric may be broken down into the proportion of nationals in professional positions versus nonprofessional staff positions, or some other disaggregation of employment positions. Figure 4.2 shows how the operator of the Chad-Cameroon pipeline project, Esso Chad, reports the number of nationals in its workforce across supervisory, skilled, semiskilled, and unskilled positions.

Figure 4.2 Head Count of Nationals in Different Positions: Esso Chad, 2009

Chad-Cameroon pipeline project
national workers employment skill levels—2009

	Supervisory		Skilled		Semiskilled		Unskilled	
	3rd Qtr	4th Qtr	3rd Qtr	4th Qtr	3rd Qtr	4th Qtr	3rd Qtr	4th Qtr
Chad	237	237	2,445	2,511	1,710	1,921	1,296	1,078
Cameroon	195	213	390	344	307	254	248	314
Project total	432	450	2,835	2,855	2,017	2,175	1,544	1,392

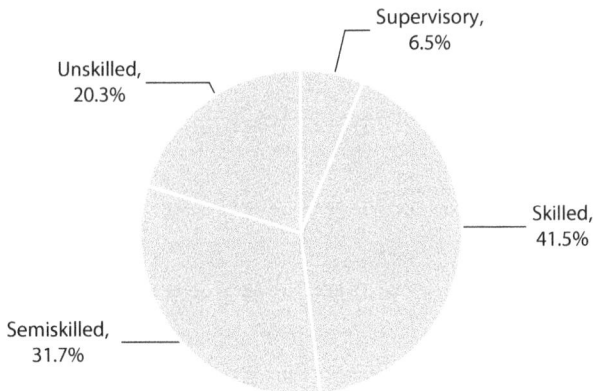

Supervisory, 6.5%
Unskilled, 20.3%
Skilled, 41.5%
Semiskilled, 31.7%

Source: Esso Chad Project Progress Report, http://www.essochad.com/Chad-English/PA/Files/27_ch09.pdf.

Other versions of this metric go further, anticipating a change—usually an increase—in the number or proportion of nationals in the workforce across time, such as across different phases in the development of an oil or gas field. A case in point is the production sharing agreement (PSA) for the Shah Deniz Prospective Area in the Azerbaijan Sector of the Caspian.[3] The PSA measures national content in the workforce using the following metrics:

• Prior to commencement of development: professionals 30–50 percent; non-professionals 70 percent
• Upon commencement of petroleum production: professionals 70 percent; nonprofessionals 85 percent
• Five years after commencement of petroleum production: professionals 90 percent; nonprofessionals 95 percent.

Finally, it is increasingly common to see composite metrics that combine head count, job position, and the promotion of nationals over time. Figure 4.3 shows an example of a local employment sustainability graph. In the example, greater weight is given to nationals in management positions compared to skilled, and to nationals in skilled positions compared to unskilled. The link between project phase and local employment levels and type is also shown. During the initial phases of a project, local employment growth is "psychological" because it refers to new employment. As the project is implemented, the number of local employees and their skills levels tend to increase. Turnover rates are also high as

Figure 4.3 Local Employment Sustainability Graph

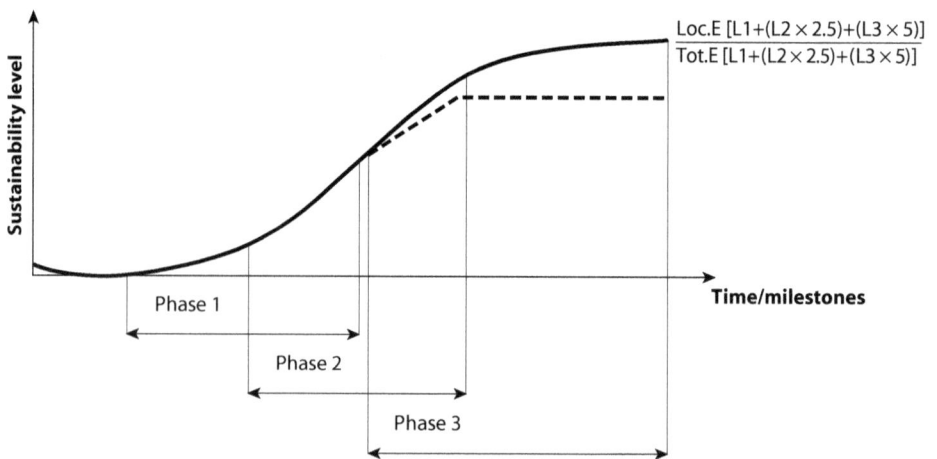

Loc.E [L1+(L2 × 2.5)+(L3 × 5)]
Tot.E [L1+(L2 × 2.5)+(L3 × 5)]

• Phase 1 = Physiological growth
• Phase 2 = Consolidation
• Phase 3 = Sustainable growth

Source: World Bank data.

the company carries out training programs and selectively assesses its workforce. In Phase 3—which may occur after five or six years from the start of the project, depending on its complexity—the transit of local employees from basic to higher skill levels finally takes place.

Nationals in Contract Execution
The proportion of total man-hours of work undertaken by national citizens in the execution of a particular contract is another way to measure the proportion of nationals in the workforce by head count. Box 4.1 provides an example of reporting national man-hours for a contract to fabricate the deck of a production platform in Trinidad and Tobago. This type of metric measures the number of nationals actually involved in a particular job. Thus it avoids the situation whereby a high level of local content is assigned to a segment of procurement expenditure because of a high national head count in the service company, when actually this figure depends heavily on nationals working in administrative positions, that is, not directly involved in the contracted work.

Company Voluntary Reporting
The metrics used in figure 4.2, figure 4.3, and box 4.1 are examples of voluntary reporting by companies. The Global Reporting Initiative (GRI)—which is used by many multinational companies to report their social, environmental and

Box 4.1

Reporting of Local Content in the Fabrication of a Production Platform Deck in Trinidad and Tobago

BG Group is the operator of two off-shore blocks in Trinidad and Tobago, one of which is the North Coast Marine Area (NCMA). This block contains six gas fields, including the Poinsettia field. Phase 3c in the development of the NCMA included a new drilling and production platform on the Poinsettia field. The platform consisted of a 10,000 ton jacket, fabricated on the Gulf coast of the United States, and a 4,200 ton deck (the topside), constructed in Trinidad by TOFCO Ltd. TOFCO Ltd is a 50/50 joint venture between CMC of Louisiana, the United States (with construction facilities in Harvey and Houma) and Welfab Limited, a Trinidadian services company. The Poinsettia topside was constructed in the TOFCO fabrication yard in La Brea, on the west coast of Trinidad. In a case study prepared by BG Group, it was reported that an estimated 99 percent of the 1.1 million hours work on the Poinsettia topsides were undertaken by Trinidadian nationals, demonstrating a particularly high level of local content in all management, technical, and administrative positions.

Source: Warner 2010.

economic performance—promotes a standardized set of voluntary reporting metrics. For the oil and gas sector, GRI indicators that relate most closely to local content with regards to employment are provided in box 4.2 below. It is important to note that although the supporting guidelines make specific reference to nationals in discussing local content, these metrics do not specifically require companies to report the head count of nationals per se within their total labor force (that is, nationals versus expatriate workers). Furthermore, the guidelines do not specify the metric to be used to measure the core indicator (for example, indicator LA1 could be measured by head count or by the share of total gross or net salaries).

Definition of National

A particular problem with head-count-based metrics for measuring local content is the ambiguity that arises in the definition of what is meant by a national. Often a national is defined as an individual with rights of citizenship, who is on the company payroll, and who is resident in the country. The definition does, however, exclude nationals working on a particular contract or project while being physically located abroad. For international oil and gas companies and

---

Box 4.2

GRI Company Voluntary Reporting Indicators for Labor

ASPECT: EMPLOYMENT			For the purposes of this Supplement, local content is defined as the added value brought to a host nation (national, regional, and local areas in that country, including communities) through the activities of the oil and gas industry
CORE	LA1	Total workforce by employment type, employment contract, and region, broken down by gender	
CORE	LA2	Total number and rate of new employee hires and employee turnover by age group, gender, and region	This may be measured (by project, affiliate and/or country aggregate) and undertaken through activities including but not limited to:
ADD	LA3	Benefits provided to full-time employees that are not provided to temporary or part-time employees, by significant locations of operation	Workforce development (international and national oil companies; contractors and subcontractors), including: (1) employment of national, regional, and local workforce [emphasis added]; (2) training of national, regional, and local workforce, and (3) training of national, regional, and local workforce;

Investments in contractor/supplier development (all oil and gas industry goods and services, including engineering and fabrication yards), including: (1) developing supplies and services locally (2) procuring supplies and services locally [emphasis added].

Source: GRI 2012.

services companies, this definition may not fully capture the extent of local employment, since some of their national staff may be working on assignments associated with their country of origin while physically located in another country, as it is often the case for engineering design work or field characterization.

The definition of employee also needs careful consideration when measuring the impact of local content, as it may or may not include full- and part-time staff provided by an employment agency (depending on whether payment was made directly or via the employment agency).

Wages Paid to Nationals

An alternative to measuring the head count of nationals in the workforce or in the execution of a particular contract is to report the salaries or wages paid by the company to national employees and other pay-rolled staff. This is often measured as the gross wage or gross salary paid to and on behalf of nationals as a percentage of total gross salaries paid to all workers. The metric captures base salary associated social taxes paid by employee and employer, as well as employee benefits and expenses, including pension contributions, housing, personal and vehicle allowances, and bonuses. A similar metric uses taxable salary, that is, gross salary, less employer's contributions and expenses, as this information is usually more readily available to companies' finance departments.

Measuring local content by head count or by wages can generate very different results. Box 4.3 compares two metrics using the hypothetical case of a company with 100 employees, 5 of whom are expatriates and 95 national citizens. In the illustration, local content measured as the proportion of nationals in the in-country workforce is 95 percent, while local content measured as the proportion of total gross wages paid to nationals is 61 percent. This would likely be the case if the wages-based metric was applied to measuring the local content contribution of a company that employs expatriate labor in its local workforce in senior management, high-paying positions, as often happens especially where high-level skills are not available in the country of operation. It is not unusual for the head count of national citizens in an oil and gas-operating company to be around 90 percent of the total in-country workforce, and for the majority of them to be in the technical, semiskilled, and manual categories, resulting in a much lower share of national salaries to total salaries paid by the company. This is especially true in countries with low economic development and less mature petroleum sectors.

Both the head count and gross wage metrics are relatively simple to administer, as they are based on information already collected by companies' human resources departments and finance departments as part of normal business operations and reporting needs. Confidence in the reliability of these data should also be reasonably high. Simplicity-to-administer and confidence-in-the-data are important attributes for metrics, and should be carefully considered in defining reporting standards or policies.[4] In addition, regulators and companies should choose the metric that more closely measures the desired outcome. For example,

Box 4.3

Example of Calculation of Local Content by Head Count versus Wages

Assumptions used in calculation:

- 100 employees in company in total (equivalent to 160,000 man-hours/year)
- 5 expatriates in management positions, average gross salary of $200k/year, excl. local expenses (total $1 million/year)
- 95 nationals in workforce, as follows:
  - 5 in management positions, average gross salary $40k/year (total = $200k/year)
  - 90 in nonmanagement positions, average gross salary $15k/year (total = $1.35 k/year).

Annual labor in manhours	Total salaries and wages in US$	Foreign workers annual man-hours	Workers in management position: annual man-hours	Foreign workers in management position: annual man-hours	Workers in non management position: annual man-hours	Foreign workers in non management position: annual manhours	Total salaries in US$ paid to all foreign workers in management position	Total wages (excluding expenses) in US$ paid to all foreign workers in nonmanagement position
160000	2,550,000	8,000	16,000	8,000	14,400	-	1,000,000	-

WORKFORCE

	Annual wages, taxes, and expatriate expenses contributed to the economy		Nationals in total workforce		Nationals in management positions		Nationals in nonmanagement positions	
	US$	%	%	Man-hours	%	Man-hours	%	Man-hours
Company #1	1,550,000	60.8	95.0	152,000	50.0	8,000	100.0	144,000

Source: World Bank data based on an open-source online local content calculator (http://localcontentsolutions.com/calculator/Default.html).

the percentage of national participation in the workforce of a company does not provide information on the extent to which nationals are able to progress in terms of career development, or information on the magnitude of local employment share of benefits. For this purpose, the share of national wages in total wages would be a much more informative metric. But this too can be misleading. Although expatriate base salaries are often paid into foreign bank accounts, and thus accumulate overseas, expatriate allowances for housing, transport, and personal expenses, as well as expatriate social taxes, will mostly accrue to the domestic economy. These expenditures should not be underestimated.[5]

Metrics for Measuring Local Content in Supply Chains

This section provides an overview of metrics commonly applied to measure local content in the procurement of goods and services by oil and gas companies.

Measurement Approaches

As shown in box 4.2 the level of supplies and services procured by a company locally is a key metric for reporting local content (GRI 2012). But, just as with national labor in the workforce, the results can vary considerably depending on the metric chosen. There are two main approaches to measuring local content within expenditure on goods and services:

- With reference to some classification of local supplier
- With reference to some classification of local goods and services

These approaches are very different. The first seeks to classify expenditure against some definition of a local, national or domestic business entity, that is, the producer or provider of the good or service. The second classifies expenditure by some measure of whether the relevant service or good is deemed to be local—and, for goods only, whether value has been added in-country.

Measuring Expenditure on Local Suppliers

Definitions used by local content regulations and oil and gas companies to classify what is spent on a local supplier usually include one or a combination of the following criteria:

- The address given in vendor registration information
- The address on a purchase order or invoice
- The geographic location of the service being provided or the production of the good being supplied
- The share of equity owned by national citizens (for example, greater than 25 percent, 50 percent, or 100 percent)
- Whether the supplier is locally incorporated
- Whether the supplier is tax registered in the country of operation, including for withholding tax purposes
- Whether the supplier employs more than a specified percentage of nationals.

With regard to regional or community suppliers, more refined definitions can include the following:

- The regional/local address in vendor registration
- The regional/local address on invoice
- Suppliers and contractors who source the majority of materials or labor from the province, district, or local communities located closest to the operation.

Box 4.4 provides some illustrative definitions for a local supplier used in the oil and gas industry. The example from Indonesia uses a single metric, that is, national ownership, while the example from Angola combines legal status with geography and national ownership. These examples underscore the importance of clarity when reporting local content, since the results can differ just as much

Box 4.4

Examples of Metrics for Defining Local Suppliers

Kazakhstan: A "Kazakh producer" is a supplier of goods and services registered in the Republic of Kazakhstan with (1) more than 95 percent local (that is, national citizenship) labor for services or (2) producing goods in Kazakhstan.[6]

Indonesia: A "domestic company" is a national company in which more than 50 percent of shares are owned by Indonesian individual(s), the government of the Republic of Indonesia, a provincial/regency/municipality government, state-owned enterprise, or provincial/regency/municipality enterprise.[7]

Angola: An "Angolan company" is an enterprise that is (1) legally established or constituted in Angola, (2) has headquarters in Angola, and (3) is totally owned by Angolan citizens or citizens have at least a 51 percent participation in the company's equity.[8]

Global Reporting Initiative "....the proportion of spending on locally-based suppliers at significant locations of operation" (GRI 2012).

with expenditure on goods and services, as with local content in the direct workforce.

Figure 4.4 illustrates the pattern of expenditure that might be expected in a typical oil and gas field development project in a low-middle-income country with a mature upstream oil and gas industry. In this example, the same expenditure on goods and services is measured as 17 percent when local suppliers are

Figure 4.4 Proportion of Annual Expenditure on Goods and Services Invoices from Suppliers

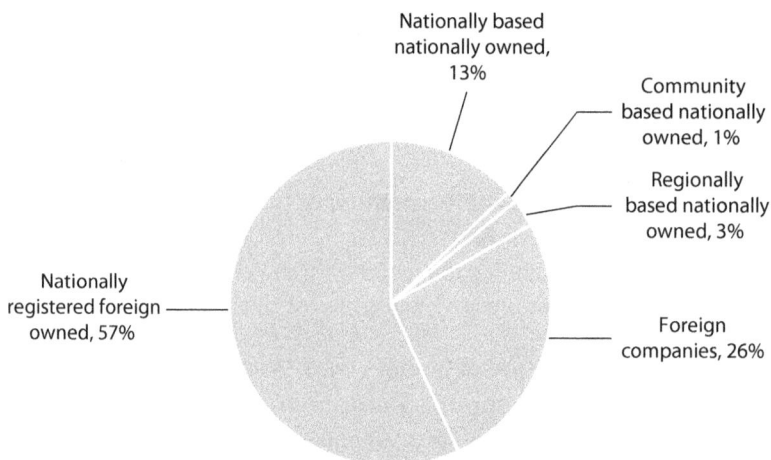

Nationally based nationally owned, 13%

Community based nationally owned, 1%

Regionally based nationally owned, 3%

Nationally registered foreign owned, 57%

Foreign companies, 26%

Source: World Bank data.

defined by national ownership, and 74 percent when measured by suppliers who are locally registered.

Another metric adopted by some companies (but less by regulators) is the number of individual contracts awarded to local suppliers. Figure 4.5 shows the relationship between a typical spread of procurement expenditure between nationally owned and international suppliers, by contract size for an oil project development in exploration phase in a frontier country. Measured by number of contracts, local content would be 36 percent (207 contracts over a total awarded of 573). But measured by value of contracts awarded to nationally owned suppliers as a proportion of the value of all contracts, local content would be around 2 percent.[9] In countries with a more mature oil and gas industry and in the field development phase of an oil project, both figures would be expected to rise steeply. It is worth noting that the estimated 2 percent does not include the portion of expenditure that might be spent with nationally owned suppliers in the supply chains of the contract holder.

Figure 4.5 Size and Number of Contracts Awarded in the Project Exploration Phase

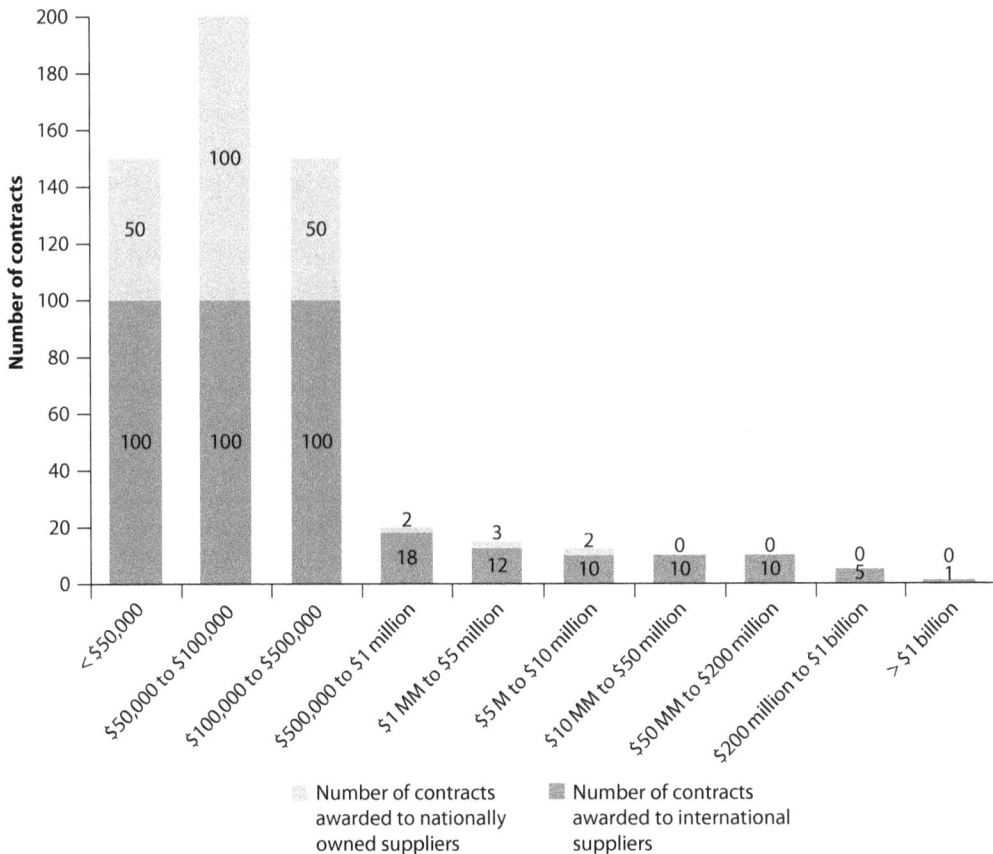

Legend:
- Number of contracts awarded to nationally owned suppliers
- Number of contracts awarded to international suppliers

Source: World Bank data.

This example illustrates that whereas a large proportion of the total number of contracts awarded in a given period or on a given phase of field development is likely go to nationally owned suppliers, when measured by the cumulative value of these contracts, the local content level may be relatively small.

Measuring Expenditure on Local Goods and Services

As noted earlier, an alternative approach to measuring and reporting local content is to classify expenditure on goods and services according to whether the service or good being purchased is itself deemed to be in some way local. To this end, some version of the "rules of origin" that classify a good as local if it originates from a particular country is commonly applied. Rules of origin were originally applied to determine whether a good or product was eligible for preferential treatment in the course of trade between nations or regional trading communities. These rules are now being applied by some regulators to formulate local content targets and reporting requirements. The implication of this method is that a company will be able to report local content only if value was added in country in order to provide a service or produce a product. In other words, a company will not report local content in procurement expenditure simply because the seller is registered or owned locally, when in fact it may be employing primarily foreign labor and reselling imported, finished, goods.

In Brazil, Mexico, Kazakhstan, and Indonesia rules of origin apply to both goods and services. Further, the same rules are also used as part of investment criteria by some national development banks. For example, the Brazilian national development bank BNDES requires 60 percent domestic content when extending finance for fixed investments in machinery and equipment (Roberts 2007).

Rules of origin for goods and products have been, and continue to be, the object of debate among members of the World Trade Organization (WTO), the European Union, the North American Free Trade Agreement (NAFTA), and Association of Southeast Asian Nations (ASEAN), as well as between the parties of various bilateral trade agreements and negotiations. A common point of contention is the choice of method for calculation and the use of thresholds to determine whether an imported product has undergone a substantive transformation in a country, such that the good is eligible for trade preferences. The main determinant of eligibility is the level of value addition achieved in the exporting country.

Calculating Value Addition: The Build-Up and Build-Down Methods. Generally, the methods for calculating value addition are of two types: build-up and build-down. The distinction is important, and lies at the heart of much of the current debate on the ambiguities and administrative complexities of local content reporting.

Build-up methods aggregate, piece-meal, the value added to the domestic economy from in-country industrial activity, that is, the value of the locally originating raw materials and components, the direct labor costs, direct overhead costs, internal transportation, and profit or mark-up.[10] The build-up methods are thus generally more accurate but also more complex to piece together, requiring data drawn from a range of company functions: procurement, finance, human resources, sales, and so on. Build-down methods subtract the value of the nonoriginating components from the total value of the good—usually the imported raw materials or semiprocessed or assembled materials and products—and assume that what remains is the value addition to the local economy. Build-down methods are less accurate than build-up methods, and more subject to assumptions, such as that all labor in the manufacturing process is local.

Calculating value addition in services follows a similar process. Under a build-up method, the base salaries paid to nationals, associated employer and employee tax contributions, and employee benefits, are commonly aggregated with the local allowances, benefits, and social taxes paid to expatriates.[11] In other words, the reporting of local content in services is built up from the individual local service components. A variant of this metric is to prorate the resulting local content figure by the proportion that an individual contract plays in the total annual revenues of the supplying entity. In some cases value addition is assumed to equal the taxable salary of nationals, although this then fails to take account of expatriates' local allowances and other compensation that remain in the country. In contrast, the build-down method applied to services identifies the nonoriginating labor content (that is, foreign labor) and deducts it from the transaction price. This approach takes the entire employee wage bill and all taxes and benefits as the starting point. It then deducts that portion paid to expatriates as base salaries and bonuses. This theoretically leaves the value of the service contributing to the domestic economy, that is, the proportion that is local content

Under conventional rules of origin for trade preferences for goods, a threshold is then applied to the originating portion—whether this is derived from a build-up or build-down method. This threshold marks the point at which a good is considered to have undergone substantive transformation, and determines whether a trade preference applies. The importance of thresholds in reporting local content in oil and gas expenditure is demonstrated by the different ways in which the formulae in Brazil and Kazakhstan have utilized rules of origin for goods (see table 4.3). For oil and gas operations governed by concession agreements pertaining to the licensing of acreage in Brazil in bidding rounds 1 to 10, reporting rules require both the application of the rule of origin and of a threshold.[12] In Kazakhstan, under the 2010 unified method, and in the more recent bidding rounds in Brazil, the formulae for reporting local content do not involve the application of a threshold.[13]

In both Brazil and Kazakhstan reporting regulations require use of the build-down method to calculate local content in goods. The metric involves deducting cost, insurance, and freight (CIF) from the sales price, along with import taxes and overseas overhead costs.

Table 4.3 Metrics to Measure Goods and Services of Domestic Origin: Examples from Brazil and Kazakhstan

An Example from Brazil (Rounds 4 and 5)	*An Example from Kazakhstan (2010)*
Step 1: Calculate % local content in goods and services	
Screening of components for evaluation	Build-Down Method—Local content metrics for goods (used in calculation of CT-KZ certificate of origin)
Subset of components subjected to evaluation, based on Pareto's 80/20 rule (inputs ranked by value) with remaining 20% and certain buld materials assumed to be 10% Brazilian without need for evaluation.	Value of direct and third-party imported components as CIF (cost, insurance, and freight) or FOB (free on board) plus foreign freight and insurance, including import duties, IPI (tax on industrial products) and
Build-Down Method—Nationalization Index for Goods (INB)	$$\frac{Cost\ of\ the\ foreign\ raw\ material\ and\ other}{Sales\ price}$$
Value of direct and third-party imported components as CIF (cost, insurance, and freight) or FOB (free on board) plus foreign freight and insurance, including import duties, IPI (tax on industrial products) and	This metric is only applied in the context of calculating the % domestic content for the purpose of preparing the CT-KZ certificate confirming that goods are produced in the Republic of Kazakhstan
$$\frac{ICMS(state\ VAT)}{Sales\ price}$$	Build-Up Method—Local content metric for services
Correction factor to take account of overheads incurred outside Brazil	$$\frac{\left(\begin{array}{c}\text{CT-KZ \% in goods used to provide the services + Share} \\ \text{of total payroll perceived by Kazakh citizenspursuant} \\ \text{to the primary contract + value of subcontract} \\ \text{performed by legal entities incorporated in Kazakhs} \\ \text{tan with more than 95\% Kazakh employees}\end{array}\right)}{Sales\ price}$$
Build-Up Method—Nationalization Index for Services (INS)	
$$\frac{\left(\begin{array}{c}\text{Imported human resources (value of foreign man hours) +} \\ \text{Imported capital goods used to provide the service (rental,} \\ \text{leasing) + Intermediate imported goods/consumables}\end{array}\right)}{Sales\ price}$$	
Step 2: Classification of local content as goods or services of domestic Origin	
Goods and services origin verification	Certification of origin
Goods	Goods
If INB> 40%, then the goods are deemed 100% Brazilian, and total sales price counts toward local content targets	% share of Kazakh content in goods, as specified in the CT-KZ certificate
Services	If there is no CT-KZ certificate of origin, then Kazakh content is deemed 0%
If INS > 80%, then services are deemed 100% Brazilian, and total service price counts toward local content targets.	

Source: Adapted from Warner 2010.

To calculate local content in services, the two countries use different methods. In Brazil, for procurement of services related to acreage awarded under rounds 4 and 5, the build-down method applies. This involves the deducting of the foreign labor component from the total contract price. In Kazakhstan, at the time of writing, the applicable method is to add the gross salary and benefits of nationals utilized in contract delivery to the total value of subcontracts awarded to nationally registered service providers whose staff includes more than 95 percent of nationals by head count. In other words, Kazakhstan uses a build-up method.

International Commerce Terms and Local Content. International commerce terms (IncoTerms) are published by the International Chamber of Commerce and widely used in international transactions.[14] The IncoTerms most relevant to calculating the nonoriginating component of procurement expenditure on goods under a build-down method are free on board (FOB) and cost, insurance, and freight (CIF).

In calculating local content, if a supplier has paid for goods FOB, then the subsequent port-to-port freight costs and associated insurance would need to be added to the FOB price before deducting this from the total sales price. For this reason usually CIF is the preferred approach to calculating local content under a build-down method, since CIF includes the nonoriginating costs up to the port of entry. In other words, CIF is the closest IncoTerm to a single measure of which proportion of the sales price is not local content. All other IncoTerms need some sort of adjustment before they can be used in the calculation of local content. Figure 4.6 illustrates how FOB with CIF are used in the calculation of local content.

The attraction of using FOB or CIF IncoTerms to calculate local content with the build-down method is their relative administrative simplicity. FOB and CIF information is identifiable in the buyer's internal documentation (for example, import declaration), and can readily be deducted from sales price to generate a reasonably accurate figure for local content.[15] On the other hand, a drawback of using Incoterms in local content reporting is that they reveal the result of price negotiations between supplier and seller—information that is often considered commercially sensitive. In Brazil this limitation is addressed through an independent third-party system of certification; local content is reported only on an aggregated basis across categories of expenditure.

Expenditure on Local Suppliers: Comparing Metrics

As shown in figure 4.7, different metrics for measuring local content in supply chains lead to different results. In this hypothetical example, a purchase order has been raised by an oil company for the supply of machine spare parts. Two scenarios are compared:

Figure 4.6 Local Content Calculation for FOB and CIF Prices

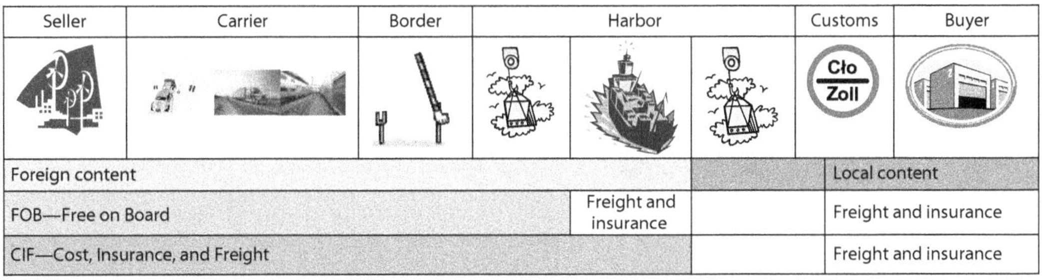

Source: World Bank data.

Figure 4.7 Effects of Different Metrics on Local Procurement Content

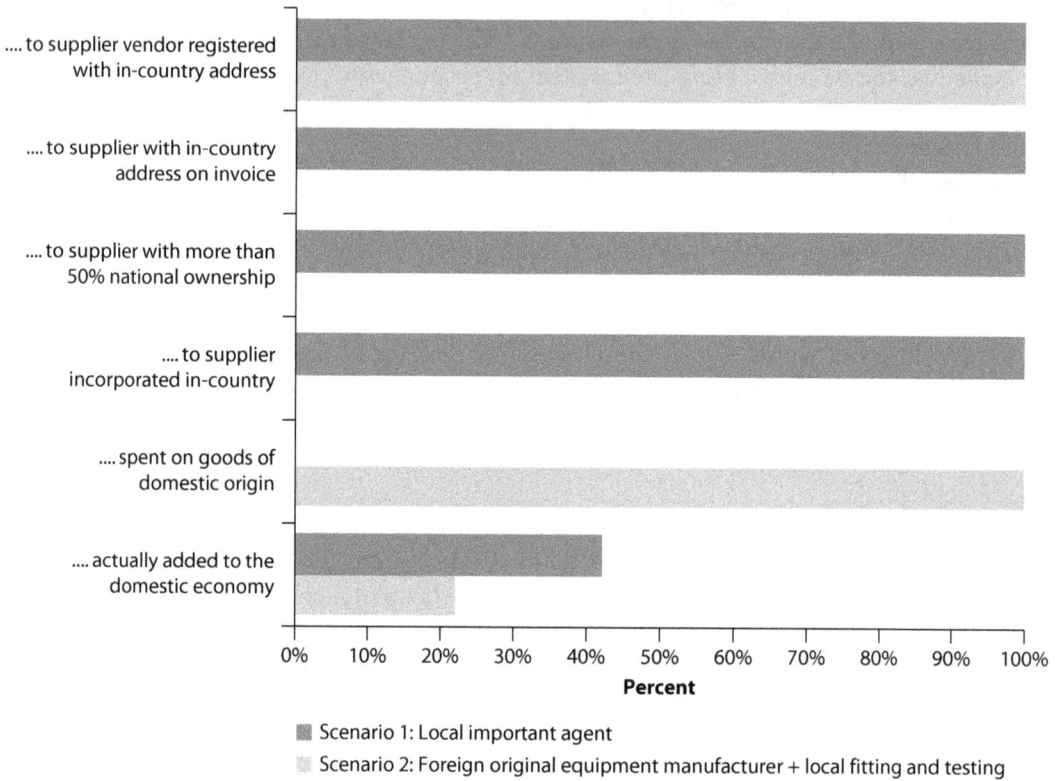

Scenario 1: Local important agent
Scenario 2: Foreign original equipment manufacturer + local fitting and testing

Source: World Bank data.

- In scenario 1, the supplier is a wholly nationally owned import agent, with its office located in-country. The agent imports and then sells goods that are already finished and packaged. He provides a temporary storage facility for the goods and transports the parts to the end user. Fitting and testing of the parts is performed by the oil company. Using a build-down method, the ex-factory cost plus freight and insurance to the port of entry (that is, the CIF price on the import declaration) is 78 percent. This leaves 22 percent as value contributed to the domestic economy.
- In scenario 2, the supplier's main office is located overseas. But the company has made recent investments in local capability to store, transport, fit, and test the parts. Using a build-up method, these in-country capabilities represent 42 percent of the purchase price. The goods are thus deemed by regulators to be of domestic origin, since more than 40 percent of the value of the sales has originated in-country.

In both scenarios each company can legitimately report 100 percent local content if the metric chosen is expenditure by the oil company with a supplier whose office address on the vendor registration form is the country in question.

But if the metric changes to the address on the invoice (which is not uncommon, since these data are readily accessible through a company's invoice payment system), then immediately the local content for the foreign company, with its financing office overseas, falls to zero, while the local import agent achieves 100 percent.

The same occurs with both equity ownership and registration. The local reseller is both wholly nationally owned and locally registered, and thus achieves 100 percent local content against either metric. In contrast, the foreign supplier has no local equity in his in-country business, and has yet to register. Thus under these two metrics this supplier would report zero local content.

Entirely the opposite effect arises using a metric that reports whether the goods being supplied are of domestic origin. In this case 100 percent of what is paid to the foreign supplier counts as local content because the proportion of the purchase price calculated as being of domestic origin is greater than the 40 percent threshold. This is so in spite of the fact that only 42 percent of the actual purchase price contributes to the local economy. In contrast, the importer adds 22 percent of the purchase price in the country through a combination of his fee, the cost of storage and inland freight costs, and his profit. Because, in aggregate, this sum is below the deemed local content threshold, the importer cannot report any local content.

Context Matters

In the previous subsection we discussed the widely different results that local content metrics can generate. It is therefore important that regulators and companies provide appropriate interpretation and background information when reporting local content results. For example, say a company's annual report contains the following statement: our company spent $950 million on procurement this year, of which 47 percent was local content. This information would be meaningless if reported without clarity on the local content metric being used, including what is meant by the term spent. Table 4.4 provides an example of the underlying data upon which the above generalized statement was based.

Table 4.4 Illustrative Data on Local Content in Expenditure on Goods and Services

	Year 2010		
	$ million Total	$ Spent on Suppliers Tax Registered In-country ($m)	Local Content (%)
Committed expenditure (spend assigned to contracts awarded in 2010)			
Services	700	$425m	61
Goods	250	$22m	9
Total	950	$447m	47
Actual expenditure (spend against invoices paid in 2010)			
Services	450	280	62
Goods	130	55	42
Total	580	335	58

Source: World Bank data.

Based on the same data, the company's report could have stated: In 2010, $950 million was committed for expenditure on goods and services, of which $447 million (47 percent) was to suppliers tax registered in-country. Of this $447 million, $425 million is for the provision of local services, and $22 million for the supply of goods. The relatively low figure of $22 million for goods is explained by the period of capital refurbishment anticipated for 2011. (A more routine figure for spending in this category during normal operations would be around 40 percent, as evidenced by actual expenditure of 42 percent against invoices from local tax-registered suppliers of goods in 2010.)

This simple example shows that, when reporting local content, companies and regulators should provide clear information on the actual metric being applied, as well as supporting data so that the trends and significance of the reported numbers are clear.

Measuring Local Content Development

While the standard metrics for measuring local content in the workforce and expenditure on local suppliers previously discussed may well show that over time the number of local jobs is increasing or local suppliers are winning more work, these data say little about whether the productivity of a workforce is improving or whether local suppliers are becoming more capable or competitive.

Metrics that measure the development of local content are as equally diverse as those available to measure its level. Table 4.2 contains examples of local content development input and output metrics. For a more comprehensive list of such metrics, the reader is referred to a recent report by the World Business Council for Sustainable Development prepared by the Dalberg consultancy firm (WBCSD 2012).

Input Metrics

The input metrics shown in table 4.2 are essentially proxy indicators for measuring the outcome or performance initiatives to develop local skills and suppliers. For example, an oil or gas operating company would expect the future earning power of its employees who receive vocational training (or the future growth prospects of community-based suppliers benefiting from a vendor development programs) to be at least equal to the cost of providing the training (or vendor development program). Likewise, levels of capital investment committed to build capability in local suppliers made by an operating company, or leveraged from international contractors or third-party financial institutions, might also be claimed as a proxy indicator for the growth potential of these suppliers.

Apart from reporting on training expenditure, it is rare to see indicators that measure local content development being adopted by either regulators or companies. Most of the commonly used metrics measure the level of content, not its sustainability or competitiveness. One notable exception is Indonesia, where BP Migas—the oil and gas sector regulator—has introduced regulations that reward local suppliers who show expenditure on developing the environmental management and health and safety standards of local material and equipment suppliers, or expenditure on promoting partnership programs to build the capability of local enterprises lower down the supply chain.[16] Documenting local content development in this manner may contribute up to an additional 15 percent of local content, which is then applied to the bid price to afford an advantage in the process of awarding contracts.[17]

Output Metrics

Output metrics are perhaps more meaningful than input metrics for reporting local content development. But to date, these have rarely been used by companies and regulators.

In order to measure the development of local suppliers, one would need to use metrics that track actual improvements in the core parameters of a local supplier competitiveness over time, that is, supplier costs, delivery times, labor productivity, quality of service or product, volume capacity, and HSE performance. Output data would need to be benchmarked against international standards. Further, their measurement would likely require additional commitments in human resources, in particular to undertake field surveys of individual suppliers. The investment needed to administer these types of metric is considerable, and probably explains their lack of uptake at present.

Two particularly meaningful output metrics that do not depend on firm-level surveys are to investigate what new contracts local suppliers have won as a result of being contracted by, or supplying to, oil or gas companies, and how the revenues of these local suppliers have grown over time. Positive trends in the two metrics would demonstrate if local suppliers are becoming more competitive and growing. But confidence in the results would be predicated on a clear cause-and-effect link between new contracts being won and the supplier support programs of the company or its lead contractors. To date there is little evidence that such metrics are being adopted.

Conclusion

In this chapter the authors explored some of the more common metrics used to measure local content in the oil and gas sector, and shed light on other metrics that are less common but nonetheless have the potential to be adopted by regulators and companies in the future.

Regarding common metrics, those for measuring local content in the workforce are largely either by head count of nationals or by the proportion of wages paid to nationals. Both metrics are relatively easy to administer and defensible with regards to the reliability of data used, although the formulae for the local proportion of total wages can differ considerably depending on the assumptions being made. The two metrics can generate very different results, and care is needed to explain clearly what is actually being measured.

With regard to metrics for measuring local procurement, most common is to report expenditure against some classification of a vendor or supplier as being local. Various criteria are used to define local. But the most common criterion, likely because of ease of administration, is to refer to the office address given in the vendor registration form or the invoice. Because using an office address to define a local vendor can lead to markedly overestimated levels of local content, some government are now mandating the use of build-up and build-down methods to measure value addition of expenditure on local goods and services.

Finally, although not common at present, it is likely that in the future regulators will mandate the use of metrics to measure the long-term development, efficiency, and competitiveness of local workforces and suppliers.

Notes

1. Ministry of Industry Regulation No. 15/16 2011: Manual on Utilization of Domestically Produced Goods and Services for Government Procurement and Local Content Calculation.

2. Employment of Foreign Citizens Non-Resident, Decree 5/95, Ministry of the Interior, Republic of Angola, http://www.sme.ao/attachments/article/209/Decree%20No.%20 5-95%20of%20April%207%20-%20Employment%20of%20Foreign%20Citizens%20 Non-resident.pdf.

3. The reader is referred to the Agreement on the Exploration, Development and Production Sharing for the Shah Deniz Prospective Area in the Azerbaijan Sector of the Caspian Sea, 1996, http://www.bp.com/liveassets/bp_internet/bp_caspian/bp_ caspian_en/STAGING/local_assets/downloads_pdfs/pq/SD_PSA.pdf.

4. An overview of the administrative simplicity and reliability of selected metrics is shown in tables 4.1 and 4.2.

5. In one economic assessment of local content in the upstream oil sector in Kazakhstan, the in-country allowances and social taxes paid to and on behalf of expatriates were— on their own—three times the total gross wages and social taxes paid to and on behalf of all national citizens in the same company (Warner 2010).

6. Decree 964/2012 on Approval of the Unified Methodology of Calculation by Organizations of Kazakhstan (Local) Content in Case of Procurement of Goods, Work and Services, Sept 2012.

7. Republic of Indonesia, BP Migas—PTK 007/Rev.1 to PTK 007/Rev.2.

8. Republic of Angola Law 14/2003 Angolan Private Entrepreneurship Promotion.

9. This is an estimate, based on taking the central value in each category of contract, plus an assumed $3 billion for a single engineering, procurement and construction (EPC) contract in the highest contract value category.

10. Annex 3 Rule of Origin to TIG ASEAN Rules of Origin, available at http://www. aseansec.org/AKFTA%20documents%20signed%20at%20aem-rok,24aug06,KL-pdf/ Annex%203%20to%20TIG%20(ROO)-%20ASEAN%20Version%20-%20 august%2006-final.pdf.

11. This excludes expatriate staff's base salaries and bonuses that are normally paid overseas.

12. Brazilian Local Content Regulation for Concession Agreements, Agencia Nacional do Petroleo, Gas Natural e Biocombustives, http://www.braziltexas.org/attachments/files/401/ANP-Marcelo.pdf.

13. Republic of Kazakhstan, Decree 964 (2010) Uniform Method of Kazakh Content Calculation by Companies when Purchasing Goods, Works and Services

14. For a full description of IncoTerms, see http://www.iccwbo.org/products-and-services/trade-facilitation/incoterms-2010/

15. This, however, assumes that the proportion of sales price that is foreign overhead and foreign mark-up is not material, which may not be the case.

16. Manual on Supply Chain Management for Production Sharing Contract Contractor—Book Two Revision-II, BPMIGAS 2011 (unofficial English translation of regulation 0003/BP00000/2011/SO).

17. Company Benefits Weightings, Appendix IX RI Regulation of the Minister of Industry 16/M-IND/PER/2/2001, 21 February 2011.

References

GRI (Global Reporting Initiative). 2012. "Sustainability Reporting Guidelines and Oil and Gas Sector Supplement, Version 3.1," 34–36. https://www.globalreporting.org/resourcelibrary/OGSS-G3.1-Complete.pdf.

Roberts, S. 2007. "National Development Banks in Sustainable Financing: Addressing Market Failures." Presentation to the Competition Commission and the University of Witwatersrand. Johannesburg, November, 22–23. http://www.authorstream.com/Presentation/Donato-45182-NDBs-MSC-SA-Roberts-National-Development-Banks-Sustainable-Financing-addressing-market-failures-Thinking-ND-rob-Education-ppt-powerpoint/

Warner, M. 2010. "Unpacking Local Content Metrics and Measurement: Local Content Solutions." Briefing No. 5, Local Content Solutions. http://www.localcontentsolutions.com/pdf/SolutionsSeries5.pdf.

WBCSD (World Business Council for Sustainable Development). 2012. *A Framework for Dialogue on National Market Participation and Competitiveness*. Geneva: WBCSD. http://www.wbcsd.org/Pages/EDocument/EDocumentDetails.aspx?ID=14421&NoSearchContextKey=true.

## CHAPTER 5

The Design and Implementation of Local Content Policies: Lessons Learned

Think global, act local.

—Patrick Geddes

The design of effective and sustainable local content policies (LCPs) and the choice of policy tools for their implementation require the definition of the economic, social, and political objectives that policy makers wish to achieve through their application. LCPs targeting the oil and gas sector need to take into account geology and geography (size of known and likely reserves, their location, development cost); level of economic diversification; structure of the labor market (unemployment rates, skills level, and distribution); access to energy; structure of the oil and gas sector (size and strength of players, level of competition, degree of integration); issues related to trade agreements and participation in economic unions; and the level of regulatory and institutional capacity. This explains why policies and tools that work well in one context may not yield the same results when used in others.

This approach—discussed in chapters 2–4 and schematized for ease of reference in figure 5.1—is now applied to the analysis of LCPs in a selected sample of petroleum-producing counties, including Angola, Brazil, Indonesia, Kazakhstan, Malaysia, and Trinidad and Tobago. The authors first summarize the main aspects of LCPs in the sample countries, and discuss issues related to the choice of policy objectives and implementation tools. Reference to other petroleum-producing countries is also made.

We then list the most common policy issues that have emerged from our analysis. Finally, we conclude by offering preliminary observations on which issues are key to the design of coherent and sustainable LCPs.

Figure 5.1 Local Content Policy Flow Chart

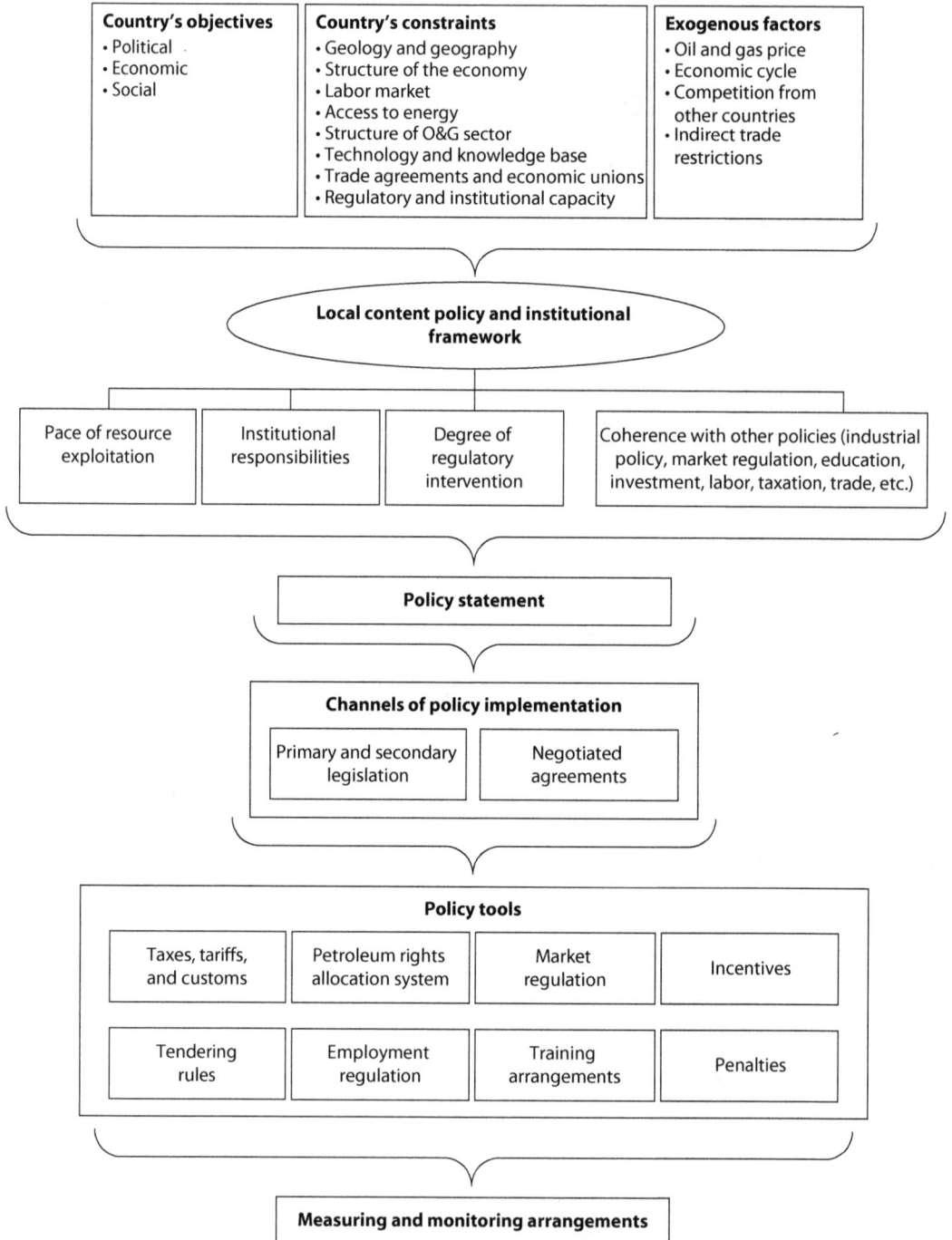

Country's objectives	Country's constraints	Exogenous factors
• Political	• Geology and geography	• Oil and gas price
• Economic	• Structure of the economy	• Economic cycle
• Social	• Labor market	• Competition from
	• Access to energy	other countries
	• Structure of O&G sector	• Indirect trade
	• Technology and knowledge base	restrictions
	• Trade agreements and economic unions	
	• Regulatory and institutional capacity	

Local content policy and institutional framework

Pace of resource exploitation	Institutional responsibilities	Degree of regulatory intervention	Coherence with other policies (industrial policy, market regulation, education, investment, labor, taxation, trade, etc.)

Policy statement

Channels of policy implementation

Primary and secondary legislation	Negotiated agreements

Policy tools

Taxes, tariffs, and customs	Petroleum rights allocation system	Market regulation	Incentives
Tendering rules	Employment regulation	Training arrangements	Penalties

Measuring and monitoring arrangements

Source: World Bank data.

Local Content Policies in a Selected Sample of Countries

Case Studies

This subsection contains a description of LCPs in a sample of petroleum-producing countries, and serves as basis for the analysis of policy design and implementation issues presented in the following subsection. The choice of case study countries, which include Angola, Brazil, Indonesia, Kazakhstan, Malaysia, and Trinidad and Tobago, has been largely driven by the availability of information, the length of each country's experience with LCPs, and the level of economic and sector development. Because LCPs that leverage petroleum activities require a medium to long time frame for any appreciable effect to be observed, new producers have not been included in our sample. Furthermore, an assessment of the relative efficiency and effectiveness of alternative LCPs, which requires the availability of detailed time series, is beyond the scope of this paper and has not been attempted.[1]

Table 5.1 summarizes: (i) each country's context, policy objectives, policy tools, and monitoring arrangements; and (ii) the main conclusions from the case studies. Detailed case studies are presented in a separate background paper downloadable from http://issuu.com/world.bank.publications/docs/local_content_policies_in_the_oil_and_gas_sector.

Lessons Learned

As argued earlier in this paper, a country's social, political, and economic objectives affect the way LCPs are defined and implemented. Since social and political objectives cannot be easily generalized, this section will focus on design issues with respect to the achievement of LCPs' economic objectives.

From an economic viewpoint, a government would want to design a LCP that:

• Is consistent with other economic development policies
• Addresses market deficiencies
• Promotes competition and the emergence of an efficient domestic economy
• Fosters technology and knowledge spillovers
• Supports the development of adequate local skills
• Minimizes compliance and administrative costs
• Develops economies of scales or localization.

In the following pages the experience of the countries included in our case study sample is used to illustrate these points. Where appropriate other country examples are also provided.

Table 5.1 Key Features of LCPs in Case Study Countries

POLICY OBJECTIVE	ANGOLA
	COUNTRY CONTEXT
• Reduce inequalities faced by domestic companies vis-à-vis foreign companies • Encourage synergy among domestic companies	**Structure of the economy:** Once a diversified economy (agriculture and manufacturing), the country gradually increased its economic reliance on extractive industries, particularly petroleum and diamonds (50% of GDP in 2010, up from 35% in 1975). Refined petroleum products, coffee, sisal, fish and fish products, timber, and cotton are the main exports beside crude oil and diamonds. Angola has a relatively young population. High unemployment rates (25%), and a weak education system (both state and privately owned) have been important drivers of LCPs **Geology:** Three major sedimentary basins lie along the coastline (Lower Congo, Dem. Rep., Kwanza, and Namibe) with different degrees of maturity. Angola has an estimated 13.5 bbl proven oil reserves (1% of the world's proven oil reserves), and produces 2.3% of the world's oil production. Over 90% of oil production is exported. Angola's natural gas reserves are estimated at 10.9 tcf. Most recent discoveries were made deep offshore **Structure of the petroleum sector:** The national oil company, Sonangol, is the concessionaire, and participates in most PSAs. Participants include most of the large and medium-sized IOCs, as well as NOCs from other countries Local industrial capacity has been created in the manufacturing of umbilicals, risers, and flowlines, which is helping to create a demand for metal working capabilities (thus potentially benefiting other sectors such as construction and infrastructure). Other local services companies provide sale, contracting, and after-sale services (Teka 2011) Angola has one refinery that meets about 50% of the domestic market needs, and plans to build a much larger refinery for export. Natural gas is currently either reinjected or flared, but plans to build an LNG plant are in place **Trade agreements:** Member of WTO since 1996, and therefore bound by the General Agreement on Tariffs and Trade (GATT). As a least-developed country, Angola obtained a seven-year grace period under the Agreement on Trade Related Investment Measures (TRIMs). Angola has not made specific commitments with respect to the energy sector under the General Agreement on Trade in Services (GATS) Angola is not a signatory to the WTO Agreement on Government Procurement Angola is a signatory to the SADAC trade protocol in 2003 that calls for reduction of tariffs and harmonization of trade policies to facilitate trade among SADAC countries. But its implementation has been delayed Customs cooperation agreements are in place with Portugal and São Tomé and Príncipe. Bilateral investment treaties are in place with several countries including China, Argentina, Portugal, South Africa, the United Kingdom, Italy, Germany, and Cape Verde

(table continues on next page)

Table 5.1 Key Features of LCPs in Case Study Countries *(continued)*

LOCAL CONTENT POLICY	Key policy elements:
Channel of policy: • Law 10/79 mandating Sonangol to employ and train nationals • Decree 20/82 on the Angolanization of the petroleum industry workforce • Law 14/03 establishing a framework for the promotion of Angolan private enterprises in all sectors of the economy • Decree 127/03 on domestic sourcing of goods and services in petroleum related activities • Local content provisions in production sharing contracts • Decree 13/10 grants protection to nationals against discriminatory hiring and remuneration practices • Petroleum sharing contracts set forth specific requirements in terms of level and area of training for Angolan workers, and extend training requirements to subcontractors providing services to the contractor for more than one year	***Labor:*** *Policies to increase the number of national workers:* • Minimum 70% Angolan citizens in the workforce by head count • Submit annual recruitment plans for the Ministry of Petroleum's approval • Protection of nationals against discriminatory hiring and remuneration practices defined in regulations *Policies designed to restrict foreign workers:* • Foreign workers may be hired only if no qualified national worker is available • Foreign nonresident contracts duration limited to 36 months • Temporary foreign workers below 90 days to be approved by Ministry of Labor *Policies designed to promote nationals' skills development:* • Angolanization targets by job grade set by the Ministry of Petroleum for groups of expatriates or on a case-by-case basis • Companies operating in the petroleum sector shall make contributions to the training and development fund based on the scope of activity • Training programs for Angolan nationals to be approved by the Ministry of Petroleum ***Sourcing of goods and services:*** *Policies that involve margins of preference:* • Goods and services not requiring heavy capital investment and with a basic, medium, or higher level of non-specialized know-how are reserved for Angolan companies. Foreign companies may take part in the initiative of Angolan companies • National private or state-owned suppliers are preferred over foreign suppliers if the price offered is no more than 10% higher than that of foreign suppliers • Companies with at least 51% Angolan ownership receive fiscal incentives, loans, subsidies, and preferential treatment in the award of oil and gas concessions **Policy tools:** • The ***national oil company,*** Sonangol, is a major instrument of local content development. It is mandated to provide national companies with: (1) preferential treatment in the award of contracts; (2) reduction of petroleum and industrial taxes; and (3) nonrefundable subsidies, loans and financial guarantees • The ***E&P licensing system:*** The bidding parameters for exploration and production rights include a "contribution for social projects," weighted at 20%. Bidders are not allowed to present joint bidding. Sonangol decides the composition of the participating interests in each block and the operatorship. A share of participating interest is reserved for Angolan companies and varies depending on the block

(table continues on next page)

Table 5.1 Key Features of LCPs in Case Study Countries *(continued)*

Incentives:

- Contribution to the training and development fund are deductible costs for the purpose of corporate income tax calculation
- Costs associated with the training of Angolan staff are allowable production costs
- Fiscal incentives, loans, and subsidies are offered to companies with at least 51% Angolan ownership

Penalties:

- Companies that breach the laws on Angolanization of the workforce are subject to monetary penalties, and are banned from entering into new contracts in the petroleum sector

Institutional responsibilities:

- The Ministry of Petroleum is responsible for: (1) the formulation of LCPs, (2) the approval of foreign workers recruitment and annual recruitment plans, and (3) approval of capacity building plans for nationals
- The Ministry of Industry publishes a list of domestic goods suppliers
- The Chamber of Commerce publishes a list of domestic service providers
- The Ministry of Public Administration (Center for Employment and Vocational Training) certifies the lack of suitable Angolan nationals as a condition for hiring foreign workers
- Sonangol: (1) negotiates LC provisions in petroleum agreements; (2) manages the licensing of petroleum rights; and (3) manages procurement aspects of LCPs through the approval of procurement activities and its influence over the selection of suppliers. The company is the main vehicle for enhancing local participation in the oil and gas sector

Measurement and monitoring:

- Monitoring of policy implementation is done by the Ministry of Petroleum with respect to the recruitment of foreign workers
- A process and methodology to measure the impact of training activities and the effective utilization of resources from training funds does not seem to be in place, particularly with respect to funds provided to universities by the Ministry of Petroleum
- Monitoring of domestic sourcing of goods and services is carried out by Sonangol

---

MAIN CONCLUSIONS

- Angola's LCPs have been in place for approximately 30 years. Over time, their scope and implementation tools have been refined to address new challenges
- Despite the longstanding training requirements applicable to companies in the oil and gas sector, higher technical-level training is still inadequate
- The effectiveness of quantitative targets to drive employment of nationals and their progression to higher technical and managerial positions is difficult to assess, given the lack of publicly available data on the outcome as well as on the rationale for the chosen benchmarks
- LCPs on domestic sourcing of goods and services have been generally effective in raising local participation, although most of the local links seem to involve basic general products, trading in imported goods, and basic services. On the other hand, Sonangol has diversified in a number of sectors more or less directly linked to the oil sector—including drilling, fabrication, transportation, industrial supplies and infrastructure, distribution, storage, services, banking, food retail and catering, civil engineering, and real estate development. In this sense, the national oil company has been the primary tool for economic diversification. However information on their efficiency and the extent to which they contribute to cascading backward links is not publicly available

(table continues on next page)

Table 5.1 Key Features of LCPs in Case Study Countries *(continued)*

	BRAZIL
POLICY OBJECTIVE	COUNTRY CONTEXT
• To increase the participation of the national industry on competitive bases • To improve national techno-logical development • To improve the level of national capabilities. • To create job opportunities for nationals and achieve growth in income	**Structure of the economy:** The world's seventh-wealthiest economy (2011 GDP \$2.2 trillion), Brazil is the largest country in area and population in Latin America and the Caribbean. Brazil enjoys a large domestic market, high level of sophistication of business, efficient financial markets, and high rates of innovation and technological adoption. The 2011 Global Competitiveness Report placed Brazil in the 53rd position out of a total of 142 countries. Brazil's GDP grew 7.5% in 2010 and 2.7% in 2011, because of the new global slowdown. The service sector is the largest component of GDP at 67.0%, followed by the industrial sector at 27.5%. Agriculture represents 5.5% of GDP (2011). The Brazilian labor force is estimated at 100.77 million, of which 10% is occupied in agriculture, 19% in the industry sector, and 71% in the service sector. By 2050 the elderly are estimated to account for 49% of the Brazilian population: an increase with impacts on the economy, the public services, and the society Brazil's strong domestic market is less vulnerable to external crisis, and Brazilians are benefiting from stable economic growth, rela-tively low inflation rates, and improvements in social well-being. On the other hand, multiple structural factors hinder the progress of the country, including inadequate infrastructure, a complex fiscal system, heavy bureaucracy, and a shortage of skilled labor. Despite important advances in institutional reforms, the quality of government services in relation to expenditures also remains relatively low compared to other middle-income countries. Inequality remains at relatively high levels for a middle-income country, and there is still a large gap in access to primary and secondary education. After having reached universal coverage in primary education, Brazil is now struggling to improve the quality and outcome of the system, especially at the basic and secondary levels **Geology:** Brazil is endowed with 15.1 billion barrels of proven oil reserves, and 16 trillion cubic feet of proven natural gas reserves. Production from onshore and shallow water basins is at a plateau or in decline, and most of the foreseen growth in production will be from deep water basins. The country's 29 sedimentary basins are spread across the north, coastal regions, and deep waters. Most of the country's inland natural gas reserves are unexploited due to limited transportation capacity. Recent presalt discoveries will potentially move the country's worldwide rank in oil reserves from fifteenth to fifth, increasing the country's reserves to 114 billion barrels **Structure of the petroleum sector:** The national oil company, Petrobras, is the dominant player. Created in 1953, Petrobras held a monopoly over the oil and gas value chain (except for retail and wholesale distribution) until 1997, when the sector was liberalized. Over the years, the company built internal capabilities through knowledge transfer from foreign experts, training programs, and in-house research activities. Petrobras remains the dominant player in the oil and gas upstream sector, with over 90% of oil and gas production. Other players include the major oil companies and local private firms **Trade agreements:** Brazil's specific commitments under GATs cover business services, communication services, construction and related engineering services, distribution services, financial services, tourism and travel related services, and transport services. Brazil is also member of the MERCOSUR, and is party to various bilateral agreements on trade and economic cooperation, including on O&G, other sectors such as commodities, aerospace, consumer electronics, and information technology

(table continues on next page)

Table 5.1 Key Features of LCPs in Case Study Countries *(continued)*

	LOCAL CONTENT POLICY	
	Channel of policy:	**Key policy elements:**
	• The petroleum law number 9478/97 sets out general local content principles	*Labor*
		There are no local content requirements with respect to employment
	• Minimum local content requirements are established in licensing round for the award of oil and gas exploration and production rights, and change over time and for different type of acreage (based on relative maturity and location)	*Sourcing of goods and services*
		• Before 2007 local content regulation imposed overall minimum targets for local procurement those operators and their partners were required to meet. Since 2007, in addition to global targets, minimum local content targets for each subcategory of expenditure are established in connection with each licensing round
	• Specific commitments are set out in petroleum contracts.	• Operators must invest 1% of each field's gross revenues on oil and gas related research and development. Up to 0.5% can be invested in operator's research facilities in Brazil. The rest shall finance research to be carried out by local universities or research institutes accredited by ANP
	• ANP Regulation No. 6/2007 Resolution No.36/2007 specify the criteria and procedures for the calculation and certification of local content	**Policy tools:**
		• Being the major local player in the oil and gas sector, Petrobras plays a crucial role in the implementation of local content policies. In addition, the company is part of a longstanding agreement with SABRESABRE—a national small business support association—for the inclusion of micro and small enterprises in the petroleum supply chain. The agreement provides for the mapping of potential business opportunities for SMEs, and the provision of training and other support services to facilitate the development of local capacity
	• ANP Regulation No. 8/2007 and Resolution No. 38/2007 specify the procedure for audit of local content certification	
	• ANP Regulation No. 9/2007 and Resolution No. 39/2007 specify the reporting procedure and format	• The **Programa de Mobilização da Indústria Nacional de Petróleo e Gás Natural** (PROMINP), created by the federal government in 2003, plays a major facilitating role by identifying challenges to the implementation of local content policies, and leading training programs. The most relevant initiatives under PROMINP include the following:
		- The Petrobras Supply Chain Financing Program, Progredir, offering competitive financing to suppliers contracted by Petrobras. The program involves the six largest banks in Brazil and is managed on an online platform
		- The national competitive diagnostic study that set the basis for series of technological, infrastructure, capabilities, and financing initiatives designed to address identified gaps in local capacity

(table continues on next page)

Table 5.1 Key Features of LCPs in Case Study Countries *(continued)*

	The E&P licensing system Minimum local content targets are established by the ANP in connection with licensing rounds for the award of exploration and production rights. Requirements are block specific (deep water, shallow water, and onshore), and phase specific (exploration and development). Bidders may bid higher local content percentages. The relative weights for local content, technical, and financial scores are set by the regulator ahead of each licensing round **Incentives and penalties** In 1999 a federal tax exemption regime (REPERTO) was launched offering tax benefits to exports of oil and gas related goods manufactured in Brazil. The incentive is expected to terminate in 2020 Raw material to be used in the domestic manufacturing of goods are exempted from social security system (COFINS), import tax (II), tax on industrial products (IPI), and social integration plan (PIS) Concessional financing from the national development bank (BNDES) to local suppliers The Merchant Marine Fund, launched by the government in December 2009, finances the construction of 17 new shipyards and the expansion of 5 existing ones Research and development projects qualify for governmental direct assistance and tax reliefs In case a higher local content level is achieved in the exploration phase, the incremental value achieved can be transferred to the development phase upon approval by ANP. In case of noncompliance, upon award of contract a fine is applied. The fine is based on a schedule linked to the nonrealized value of local investment. But concessions agreements allow the concessionaire to request ANP to waive local content requirements on items in case of excessively high prices, delivery times or absence of technology
	Institutional responsibilities: Conselho Nacional de Politica Energetica establishes guidelines for local content policies in coordination with the Ministry of Mines and Energy Regulatory activities fall under the responsibilities of Agecia Nacional do Petroleo, which sets the minimum local content requirements; defines criteria, accredits, and audits certification entities; accredits research and development institutions; issues templates for local content reporting; checks local content commitments and apply penalties in case of incompliance; and runs training programs, funded by revenues from royalties Banco Nacional de Desenvolvimento Economico e Socialal also sets minimum local content requirements for activities that they finance Several independent institutions, of which National Organization of the Petroleum Industry (ONIP) is the largest, carry out vendors certification programs, training, and advocacy activities

(table continues on next page)

Table 5.1 **Key Features of LCPs in Case Study Countries** (continued)

- The governing body of the PROMINP includes the Minister of Mining and Energy, the Minister of Development, Industry, and Trade Ministry, President and Services Director of Petrobras, the President of BNDES, the President of ONIP and the President of the Brazilian Petroleum Institute

Measurement and monitoring:

Prior to 2005 companies was required to state the origin of sourced goods and services without providing supporting evidence. From 2005, local content is measured on expenditure. Annex III to Regulation 6/2007—a local content primer—includes definitions related to local content and details the methodology for calculating the level of local content for equipment and goods, equipment and goods for temporary use, services, systems, and subsystems

Monitoring activities are carried out by the ANP

- Local content reporting happens on a quarterly basis
- Reporting is block specific for the exploration phase and area specific for the development phase
- Templates are provided by ANP and are standardized for each phase (that is, exploration and development)
- Auditing takes place at the end of the exploration phase as well as the development phase

MAIN CONCLUSIONS

The strong local content policy framework and regulations have driven an increasing share of local employment, goods and services, and are helping to reestablish Brazil as a shipbuilding nation. The development of local content relied heavily on and was driven by Petrobras' activities and development plans. Complementary trade and investment regulation were also put in place to shore up inward investment. Brazilian regulations mandate targets for goods and services of domestic origin. In this sense, they encourage the emergence of a competitive local supply industry by incentivizing inward investment by international suppliers and service contractors that strive to meet these targets. But industry observers have pointed at bottlenecks and inefficiency exacerbated by ambitious targets.

INDONESIA

POLICY OBJECTIVE	COUNTRY CONTEXT
• To develop local capability in the oil field services and equipment sectors so as to enable domestic companies to compete nationally, regionally, and internationally	**Structure of the economy:** Indonesia continues to post significant economic growth. As of April 2012, the country's economy is expected to grow by 6.1% in 2012 and increase to 6.4% in 2013. The country's GDP per capita has steadily risen from $773 in the year 2000 to $3,495 in 2011. The key contributors to Indonesia's GDP were the manufacturing and service sectors (respectively, a 45% and 38% share). Foreign direct investment has historically been vital to Indonesia's economic development. Inflows were particularly strong in 2011, reaching $18.9 billion (an increase of $13.9 billion from 2010), driven by low labor cost, tax incentives, a reduction in bureaucratic procedures, and an improvement in the country's macroeconomic stability. Petroleum and mining have dominated exports commodities over the past 10 years. Employment growth has been slower than population growth. Public services remain inadequate by middle-income standards. Indonesia is also doing poorly in a number of health- and infrastructure-related indicators. The primary resource sector absorbs the largest share of employment, followed by labor-intensive services (respectively, 45% and 30.7% of total employment in 2008). The low-cost labor force is characterized by an overall shortage of skilled labor, and by rigid market regulations. Compared to regional averages, Indonesia ranks 4th lowest in terms of enrollment rates in tertiary education (23% in 2010) and average workers compensation.

(table continues on next page)

Table 5.1 Key Features of LCPs in Case Study Countries *(continued)*

Thanks to recent reforms—decentralization, simplification of bureaucracy, and reducing corruption—the business environment has improved, although it remains below its regional peers. Indonesia has formulated a long-term development plan that spans 2005–25. It is segmented into five-year medium-term plans, each with different development priorities. The current medium-term development plan covering 2009–14 is the second phase and focuses on promoting the quality of human resources, developing science and technology, and strengthening economic competitiveness.

Geology:

Indonesia's 11 petroleum basins are spread all over its territory, both onshore and offshore. While oil reserves have been declining since the early 1980s (reaching 4 billion barrels in 2011) natural gas reserves increased from 0.8 trillion cubic meters in 1890 to 3.1 trillion cubic meters in 2011. Most of the currently producing fields are locate onshore and in shallow waters

Structure of the petroleum sector:

The petroleum sector plays a key role in the Indonesian economy, accounting for over 7% of GDP and 25% of revenue in 2010. In 2004 the country became a net oil importer and began a shift toward natural gas (of which production has been increasing) for energy generation. Several attempts have been made to slow the decline in oil reserves, including the use of incentives for enhanced oil recovery, deep-water exploration, and the offering of new exploration acreage. The oil upstream sector is dominated by international oil companies (Chevron, BP, ConocoPhillips, ExxonMobil, Total, PetroChina, and CNOOC) operating pursuant to production sharing contracts. The licensing of oil and gas exploration and production rights is done through competitive tenders. Indonesia's refining capacity is distributed over nine plants (some are aging with very limited output), of which eight are operated by Pertamina

Trade agreements:

Indonesia joined the WTO in January of 1995. Under the GATS agreement, Indonesia has made commitments for professional and business services, telecommunications, construction and engineering services, educational services, financial services, health services, tourism and maritime cargo handling. But several limitations and exemptions apply, including with respect to banking services, movement of semiskilled personnel, employment of low-skilled personnel from other countries, preferential short listing in international competitive bidding for construction services in government funded tenders. Indonesia is not a signatory to the WTO Agreement on Government Procurement

LOCAL CONTENT POLICY	
Channel of policy:	*Policies to increase the number of national workers:*
• Oil and Gas Law No. 22/2001 segregating regulatory roles and commercial operations • Presidential Regulation No. 54/2010 on procurement of domestic goods and services	• The recruitment of domestic workers requires the regulator's approval. Salary and benefits that can be offered by companies are controlled and capped by the regulator • Domestic companies operating in the downstream sector are required to give priority to local employment, which shall be done in coordination with the regional government and shall favor employment in the area of operation

(table continues on next page)

Table 5.1 Key Features of LCPs in Case Study Countries *(continued)*

• Supply Chain Management Manual PTK 007/2009 as revised in 2011
• The 2005 Guidelines for Human Resource Management of BPMIGAS and revision of 2008
• Ministry of Industry Regulation No. 15–16/2011 on local content calculation;
• Investment Law No. 25/2007 (applicable only to limited liability companies domiciled in Indonesia and owned by Indonesian investors)
• Regulation No. 258/PMK.011/2011 on caps applicable to expatriate costs;
• Company Law No. 40/2007
• Joint Cooperation Contracts (that is, Production Sharing Contracts, Technical Assistance Contracts, Joint Operation Agreements, Enhanced Oil Recovery Contracts, and Technical Evaluation Agreements) for upstream activities
	Policies designed to restrict foreign workers:
	• The use of expatriate personnel is allowed for certain positions and areas of expertise that cannot be fulfilled by Indonesian personnel. These positions are controlled by the regulator, and Indonesianization plans for these positions are reviewed annually. Specific regulations detail the procedure to be followed, including the obtaining of approval from the regulator
	• Expatriates costs are cost recoverable under joint cooperation contracts, up to a maximum amount determined by the Ministry of Finance
	
	Policies designed to promote nationals' skills development:
	• Targets for the recruitment of Indonesian workers are set by skill level and phase of project development
	• Companies are required to establish and deliver training programs designed to achieve the local target levels
	
	Sourcing of goods and services
	Policies that involve a margin of preference for domestic suppliers:
	• Tender price normalization is based on percentage local content levels proposed in bids. Additional price premia are granted in conjunction with the company status (domestic or foreign) and the activity's contribution to the development of the local supply chain. Price formulas for goods and services are detailed in the regulations
	
	Mandated targets for procurement of local goods and services:
	• Priority is given to domestic companies in the procurement of services. Bidders must commit to a minimum 35% local content for contracts whose value is above $100,000 (or a minimum 30% if less than three bidders are able to commit to 35%); special procurement procedures apply for engineering, procurement and construction services;
	• Minimum local content levels for goods vary with the type of goods and the suppliers' local content levels. More specifically:
	  – For "mandatory goods" (that is, primary goods for exploration and production where there exists at least one domestic manufacturer who has a minimum local content plus company benefit weight [BMP] level of 40%), restricted tender lists are used that include suppliers that have a demonstrated minimum 15% local content. This procurement rule applies to all contracts independent of the contract value
	  – For "maximized goods" (that is, primary goods that are produced domestically where there exists at least one domestic manufacturer who has a minimum local content level of 25% and no domestic manufacturer with a local content plus BMP of 40%, and supporting goods where there exists at least one domestic manufacturer who has a minimum local content level of 25%), restricted tenders are used for primary goods, and open tenders for supporting goods, both open to domestic manufacturers that have achieved at least 10% local content. This procurement rule applies to contracts whose value is above $100,000

Table 5.1 Key Features of LCPs in Case Study Countries *(continued)*

- For "empowered goods" (that is, goods that are produced locally by at least one domestic manufacturer that has at least 5% local content where there are no local suppliers that can demonstrate at least 25% local content), restricted tender lists are used that include all domestic suppliers that have at least 5% local content. This procurement rule applies to contracts whose value is above $100,000

Policy tools:

The E&P licensing system

- Minimum local content targets are not part of the criteria for the award of oil and gas exploration and production rights. Indeed local content provisions set forth in the oil and gas law and implementing regulation apply to all companies, local or foreign

Incentives and penalties

- Administrative and financial penalties are applied to providers of goods and services that fail to deliver the local content targets specified in their contracts, including a one-year exclusion from participating in future tenders related to the same petroleum sharing agreement (PSA). If failure to deliver local content targets affects more than one PSA, the supplier of goods or services is blacklisted. Financial penalties vary depending on whether the achieved local content level would have changed the ranking of successful bidders or not

- In assessing implementation of contractual provisions, suppliers may benefit from BMP when they invest in developing the local supply industry (that is, empowering local small and micro enterprises, developing local capability in environment, safety and health management, investing on community development, and developing local after-sales services). BMP can increase a contract's local content level by up to 15%.

- For services, any of the bidding requirements (that is, local content, value of contract implemented by domestic company, amount of physical work carried out in Indonesia) may be compensated by a loan from a state-owned enterprise (BUMN) or a regional government–owned enterprise (BUMD). Detailed rules are laid out in the procurement guidelines issued by BPMIGAS

- Investment Law No.40/2007 provides exemption or relief of import duty on imported capital goods, machines, or equipment for production needs in the downstream sector; and/or exemption or postponement of value- added tax on such capital goods or equipment. These facilities are only available for Indonesian investors only (so-called PT companies)

(table continues on next page)

Table 5.1 Key Features of LCPs in Case Study Countries *(continued)*

Institutional responsibilities:

- The Ministry of Energy and Mineral Resources is charged, among other things, with creating and implementing Indonesia's energy policy, ensuring that business activities reflect existing laws, and awarding contracts. The Directorate General of Oil and Gas of the Ministry of Energy and Mineral Resources is tasked with the offering of exploration and production blocks, lifting calculation and division between local and central government, and preparing oil and gas policies. Prior to 2001 these functions were carried out by Pertamina, the national oil company

- The Executive Agency for Upstream Oil and Gas Business Activities (BP MIGAS)—established in 2002 as a nonprofit state-owned legal entity—controls upstream activities and managers petroleum contracts on behalf of the government. BP MIGAS reports to the President of the Republic, and works in coordination with the Ministry of Energy and Mineral Resources. BPMIGAS is responsible for the design and monitoring of implementation of local content policies in the upstream oil and gas sector

- The Executive Agency for Downstream Oil and Gas Business Activities (BPH MIGAS), established in 2002, regulates and supervises all distribution and trading activities, including the availability, allocation, transportation and marketing of natural gas for domestic and international needs. BPHMIGAS supervises fuel oil distribution and transportation of gas by pipelines operated by domestic companies

- Regional governments are involved in the approval of field development plans through the issuance of local permits and land rights

- Pertamina was created in 1968 to consolidate the management and control of oil and gas activities. It was assigned with the full spectrum of responsibilities in exploration, production, processing, refining, transportation, and marketing of oil and gas products. By means of the oil and gas law no. 44 of 1960, and the later law no. 8 of 1971, the national oil company became solely responsible for all petroleum activities in the country. The company was restructured pursuant to the Oil and Gas Law No. 22/2001, and later transformed into a limited liability company—PT Pertamina—with the majority of shares owned by the state, with a view to privatizing it (Decree No. 31/2003)

Measurement and monitoring:

- Production sharing contractors must align their local content targets with BP MIGAS. Specific templates have been developed by the regulator that provided for local content targets to be set by activity

- Contractors submit monthly report to BP MIGAS following the format and instructions contained in BP MIGAS procurement guidelines

- The Ministry of Trade issues local content certificates to certify the level of local content for goods. For services, local content is computed as the ratio of the cost of the service net of foreign components to the total cost of the service. The percentage local content is set with respect to the place of origin and the ownership of the producer (for example, goods that are produced locally by company that is wholly owned by Indonesians receive 100% local content, while they would receive only a 75% if 75% of the company was owned by foreign investors or if they were produced abroad by a company wholly owned by Indonesian investors). The measurement of local content includes the second- and third- tier contractors (detailed rules apply to the determination of LC for second- and third-tier suppliers) Similar criteria apply for measuring local content in services

- Monitoring of compliance is made by BP MIGAS annually

(table continues on next page)

Table 5.1 Key Features of LCPs in Case Study Countries *(continued)*

MAIN CONCLUSIONS
Indonesia's assertive regulatory framework aims to create opportunities for the development of local human and industrial capacity in a wide range of activities that provide input and utilize the output of the petroleum sector. This has been done through a complex set licenses and business permits, minimum employment targets, procurement limitations, and investment and company regulation. This policy, coupled with state direct state participation in all links of the value chain, has been in use, with various degrees of flexibility, since the early 1970s. Nonetheless, compared to its regional neighbors that enjoy less important oil and gas endowments, Indonesia's LCPs would seem to have been less effective in generating spillover effects. Most local companies are small, operate a basic technological level, and lack the industrial capacity and financial strength to become dominant suppliers to the local oil and gas industry, set aside to compete internationally. The complex regulatory environment may be among the factors that contributed to hindering the normal market processes that lead to the emergence of efficient and sustainable local manufacturing and technological capacity

KAZAKHSTAN	
POLICY OBJECTIVE	**COUNTRY CONTEXT**
• To support economic diversification • To reduce economic dependency on the petroleum sector	**Structure of the economy:** An upper-middle-income country, Kazakhstan's per capita GDP was $11,357 in 2011. Despite solid macroeconomic indicators, Kazakhstan's economy suffers from an overreliance on oil and extractive industries. Kazakhstan's economy is export-oriented. Petroleum products have increasingly dominated Kazakhstan's economy, accounting for approximately 70% of total exports since 2005. The industrial sector rests on the extraction and processing of natural resources and also on a relatively small machine-building sector. This sector specializes in construction equipment, tractors, agricultural machinery, and transportation equipment such as small buses and railroad cars. In response, Kazakhstan has embarked on an ambitious program of diversification, innovation, investment in human capital, and international trade integration for job creation Increasing emphasis is being put on strengthening governance, the business-enabling environment, and private enterprise. Key policy initiatives include measures to improve the quality of public services and to address skill shortages of the workforce, in particular to generate employment in the local economy through the promotion of small and medium enterprises **Geology:** Kazakhstan has a relatively immature but large oil and gas resource base. Most of the country's growth in production comes from offshore fields, as onshore ones are mostly mature or declining. Kazakhstan is a net exporter of both oil and gas. The main oil fields and reserves are in the western part of the country. At the end of 2011 oil Kazakhstan's proved oil reserves were estimated at 30.0 billion barrels, representing 1.8% of the world's reserves. The Tengiz, Kashagan, and Karachaganak fields contain over 50% of the country's reserves. Natural gas reserves were estimated at 66.4 trillion cubic feet at the end of 2011 (approximately 1% of the world's natural gas reserves)

(table continues on next page)

Table 5.1 Key Features of LCPs in Case Study Countries *(continued)*

Structure of the petroleum sector:

Rapid growth of Kazakhstan's oil and gas industry occurred after the country became independent in 1991 and opened the industry to foreign investors. By the early 2000s, the oil and gas industry was the major driver of the country's economy, accounting for about 62% of export earnings and close to 40% of the government's revenue. Although the national oil company—Kazmunaigaz—is an important player and participates in most field developments, the majority of production comes from private oil companies. The Kazakh government aims to use oil and gas revenues to spur overall economic development. To this end, it created the National Fund of Kazakhstan in 2000 as a stabilization mechanism to protect the economy from oil, gas and metals price volatility, and a strong national oil and gas company that would dominate the country's hydrocarbon sector (Olcott 2007). Kazakhstan's oil and gas sector has benefitted from strong foreign demand, comparatively strong domestic demand, a crossroads geographic location, a favorable foreign investment climate, and multiple joint ventures with western and eastern oil companies. The sector value chain is relatively complex. The upstream segment is dominated by international oil companies, while local companies dominate the downstream

Trade agreements:

Kazakhstan is a member of the Eurasian Economic Community (EAEC) and has entered into bilateral free trade agreements with most member countries, mostly in areas related to common customs and tariff regulation, indirect tax collection on trade, and general economic cooperation. The country is not a WTO member, and negotiation on its accession has been going on for over 15 years. In addition, Kazakhstan is signatory to various bilateral free trade agreements covering various areas, including facilitation of investments in the oil and gas sector

LOCAL CONTENT POLICY	
Channels of policy: • Law 291-IV/2010 on subsoil and subsoil users • Law 156-IV/2009 on public procurement • Decree 1139/2007 on the rules for the procurement of goods, works, and services for subsoil users • Decrees 965/2010 and 1018/2010 on reporting forms • Decree 1135/2010 on state program for local content development • Decrees 367/2010 and 964/2010 on the measurement of local content and the unified calculation method • Decree 45/2012 on expatriate workforce quota and work permit rules • PSAs, which contain local content obligations specific to the project/area of operation	**Key policy elements:** *Labor* *Policies to increase the number of national workers:* • Expatriate workforce quota and work permit rules mandate that medium and large businesses have 90% local content in workforce for technical personnel and 70% for company executives as of January 2012. Exemptions apply, including the three largest hydrocarbon projects—Tengiz, Karachaganak, and Kashagan—for three years, and small companies having up to 50 employees • Protection of nationals against discriminatory hiring and remuneration practices *Policies designed to restrict foreign workers:* • Geographical ring-fencing of expatriates' work permits, restricting mobility of expatriate workers across administrative territorial units *Policies designed to promote nationals' skills development:* • Minimum funding must be allocated to the training and education of Kazakh workers involved in the execution of the relevant petroleum contract, as well as other personnel specified by the Ministry of Oil and Gas

(table continues on next page)

Table 5.1 Key Features of LCPs in Case Study Countries *(continued)*

Sourcing of goods and services
Policies that involve margins of preference:
• Tender organizers must reduce the price offered by holders of CT-KZ certificate by 20%, provided their goods, works, and services correspond to the tender requirements and Republic of Kazakhstan technical regulations law (that is, Kazakh producers of works and services are understood as either citizens of Kazakhstan or legal entities registered in Kazakhstan whose staff includes no less than 95% Kazakh citizens; a Kazakh producer of goods is a legal entity registered in Kazakhstan that produces goods of Kazakhstan origin as confirmed by a certificate of origin issued by the Kazakhstan Chamber of Commerce and Industry. Owners of Kazakhstan legal entity may be local or foreign for the purposes of obtaining "Kazakhstan producer" status)
Guideline targets for procurement of local goods and services (no sanctions for noncompliance):
• Local content in public procurement shall be a minimum of 20% for goods and 15% for services and construction. A company with more than 50% foreign shareholding is considered as foreign and therefore excluded from participation in public procurement tenders, unless it fulfills all of the following criteria making it a domestic producer
• Kazakh content in private companies procurement shall be:
– Minimum 82.5% for services
– Minimum 11% for goods
Policy tools:
• Legislation requires that production sharing agreements include at least 50% to be held by the national oil company KazMunaiGaz, and requires companies to submit their local procurement plans to the government for review. The company has set local content goals, and actively promotes local content development in its activities. These measures are detailed in the Program of the NC KazMunaiGaz JSC for the Development of Kazakhstan's Content for 2011–15
• The E&P licensing system
• The Unified Register of Domestic Producers and Foreign Investors created to improve transparency and reduce information asymmetry among potential suppliers

(table continues on next page)

Table 5.1 Key Features of LCPs in Case Study Countries *(continued)*

- The Subsoil Users Report Acceptance System is an online system for the management of the procurement processes of subsoil users and their contractors. It contains all procurement information from expression of interest to contract award

  Incentives

  In addition to the positive price discrimination in favor of local companies, multiple measures are taken to support local suppliers (that is, interest-free loans, advance payments for Kazakh contractors' equipment and personnel mobilization, support in certification, and technology transfer activities)

  Penalties

  - Law 291-IV/2010 provides for petroleum contracts to contain the size of penalties (fines, penalties) for failure or improper execution of commitments on the local content in goods, works, services and personnel
  - Noncompliance with procurement rules under decree 1139/2007 is subject to a monetary fine equal to 30% of the value of the violation for violations below 50% of the annual investment commitment, and contract termination for violation, with a value equates to 50% or more of the company's annual investment commitment

Institutional responsibilities:

- The Ministry of Oil and Gas and the Ministry of New Technologies are responsible for policy design
- The Kazakhstan Contract Agency (KRA) is tasked with promoting local content in the oil and gas value chain; oversee the Unified Register of Domestic Producers and Foreign Investors; assist local manufacturers in meeting industry standards and requirements; and carry out local content implementation analysis
- The Expert Council on Local Content participates in (1) the assessment of local content implementation for major projects and (2) the development of working programs for Tengiz, Kashagan, and Karachaganak, and sees to the interest of domestic suppliers. The council is under the supervision of the Ministry of Oil and comprises representatives of industry associations, suppliers of goods and services, subsoil users, and government policy experts
- The Technical Regulation and Metrology Committee is responsible for issuing the certificate of domestic producer

Measurement and monitoring:

- Specific formulae for the calculation of local content in goods, works, and services are set forth in decree 367/2010 (unified method for calculating local content)
- Subsoil users are required to file quarterly and annual reports in the KRA Register detailing their: (1) medium- and long-term procurement plans; (2) local content in goods, works and services; (3) local employment; and (4) training performance
- Local content in employment is monitored through the work permit applications and the subsoil users reports to the KRA
- Educational budgets are monitored by KRA. Unspent amounts are carried forward and must be spent before the end of the relevant petroleum contract

(table continues on next page)

Table 5.1 Key Features of LCPs in Case Study Countries *(continued)*

MAIN CONCLUSIONS

The level of local content in employment, works, goods, and services appears to have improved after the introduction of the unified methodology and certification process. LCPs in Kazakhstan extend beyond the first tier of contractors to include subcontractors, thus triggering both direct and indirect economic links

While local content in goods remains relatively low (12% in 2011), local content in works and services was respectively 58% and 69% in 2011. The highest levels of local content have been reached in services that require local knowledge and/or localization for effective and efficient execution, such as legal and insurance services, transportation, industrial waste management, permits and approvals, custom clearance services, and so on. Similar considerations apply to works. With respect to goods, high levels of local content have been observed with respect to the production of goods that require comparatively lower levels of technology and/or capital investment

KazMunaiGaz is the cornerstone of LCP implementation. The company actively promotes local content development through supply chain management and supplier capacity building. Specific targets and activities are outlined in the Program of the NC KazMunaiGaz JSC for the Development of Kazakhstan's Content for 2011–15

Although local content has been rapidly increasing, challenges remain with respect to the ability of industry to comply with the new local content requirements. These include the following: (1) a shortage of suppliers with specialized capacity to construct products in demand by subsurface users; (2) lower technological capacity among local suppliers than required by industry demand; (3) insufficient number of qualified local workers; and (4) insufficient investments directed toward the development of SMEs

Available data focus on reporting the level of local content for eligible activities (that is, they exclude large projects and other exempted activities). Analysis of local suppliers' efficiency gains does not seem to have been carried out by the regulator or at least is not publicly available

---

MALAYSIA

POLICY OBJECTIVE	COUNTRY CONTEXT
• Strengthen value-creating activities across the oil and gas value chain • Transform Malaysia into a hub for oil field services and equipment	**Structure of the economy:** Malaysia is an upper-middle-income economy with a gross national income of $9,977 per capita in 2011. It is a highly open economy (exports comprise almost 100% of GDP) and a leading exporter of electrical appliances, electronic parts and components, palm oil, and natural gas. Malaysia is also externally competitive, ranking 21st (out of 183 economies) in the International Finance Corporation 2011 ranking of ease of doing business in the world. Malaysia has progressed from being a producer of raw materials, such as tin and rubber, in the 1970s to being a multisector economy. Along with the promotion of the country's manufacturing base and exports, Malaysian governments have been focusing on the promotion of foreign investments through a transparent, competitive, and relatively well-developed tax system, as well as targeted incentives in a wide range of economic activities including manufacturing, tourism, environment protection, training and research, transport, and communication. Unemployment is relatively low compared to regional averages (around 4% over the past 10 years), and the share of secondary and tertiary educated workers has increased considerably over the past two decades (reaching 56% of the total workforce in 2010). In 2010 Malaysia launched the Economic Transformation Program (ETP), which aims for the country to reach high-income status by 2020 while ensuring that growth is also sustainable and inclusive. The ETP envisions economic growth that is primarily driven by the private sector and which moves the Malaysian economy into higher value-added activities in both industry and services. Three of the twelve sectoral policies under ETP fall within the scope of petroleum sector LCPs. These policies aim to increase the competitiveness of Malaysia's oil field services and equipment subsector with the objective to become a regional hub in 2017

(table continues on next page)

111

Table 5.1 Key Features of LCPs in Case Study Countries *(continued)*

Geology:

Malaysia's continental shelf is made up of six major sedimentary basins located in peninsular Malaysia, Sarawak, and Sabah. At the end of 2011 Malaysia's oil and gas reserves stood at 5.9 billion barrels and 86 trillion cubic feet respectively. Significant discoveries were made in the shelf and deep water. Most fields have been producing for over 30 years, and production levels are declining fast. Maintaining the reserve base has been a key pillar of Malaysia's oil and gas sector policy, which focuses on ensuring long-term security of supplies while providing affordable fuel to local consumers. Deep-water exploration and enhanced recovery in mature fields are therefore critical areas of policy focus

Structure of the petroleum sector:

Malaysia is a resource-rich country in geographical proximity to dynamic economies dependent on imported fuel, such as Japan, Korea, Rep., Singapore, and Taiwan. The 26th-largest producer of crude oil, and the 14th-largest producer of natural gas in the world, it is one of the leading LNG developers and exporters. The petroleum sector has been a driver of economic expansion for decades, but it has never played a dominant role in Malaysian economy. The national oil company, Petronas, is the largest single contributor to the government tax revenue, accounting for over 40% of tax revenue in 2010. Despite the creation of Petronas in 1974, Malaysia has continued to invite private companies to participate in the hydrocarbon sector and has benefited from access to risk capital and management and technology practices

To strengthen local skills Petronas has established several technical and management-oriented universities. One of its two training units—Institut Teknologi Petroleum Petronas (INSTEP), established in 1981—has been the major source of technically competent skilled manpower for the company and for private companies operating in the country. In 1989 Petronas established PERMATA, which provides mainly management-training programs and courses for its employees

Trade agreements:

Malaysia is a WTO member, and has entered into a number of regional and bilateral free trade agreements (Japan, Pakistan, New Zealand, India, Chile, and Australia). Malaysia is also a member of the ASEAN free trade area. Malaysia's trade agreements include investment, trade facilitation, and intellectual property rights, as well as economic cooperation in areas comprising competition policy, standards and conformity assessment, information and communication technology, science and technology, education and training, research and development, financial cooperation, small and medium enterprises development, and paperless trading. Malaysia has made commitments under the GATS in the following sectors: business and professional services, communications services, construction and related services, financial services, transportation services, health-related social services, tourism and travel-related services, and recreational and cultural services. Malaysia is not a signatory of the WTO Government Procurement Agreement (GPA). Public procurement policies are used to encourage greater participation of Bumiputra in the economy, transfer technology to local industries, reduce the outflow of foreign exchange, create opportunities for local companies in the services sector, and enhance Malaysia's export capabilities

(table continues on next page)

Table 5.1 Key Features of LCPs in Case Study Countries *(continued)*

LOCAL CONTENT POLICY	

Channel of policy:
 	
• Petroleum Mining Act 1966
• Petroleum Development Act 1974
• Petroleum sharing contracts
• Economic Transformation Program 2010
• Companies Act 1965
	Key policy elements:
	
	Labor
	
	Policies to increase the number of national workers:
	
	• Malaysia's PSA terms encourage contractors to maximize the employment of nationals. There are no minimum targets (general or position-based) in Pecs or regulations
	
	Policies designed to restrict foreign workers:
	
	• Malaysian company law links the size of paid capital to the number and type of expatriate work visa that may be requested and obtained by a company
	
	Policies designed to promote nationals' skills development:
	
	• PSA terms require contractors to:
	
	  – Train Malaysian personnel with the objective to replace the expatriate workforce. This includes minimum monetary commitment to training that is contract specific
	
	  – Train Petronas' personnel upon request
	
	• PSA terms oblige contractors to an annual research contribution of 0.5% of the sum of cost oil and their share of profit oil.
	
	Sourcing of goods and services
	
	Policies that involve margins of preference:
	
	• PSAs require petroleum companies to acquire all materials and supplies from Malaysian-registered companies or to purchase them directly from the manufacturer when no Malaysian-registered company is available to provide the required material or perform the service
	
	• The law reserves domestic shipping for Malaysian registered vessels. Foreigners are permitted to hold a 70% stake in shipping and logistics companies and 49% in forwarding agencies. The limitation also applies to vessels that support oil and gas operations
	
	• Restrictions based on citizenship or permanent residency apply to legal services, engineering services, taxation and accounting services, professional services, telecommunications, advertising, financial and insurance services, and banking services
	
	• The law mandates local incorporation of foreign companies and a minimum share of domestic equity holding
	
	Local content leveraged during tendering process:
	
	• Companies that wish to participate in any business or service to supply equipment, facilities, and services to oil and gas upstream companies must obtain a license from Petronas. Non-Malaysian firms are permitted to participate in oil services either in partnership with local firms or as contractors. They are restricted to a 30% equity stake if they are incorporated locally

(table continues on next page)

Table 5.1 Key Features of LCPs in Case Study Countries *(continued)*

	Policy tools:
	• The Petroleum Development Act 1974 grants Petronas the exclusive rights, powers, liberties, and privileges to explore, exploit, win, and obtain petroleum, whether onshore or offshore of Malaysia
	• Petronas has been the main tool for the development of local capabilities and an industrial base to support oil and gas exploration and production since the 1970s. Focus on operatorship, technical skills, and the development of the local supply industry allowed Petronas to improve its efficiency while fulfilling its national mission objectives
	• The 2010 **Economic Transformation Program** is the main tool for coordination of sectoral economic development policies
	Incentives
	• Tax incentives are provided under the Income Tax Act and Customs Act of 1967, Sales Tax Act of 1972, Excise Act of 1976, Promotion of Investments Act of 1986 and Free Zones Act of 1990. The main incentives include pioneer status, investment tax allowance, reinvestment allowance, industrial adjustment allowance, research and development incentives, industrial building allowance, incentive for approved overseas investments, incentives for overseas construction projects, and operational headquarters incentives
	• A five-year partial exemption from the payment of income tax is granted to manufacturing companies with "pioneer status" (companies promoting products or activities in industries or parts of Malaysia to which the government places a high priority). Manufacturing companies with "investment tax allowance" status (those on which the government places a priority, but not as high as pioneer status) are entitled to an allowance of 60% of their qualifying capital expenditure (factory, plant, machinery, or other equipment used for the approved project) incurred within five years from the date the first qualifying capital expenditure is incurred. Government priorities include the levels of value-added, technology used, and industrial links. To qualify for any of these exemptions, companies must spend at least 1% of their gross sales on domestic research and development, and at least 15% of the company's workforce should have scientific and technical background with a minimum five years of experience
	• Tax and regulatory exemptions are provided to companies that obtain Multimedia Super Corridor (MSC) status, a government scheme to foster the growth of research, development, and other high-technology activities in Malaysia. Foreign investors who obtain MSC status receive tax and regulatory exemptions as well as public service commitments in exchange for a commitment of substantial technology transfer. To obtain MSC status the number and qualification of knowledge workers employed by the applicant company is one of the key criteria. If the Malaysian company does not intend to appoint local knowledge workers and does not have enough paid up capital to obtain employment passes for foreign workers, the company has to source foreign workers based on professional visit passes. The holder of a professional visit pass is not considered a "direct employee" of the company. Therefore he/she cannot be deemed a knowledge worker of the company, and does not count toward obtaining MSC status
	• Fiscal incentives are linked to performance requirements in the form of export targets, local content requirements, and technology transfers, which are specific to every manufacturing license

(table continues on next page)

114

Table 5.1 Key Features of LCPs in Case Study Countries *(continued)*

- Malaysian company law links the size of paid capital to the number and type of expatriate work visas
- Fiscal incentives granted to both foreign and domestic investors historically have been subject to performance requirements, usually in the form of export targets, local content requirements, and technology transfer. Performance requirements are usually written into the individual manufacturing licenses of local and foreign investors
- Fiscal incentives are offered to companies and universities involved in the Pilot Internship Program For Engineering Consultancy Services and the National Talent Enhancement Program aimed to provide field exposure to engineering students

Penalties:

- Companies that obtain tax exemptions and fail to implement the agreed program of activities loose the extended exemptions and risk losing their license to operate

Institutional responsibilities:

- The Economic Planning Unit sets Malaysia's energy policy, and the Implementation and Coordination Unit oversees its implementation. Both units report directly to the prime minister
- The national oil company, Petronas, has regulatory functions for petroleum upstream, as well as commercial operations spanning the entire value chain. Petronas is the sole holder of petroleum exploration and production rights, and reports directly to the prime minister's office. Petronas has two special units that are tasked with the design and implementation of local content related initiatives: the Supply Chain Management Unit and the Education Unit
- The Ministry of International Trade and Industry and the Ministry of Domestic Trade and Consumer Affairs regulate, respectively, the downstream (including petrochemicals) and the midstream sectors
- The Malaysian Industrial Development Authority charged with responsibility for the promotion and coordination of industrial development in Malaysia
- The Oil Field Service Unit—Malaysia Petroleum Resources Corporation (MPRC), created in 2011 as part of the measures envisaged under the ETP, is tasked with the promotion of the oil and gas industry locally and overseas. The MPRC oversees and make recommendations on policies, business regulation, and fiscal incentives for the oil and gas industry
- The Performance Management Delivery Unit, PEMANDU, oversees the implementation and assesses the progress of the Economic Transformation Program and the Government Transformation Program. The unit was established in 2011

Measurement and monitoring:

- Reports on the level and trend of local content, or on the monitoring of local content obligations under PSAs are not publicly available. But PEMANDU tracks progress toward the achievement of the Economic Transformation Program's targets. KPI indicators have been set to track progress toward: (1) attracting multinationals to bring their global oil field service and equipment operations to Malaysia, (2) Consolidating domestic fabrication sector, and (3) developing engineering, procurement, and installation capacity through strategic partnerships and JVs

(table continues on next page)

115

Table 5.1 Key Features of LCPs in Case Study Countries *(continued)*

MAIN CONCLUSIONS

Given that the Petroleum Act of 1974 gives Petronas exclusive rights and powers over Malaysia's hydrocarbon resources, the NOC has been the main vehicle for its country's LCPs, which translate into contractual obligations under PSAs that Petronas negotiates and enters into with participating petroleum companies. In addition, Petronas has invested in creating a skilled workforce, developing technology, and supporting the local supply industry. LCPs in the oil and gas sector are an integral part of Malaysia' economic transformation plan, thus ensuring coherence between sector specific and cross-sectoral policies. LCPs are designed to improve the performance and competitiveness of local enterprises and strengthen local skills through a mixture of mandatory requirements and incentives to both local and foreign investors. Analyses of LCPs impact and effectiveness on local development are, however, not publicly available

	TRINIDAD AND TOBAGO
POLICY OBJECTIVE	**COUNTRY CONTEXT**
The objectives of LCPs are to maximize: • the level of participation of nationals, enterprises, technology and capital; and • the value to the country from its assets through the development and increasing use of local goods and services, people, businesses and financing within and outside Trinidad and Tobago	**Structure of the economy:** Since the early 1960s Trinidad and Tobago's economy has been characterized by its heavy dependence on the production and export of petroleum and gas. Between 1973 and 1982 high oil windfall afforded rises in income, expansion of public sector employment, and improvement in physical infrastructure and living conditions. But a large share of expenditure was not sustainable, including subsidies and high public sector salaries. The high wages in the public sector inflated labor costs throughout the economy, undermining competitiveness in the nonoil sector. Only a small number of the jobs created were in the more long-term goods-producing sectors. When international oil prices declined in the 1980s, the economy contracted sharply. This and the lack of development in growth areas made high levels of public expenditure unsustainable. The rising unemployment, decline in the real value of social sector spending, and retrenchment of workers in both the public and private sector led to an increase in poverty. To overcome persistent unemployment the government set out to diversify the economy away from the petroleum sector. Several priorities were identified: (1) maintaining macroeconomic stability and insulating the economy from oil price volatility; (2) promoting economic diversification and private sector development; (3) improving infrastructure, including through encouraging private sector participation; and (4) strengthening the public sector's institutional capacity to facilitate economic development. Over the last decade Trinidad and Tobago has experienced strong economic growth, mainly driven by natural resources and related inward investment. Between 2000 and 2007 growth averaged slightly over 8%, almost twice the regional average for that period, then GDP contracted during 2009–11. Growth had been fueled by investments in liquefied natural gas, petrochemicals, and steel. The energy sector dominates the economy, followed by the manufacturing, construction, and financial sectors. The oil and gas sector has historically contributed about 40% of GDP and 80% of exports, but only 3% of employment. The country still faces a wide range of socioeconomic challenges, including sustainable development beyond the petroleum sector. Trinidad has a relatively small local workforce with relatively high average years of education compared to other developing countries **Geology:** Oil production started in the early part of the 20th century. Overall the country is a mature petroleum province, with future development expected to come from deep-water areas in the east and north, and shallow water marginal fields. In 2010 the country's oil reserves stood at 830 million barrels, while natural gas reserves were estimated to be 12.9 Tcf

(table continues on next page)

Table 5.1 Key Features of LCPs in Case Study Countries *(continued)*

Structure of the petroleum sector:

The petroleum sector is dominated by subsidiaries of large international oil companies. Exploration and production activities are carried out under the terms of production sharing agreements. The Petroleum Company of Trinidad and Tobago Limited (Petrotrin), wholly owned by the government, was incorporated in 1993, and mandated to engage in petroleum activities along the sector value chain. Petrotrin owns and operates the only refinery in the country. The National Gas Company of Trinidad and Tobago (NGC) was established in 1975, and is engaged in the purchase, transportation, and distribution of natural gas to industrial users. In addition it participates in the Atlantic LNG company. Approximately 50% of natural gas production is used locally, mainly by the petrochemical industry, and for power generation. Local petroleum products requirements are satisfied through the only refinery, owned by Petrotrin

Trade agreements:

Trinidad and Tobago and the United States are party to a bilateral agreement on the Encouragement and Reciprocal Protection of Investment that, according to the Ministry of Energy and Energy Affairs, would need to be partially renegotiated to be consistent with the government's local content policy. Local content policies are also at odds with the CARICOM treaty that requires the inclusion of CARICOM nationals in local content policies. Trinidad and Tobago is also a WTO member since March 1995, and grants most favored nation treatment to all its trading partners

LOCAL CONTENT POLICY	
Channel of policy: • The Petroleum Act Chapter 62:01 and implementing regulations • The Fiscal Incentives Act, chapter 85:04 as amended, which grants fiscal incentives to qualified companies in areas that are considered important to economic development • The Foreign Investment Act, chapter 70:07 • The Unemployment Levy Act chapter 75:03, that provides for training and relief employment for the unemployed • The Petroleum Production Levy and Subsidy Act chapter 62:02, used to fund subsidies on petroleum products • Local Content Policy Framework • Production sharing contracts	**Key policy elements:** *Labor* *Policies to increase the number of national workers:* • Priority given to the employment of national workers *Policies designed to restrict foreign workers:* • Work permits are issued by the Minister of National Security in cases where foreign employment does not preclude employment opportunity to suitable local candidates *Policies designed to promote nationals' skills development:* • PSAs mandate the contractor to provide training to national workers in line with the contractor's performance standards • Contractors shall develop and implement training programs that enable nationals to replace foreign workers • Upon issuance of a work permit, a local successor to the expatriate shall be appointed ***Sourcing of goods and services*** *Policies that involve margins of preference:* • Production sharing contracts require the contractor to maximize the use of local goods, services, and financing. But there is no explicit margin of domestic preference

(table continues on next page)

Table 5.1 Key Features of LCPs in Case Study Countries *(continued)*

Local content leveraged during tendering process:

- Contracts shall be unbundled as much as economically and practically feasible to match the timing, financial, and human capability of local enterprises
- Contracts shall be advertised locally to ensure access of local companies to all tenders
- Tender evaluation processes shall discriminate in favor of local value-added
- Seismic processing work shall be undertaken in-country
- In the award of subcontracts reasonable preference will be given to qualified local contractors or suppliers who meet the quality, cost, and schedule requirements
- National Policy Guidelines for the Utilization of Local Goods and Services for Government and Government-related projects

Policy tools:

- Work permit procedures to ensure that foreign employment does not prevent local employment when relevant skills are available, and succession plans are in place to transfer the position to a national when foreign employment is necessary.
- Field development plan must include the percentage local content that the operator plans on achieving

Incentives

- Investment incentives are coordinated through the Industrial Development Division of the Tourism and Industrial Development Company of Trinidad & Tobago Limited (TIDCO). These may include training subsidies for developing new skills, export credit insurance, and exemption from value-added tax on inputs for companies exporting 80% of production
- The Fiscal Incentives Act allows for the granting of a tax holiday (or partial holiday) for periods up to ten years for the manufacture of approved products by approved enterprises. These fall into separate classifications including the following: highly capital intensive enterprises investing in excess of TT$50 million ($8.3million); export enclaves, where products are manufactured exclusively for export; and enterprises using a significant portion of local inputs. These concessions are discretionary and require applications to the Ministry of Trade and Industry via TIDCO. Recent precedents include the grant of five-year tax holidays to major petrochemical plants in Point Lisas
- The Income Tax Act provides for several special classes of company that are entitled to a tax credit of 15% of their chargeable income for seven years. This reduces their effective tax rate to 20% from the statutory rate of 35%. These special classes of company include the following: approved small companies, approved companies trading in a regional development area, and approved activity companies. Special companies must be locally incorporated and owned. The approval process is via TIDCO except for approved small companies, which is via the Small Business Development Company Limited

(table continues on next page)

Table 5.1 Key Features of LCPs in Case Study Countries *(continued)*

	• Approved enterprises will also be granted exemption from customs duties and VAT on the construction of approved projects. These projects have usually been large-scale manufacturing within one of the three classifications, and are available only to locally incorporated companies **Penalties** There are no penalties for lack of compliance with the local content policy or local content plans proposed by contractors and approved by the Ministry of Energy and Energy Industries
Institutional responsibilities:	• The Permanent Committee on Local Content was created in April 2004 to "monitor the various activities in the energy sector to ensure that, as far as possible, all energy projects include opportunities for the development of the expertise of nationals and maximize the level of local content and local participation." The committee develops policies and strategies that ensure the transfer of knowledge and technology that improve local capabilities, in addition to business and the capital market; update local content and participation policies, as required; and ensure compliance with set policies • The Work Permit Advisory Committee, chaired by the Permanent Secretary of the Ministry of National Security, supports local content objectives by ensuring that nationals/residents are not denied employment opportunities because of expatriate employment. Where expatriate employment is necessary the committee assigns an understudy to the expatriate, in order to facilitate the transfer of knowledge and expertise to the local workforce • The Energy Research and Planning Division of the Ministry of Energy and Energy Industries acts as the focal point for the Permanent Committee; identifies critical skills in the energy sector and manages the related database; and advises on policies related to work permits • The Energy Chamber of Trinidad and Tobago is an independent body tasked with identifying local content opportunities—in country and abroad—and sharing the information with local companies; developing the local content measurement methodology; and encouraging cooperation between local and foreign companies
Measurement and monitoring:	• There are no measurement guidelines but more recent production sharing contracts provide for the contractor to use all reasonable endeavors to ensure that local contractors or suppliers and nonlocal contractors and suppliers maintain records to facilitate monitoring of local content by the government, and must certify the cost of local materials, labor, and services used with supporting documentation, all of which will be subject to audit • Operators are asked to report on their local content activities to the Ministry of Energy and Energy Industries on a quarterly basis • Training and development programs shall be approved by the Ministry of Energy and Energy Industries and progress shall be reported quarterly

(table continues on next page)

Table 5.1 Key Features of LCPs in Case Study Countries *(continued)*

MAIN CONCLUSIONS
Trinidad and Tobago's LCP is predicated on maximizing citizens' ownership, control, and financing of all activities along the energy resources sector, both locally and internationally. This approach was launched in 2004 with the adoption of the local content and local participation framework. According to official sources, the general principle that had been previously incorporated in PSAs that called for the preferencing of local goods and services whenever comparable to imported ones was inadequate to develop local capability given due to the knowledge and efficiency gaps between local and foreign companies. The Vision 2020 Energy Subcommittee Report recognizes the importance of this issue, and outlines specific objectives and initiatives to achieve local content goals. Nonetheless the implementation of the new LCP has been mostly left to the private sector. With the exception of general principles under the most recent PSAs, the new LCPs have not been detailed in regulations and/or implementing guidelines, and measures of local content have not been specified. There are no publicly available statistics on the evolution of local content in Trinidad and Tobago. But efforts are ongoing to incorporate the LCP principles in the regulatory framework, as well as to strengthen the government capacity to monitor and measure policy implementation.

Source: World Bank data.

Note: GDP = gross domestic product; LNG = liquefied natural gas; WTO = World Trade Organization; E&P = exploration and production; LC = local content; LCP = local content policies; O&G = oil and gas; PROMINP = Programa de Mobilização da Indústria Nacional de Petróleo e Gás Natural; GATS = General Agreement on Trade in Services; ASEAN = Association of Southeast Asian Nations; PSA = production sharing agreement; KPI = key performance indicator; NOC = national oil company; CARICOM = Caribbean Community; VAT = value added tax.

Consistency with Other Economic Development Policies

LCPs in the oil and gas sector have a wide range of objectives. The creation of local employment and the transfer of technology are among the most common. Other objectives may include the generation of value-added in the domestic supply sector, economic diversification, addressing regional or local socioeconomic development imbalances, the creation of competitive advantages, and the correction of market failures.

As discussed in chapter 2, LCPs are part of a broader category of policy interventions aimed to strengthen the productive structure of a particular economy. Therefore their success also depends on their interaction and coherence with broader economic development policies and related implementation tools. For example increasing local employment may require an improvement in the quality of education, changes in labor mobility, improvement in infrastructure, and so on. And fostering economic diversification may require stable macro-economic policies, attracting foreign investment, negotiating trade agreements, improving the financial market, and so on. Box 5.1 illustrates an example of integration between petroleum sector LCPs and overall economic development policy.

Box 5.1

LCPs as Part of a Country's Broader Economic Policy

Malaysia's petroleum sector dates back to 1910, when Shell Oil discovered oil in Sarawak. Prior to the creation of the national oil company in 1974, international oil companies (IOCs) played a central role in sector development. The establishment of the national oil company in 1974 gave additional impulse to a local content agenda aimed at developing local capabilities, strengthening the government control over the sector, and driving the creation of economic links from petroleum exploration and exploitation. Malaysia's governments have traditionally taken a proactive role in economic development and industrialization since independence in 1957. Successive governments have adopted five-year plans, each with set targets for developing the country's key economic, social, and environmental segments. These plans focused primarily on diversifying the country's economic base by transforming it from an agriculture-dominated economy to a more industrial and export-oriented one. Sectoral policy integration was further strengthened in 2010 with the launch of the Economic Transformation Program (ETP) that aims to transform Malaysia into a high-income country by 2020. The ETP includes 12 National Key Economic Areas (NKRAs), among which the petroleum and energy sector plays a critical role. Economic activities that are categorized as NKRAs will be prioritized in government planning and funds allocation. Policies will be amended to facilitate fast-track implementation of such activities, including liberalizing the market and removal of bottlenecks. The private sector is highly involved in the planning of transformation activities under the ETP since 92 percent of total investments are expected to originate from this sector. The Performance Management and Delivery Unit (Pemandu) is entrusted with the monitoring of implementation and associated regulatory intervention.

(box continues on next page)

Box 5.1   LCPs as Part of a Country's Broader Economic Policy *(continued)*

Petroleum sector NKRAs under the ETP aim at further developing value-adding activities along the oil and gas value chain. In particular, the government aims to increase the competitiveness of its domestic oil field services and equipment (OFSE) industry, building on existing regional competitive advantages to become a regional hub by 2017. Under the ETP, petroleum sector policies are interlinked with other sector-specific and cross-sectoral policies. Four of the six cross-sectoral strategic reform initiatives envisaged under the ETP are particularly relevant to the development of backward links from the petroleum sector. These include the following:

- The implementation of competition laws, adoption of international standards, and a liberalization of services program, which shall all contribute to making local industries competitive in the international arena and attract FDI
- The reform of public finance through the adoption of efficient broad-based taxes and reforming fiscal policies and institutions
- The improvement of the performance of public services and transformation of the role of the government into a lean, efficient, and facilitative one
- The development of the country's human capital
- The streamlining of the government's role in business (PEMANDU 2010).

Each NKRA is associated with well-defined targets and key performance indicators (KPIs). Since the policy goal envisaged for the petroleum sector is to transform Malaysia into a regional hub for OFSE, a strict measure of local content levels would fall short of the government's objective. Instead the following three KPIs are monitored:

- The amount of investment made by OFSE multinationals
- The number of successful merger of fabricators
- The number of JVs between multinationals and local OFSE companies.

Since most of the investment required to implement the activities envisaged under the ETP will come from the private sector, the government role focuses on creating an enabling environment through legal and regulatory reforms, fiscal and nonfiscal incentives, and trade-related measures.

The new local content policy represent a considerable change compared to earlier approaches whereby regulation focused on maximizing local content levels, and not so much on value addition, competitive advantage, and sustainable growth.

Addressing Market Deficiencies

Overall the oil and gas sector is characterized by high capital investment, specialized input, and technological complexity, which are often a barrier to local participation. Furthermore, as shown in table 5.2 new entrants are faced with

Table 5.2 Market Concentration in the Oil and Gas Upstream Sector

Segment	Sub-Segment	Market Size ($ bn)	CAGR, % (1999–2007)	HHI	Top 3 Players
Information on reservoir	Seismic services	12.6	14.4%	1,523	WesternGeco (Schlumberger, CGG Veritaas, Oil Geo-Service)
Drilling agreement	Onshore and offshore drilling agreements	57	18.2%	875	Transocean Inc., Noble Drilling, Diamond Offshore
	Drill bits	3.3		2,289	Baker Hughes, Smith International, National Oilwell Varco
	Drilling muds	7.8		2,317	Smith International, Halliburton, Baker Hughes
	Solid control	2.8		1,684	Smith International, National Oilwell Varco, Socomi Oiltools
	Well tools	1.6		1,911	National Oilwell Varco, Weatherford, Smith International
Drilling services and associated equipment	Rent of tools and fishing services	5.5	17.8%	967	Weatherford, Smith International, Oil States International
	Directional drilling	8.2		1,755	Schlumberger, Baker Hughes, Halliburton
	Logging drilling the filling	2.2		2,694	Schlumberger, Halliburton, Baker Hughes
	Conventional logging	9.6		2,477	Schlumberger, Halliburton, Baker Hughes
	Registration of muds	0.9		2,268	Geoservices, Baker Hughes, Halliburton
	Steel pipe or coating and production piping (OCTG)	16.2		1,743	Tenaris, Vallourec, U.S. Steel
	Coating services and installation of production piping	2.3		1,136	Weatherford, Frank's CC&R, BJ Services
	Flexible continuum piping services	–		1,171	Schlumberger, Halliburton, BJ Services
Well lining and completion	Piping inspection and coating	2.8	18.0%	5,035	National Oilwell Varco, Smith International
	Pressure pumping services	20.6		1,972	Halliburton, Schlumberger, BJ Services
	Coating and cementing equipment	0.7		2,210	Weatherford, Halliburton, Davis-Lynch
	Completion equipment	6.8		1,954	Baker Hughes, Halliburton, Schlumberger
	Production tests	1.5		2,425	Schlumberger, Expro International
	Subsea equipment	9.4		1,381	FMC, Technip, Aker
	Surface equipment	3.2		1,571	Cameron, FMC, Vetco
Production and maintenance	Artificial lift	5.9		1,184	Weatherford, Schlumberger, Baker Hughes (Centrilift)
	Well servicing	4.1	16.3%	780	Key Energy, Nabors, Basic Energy
	Specialty chemicals	3.6		2,254	Baker Hughes (Petrolite), Nalco, Champion Technologies
	Contract compression services	2.4		3,482	Exterran Holdings, Compressor, J-W

☐ HHI < 100 Competitive Index   ▨ 100 ≤ HHI < 1500 Unconcentrated Index   ▨ 1500 ≤ HHI < 2500 Moderate Concentration   ■ 2500 ≤ HHI High Concentration

Source: BNDES 2009.

Note: The calculations assume a lower bound for the HHI as it is assumed that all companies under "other" have infinitely small market shares. HHI = Herfindahl-Hirschman Index. The HHI measures the degree of concentration in a market. The index assumes all firms (N in number) have an equal market share (i.e., equal market power), and is calculated as $N * (1/N)^2$. CAGR = compound annual growth rate.

a relatively high level of market concentration, necessary to achieve economies of scale and competitiveness. In countries with little existing capacity, LCPs are more likely to succeed if they aim to support the development of subsectors with relatively low entry barriers, where local participation can develop quickly and efficiently, especially if high aggregated demand is expected. Some business sectors, such as coating and piping services, fishing services, solid waste management, supply vessels, and basic wireline services, have relatively low technological complexity and require limited capital investment. The operating leverage in these business sectors is such that limited turnovers should be sufficient to cover costs and generate a profit.

But major international contractors often have long-term sourcing arrangements for key equipment and supplies. These arrangements normally allow the contractor to secure lower prices, and provide assurance on the quality and reliability of supplies. Global supply chains are often so well integrated that even where local capability is available, local suppliers may be locked out from the opportunity to tender. Where domestic supply capability is available or can be developed to meet long-term demand, policy makers should consider facilitating the integration of local suppliers in contractors' procurement strategies. This could be done through a combination of incentives and mandatory requirements for contractors, and may need to be accompanied by other policy interventions designed to address specific bottlenecks and inefficiency (for example, infrastructure investment, education, and administrative processes). Box 5.2 outlines alternative approaches to fostering the development of local supply chains.

Box 5.2

LCPs in Support of the Local Supply Sector

At the end of 2003 the Ministry of Mines and Energy and Petrobras launched the Programa de Mobilização da Indústria Nacional de Petróleo e Gás Natural (PROMINP) in **Brazil**. The objective of the program is to "maximize good and services national industry content, within competitive and sustainable basis, in the implantation of oil and gas projects in Brazil and abroad." To this end PROMINP carried out a national competitiveness diagnostic study to identify current and projected local supplier capability. This was compared to expected aggregate demand for oil and gas projects over a 20-year period, and an action plan was prepared to address competitiveness and capacity gaps.[a] Contracting strategies were then devised, taking into account the relevance of each subsector to the oil and gas industry, the level of local production capacity, and the competitiveness of the subsector. For example: (1) where local supply capacity existed but was inadequate—such as in marine vessel fabrication, cranes and valve manufacture, and engineering services—strategies were designed to

(box continues on next page)

Box 5.2 LCPs in Support of the Local Supply Sector *(continued)*

incentivize foreign contractors to partner with Brazilian firms; and (2) where local capacity did not exist or could not be developed—as in the manufacturing of centrifugal compressors, diesel engines, and instrumentation equipment—international firms were encouraged to establish subsidiaries in Brazil, including by bundling together work packages and using repeatable designs (for example in the construction of floating production, storage and offloading vessels, and manufacturing of certain materials and equipment) to increase the returns and reduce the commercial risks to investment in Brazil. Since its inception, PROMINP has significantly raised the participation of local suppliers in the oil and gas sector, from 57 percent in 2003 to over 75 percent in 2009. This represented an additional value of $17.8 billion for goods and services purchased in Brazil, and an estimated 755,000 new jobs. Local content participation was expected to increase from $35 billion in the years 2003–07 to $190 billion for the years 2009–13 (PROMINP 2010).

Indonesia has been an oil and gas producer for over 150 years, and is the second-largest exporter of liquefied natural gas (LNG). Since the early 1970s Indonesia has adopted an assertive approach to sector regulation, with the aim to develop local manufacturing capacity and improve the skill profile of its workforce. But its supply industry remains rather fragmented, with a large number of small local enterprises that lack the industrial and financial capacity to become leading local suppliers, and to effectively compete internationally. Local content in Indonesia has focused largely on local employment and local ownership. Technology and technological advances were not central factors in the awards of petroleum rights and related industrial policy choices. Given the technology-driven and capital-intensive nature of the petroleum sector, these policies have possibly resulted in lower local content levels than its regional neighbors with less hydrocarbon endowments. Notwithstanding the setting of mandatory minimum local content targets, industry observers suggest that, in practice, local content ranges between 10 percent and 20 percent (EEPC 2002).

a. The reader is referred to Local Content Policies in the Oil and Gas Sector: Case Studies, downloadable from http://issuu.com/world.bank.publications/docs/local_content_policies_in_the_oil_and_gas_sector.

Another type of market inefficiency is the existence of information asymmetry: a condition in which some market participants do not have access to the information that they need for their decision-making process. The effects of information asymmetry in markets have been analyzed and documented in a large range of contexts. Existing literature shows that information asymmetry leads to market inefficiency or market failure. Even in countries that mandate minimum targets for the procurement of local goods and services, qualified local suppliers may not be aware of current and/or future market opportunities because companies' tender processes and procedures may be designed to target established international suppliers. Furthermore, even if local suppliers should be aware of current supply opportunities, the lack of visibility with respect to forward demand would negatively impact their ability to assess and make investments in upgrading their processes and plants so as to become efficient competitors. Regulation can solve this problem at a reasonably low cost. Box 5.3 provides an example of regulatory intervention to improve transparency and access to information for suppliers in the oil and gas sector.

Nonregulatory interventions may, however, be equally effective in addressing market inefficiency due to imperfect information among market operators. Box 5.4 provides examples of government-lead nonregulatory approaches to addressing information asymmetry between local and foreign suppliers.

Box 5.3

Addressing Information Asymmetry through Regulation

The **Kazakhstan** Contract Agency (KCA) was created in November 2002 to (1) promote local content through the involvement of Kazakhstan producers of goods, works, and services into the oil and gas supply sector; (2) manage, document, and analyze local content operations in the procurements of subsoil users and update the Unified Register of Domestic Producers and Foreign Investors (KCA Register); and (3) assist local manufacturers in meeting industry standards and requirements (KCA 2012). The KCA Register, which was automated in 2010, makes procurement processes transparent to both local and international suppliers. Subsoil users (oil and gas companies) are required to upload all procurement information and documents through the Subsoil User Report Acceptance System (SURAC) for each tender (MOG 2012). SURAC tracks information on the whole procurement process from the initial call for tender of goods, works, and services, through contract specifications, and up to the award. All information uploaded in SURAC is authenticated through electronic digital signatures. All subsoil users and their subcontractors are mandated to publish in the KCA register their procurement calendars for all upcoming and planned demand for goods, works, and services. The use of an electronic platform has greatly increased the transparency of tendering processes, reduced disputes over noncompliance with local content obligations, and substantially increased the participation of local suppliers. Information on tenders is also published in the main local journals. Registration and participation is open to all companies and individuals, whether national or foreign. In 2012, the KCA announced that 99 percent of subsoil users were adhering to the reporting and publishing obligations for the procurement of goods, works, and services. This represents a substantial increase from 2008, when only 50 percent of subsoil users were considered by KRA as compliant with reporting regulations. In addition, 98 percent of the subsoil users published their future procurement plans, compared to 45 percent in 2008. The total value of the transactions in goods, works, and services was about $8.3 billion in 2011, nearly double the 2010 level ($4.7 billion), and over four times the 2005 level ($2 billion).

Box 5.4

Nonregulatory Government-Led Measures to Address Information Asymmetry

In **Brazil** the Program for the Mobilization of the Oil and Gas Industry (PROMINP) is a major element of the government's local content policy (LCP). The program was established in 2003 to "maximize goods and services national industry content, within competitive and sustainable basis, in the implantation of oil and gas projects in Brazil and abroad." PROMINP is a multistakeholder initiative coordinated by the Ministry of Mines and Energy and composed at the steering committee level by the Minister of Mining and Energy, the Minister of Development, Industry, and Trade Ministry, President and Services Director of Petrobras, the President of BNDES, the President of ONIP, and the President of the Brazilian Petroleum Institute. Reporting to the steering committee is an executive committee and four sectoral committees. In 2009 PROMINP launched the Site Opportunities Supply Chain of Petroleum and Natural Gas in order to provide for market information about the demand for materials, equipment, and components required to carry out oil and gas projects, and encourage interaction between buyers and suppliers. The site allows micro, small, medium, and large companies to learn about supply opportunities. By registering on the platform, suppliers can also disclose the major products and services that they are able to provide, making it visible to the entire supply chain. In addition to local suppliers, national companies, government agencies, suppliers associations, and oil and gas companies can register on the Portal. The Portal is not open to importers of goods and foreign suppliers. Registration is voluntary. Furthermore PROMINP engineered the creation of the Petrobras Supply Chain Financing Program, PROGREDIR, offering competitive financing to suppliers contracted by Petrobras. The program involves the six largest banks in Brazil and is managed on an online platform. The inception of PROMINP is believed to be the driver behind the boost in the participation of the domestic industry in investments from 57.3 percent in 2003 to 74.3 percent in 2010 (PROMINP 2011).

The Petro Arctic Supplier Association (PASA) was created in 1997 in connection with the Snøhvit LNG project, located on Melkøya Island, in **Norway**, and connected to the development of three gas fields located in the Barents Sea. The project operator, Statoil, and the Norwegian government were looking at ways to increase local participation from an area that had traditionally depended on fishery, so as to facilitate the transition toward a more diversified regional economy. PASA is funded by its members, and works in cooperation with Statoil, local and regional authorities, contractors, and subcontractors. The association facilitates information exchange between developers and regional business by providing updates on project progress, and qualification and training programs. Through PASA, members can be notified about the progress of a project and many specific requests for the supply of goods and services are channeled through the association's secretariat. Among the member companies, some have considerable experience in supplying the offshore industry. But most companies are small and medium-sized north Norwegian enterprises without specific experience in the oil and gas sector.[a]

(box continues on next page)

Box 5.4 Nonregulatory Government-Led Measures to Address Information Asymmetry
(continued)

The **South African** Oil & Gas Alliance (SAOGA) is a nonprofit organization established by the provincial government of the Western Cape to support and promote the growth of local industry in the upstream oil and gas sector. SAOGA is also the membership organization for approximately 170 local upstream suppliers. Membership is restricted to companies with a South African presence. The three main strategic imperatives of the organization are to (1) build local industry by facilitating infrastructure projects and access and through skills development and training programs, suppliers development and certification programs, and public policy intervention; (2) carry out marketing and business development activities on behalf of member companies by organizing trade missions and conference trips, running networking and matching events, publishing a suppliers directory, and identifying opportunities through market research and liaison with procurement managers; and (3) promote investment in South Africa by attracting international upstream supplier companies to establish local branches or partner with local companies. In line with its basic mandate to promote the development of a South African-based upstream supplier base, SAOGA provides assistance to foreign companies that do not wish to establish in South Africa in cases where some benefit to the local supplier base can be established.[b]

a. PASA portal can be accessed through http://www.petroarctic.no/index.php?page_id=1235.

b. Additional information can be found at http://www.saoga.org.za/content/overview-saoga.

Multinational companies have an incentive to develop local supply systems to reduce their operating costs, build competitive advantages, remove market inefficiencies, lower uncertainties about costs and prices, and secure a license to operate. To this end many have introduced changes in their supply chain management systems—to the flows of goods and services, information, and money between interrelated partners—independent of local content requirements. Some of these changes have to do with facilitating access to information by local companies. Box 5.5 provides an example of industry-led initiatives to improve access of local suppliers to procurement processes.

Box 5.5

Industry-Led Initiatives to Improve Local Suppliers' Participation in Tender Processes

Local content policies in Angola specify minimum local employment targets, grant margins of preference to local suppliers of goods, works, and services, and reserve some sectors for Angolan companies (see appendix E). But local supply capacity is scarce, and companies

(box continues on next page)

Box 5.5 Industry-Led Initiatives to Improve Local Suppliers' Participation in Tender Processes (*continued*)

were finding it difficult to implement local content requirements while maintaining the efficiency of their operations. To address the barrier, in 2003 an international nongovernmental organization—CDC Development Solutions—started working with operators and the authorities to develop solutions to improve the capacity and competitiveness of local suppliers so that they could become suppliers and contractors of the oil industry. A gap analysis of existing small- and medium-sized enterprises was carried out, and the following measures were identified to enable local business development:

- Training programs geared toward the oil industry's business, administrative, and health, safety, and environmental (HSE) requirements, along with complementary capacity building trainings
- On-site consulting to assist businesses to develop and implement quality improvement plans, management upgrades, technology transfers, and HSE management systems
- Information and outreach to both research the demand for goods and services of oil companies and major contractors and publish that information (the unit would also house a database listing local companies possessing the capacity to serve the oil and gas industry and facilitate links between SME businesses)
- An Enterprise Development Center (EDC) to house the consulting and training assistance available
- Credit links through the development of working relationships with institutions and organizations offering credit to local businesses
- Active industry engagement to insure the program's success.[a]

A comprehensive implementation strategy was developed by CDC, initially with the support of British Petroleum and the Ministry of Petroleum. A couple of years later the Centro de Apoio Empresarial (CAE) was established with the support and funding of the national oil company, Sonangol, British Petroleum, Exxon Mobil, Total, and Chevron. CAE's support ranged from assisting local SMEs with financial analysis, the preparation of bids, and training on specific elements associated with the provision of goods and services to the oil industry. CAE beneficiaries were restricted to wholly owned or majority owned Angolan companies. A company directory was created including certified local companies and an assessment of their services and capacity. In 2010, CAE extended its range of services to include the provision of assistance to qualified SMEs in accessing financing to help address barriers to local SMEs development and growth (the A2F Program). The program was successful in raising awareness of financial services, and helped SME to create innovative investment and lending models (Levett and Chandler 2012). Since its inception the CAE has generated approximately 2,700 jobs; certified 132 companies in various sectors; and delivered over 1,700 training courses. Furthermore, participant SMEs have won over 300 contracts, mostly in the oil and gas sector, and mostly in tenders run by international oil companies.[b]

(box continues on next page)

Box 5.5 Industry-Led Initiatives to Improve Local Suppliers' Participation in Tender Processes
(continued)

CEA's inception strategy included a plan to transfer, employ, train, mentor, and empower Angolan staff, with the ultimate goal of transitioning the program entirely to Angolan leadership. Angolan staff holds all but two key leadership roles, which CDS expect to transition in the short term.

Lessons learned from CAE's experience include the following:

- CAE provided a way to catalyze oil companies' local procurement efforts into a common platform, providing uniformity of approach and the scale necessary to make the initiative relevant. The approval of the Angolan authorities, and Sonangol's support was critical to the success of the program, ensuring the necessary level of coordination among private companies initiatives and government actions.
- CAE facilitated the exchange of information and ideas between buyers and suppliers on ways to streamline supply chains. The A2F program was a crucial element of CAE's success, enabling local SMEs to access financing opportunities to support investment in capacity and processes necessary to participate in larger oil and gas contracts and become competitive going forward.
- The early involvement of all stakeholders was important to the design of the correct design of the program, as well as to manage expectations.
- Although inefficiencies may still cause local suppliers to be less competitive than international ones, costs are expected to fall with rising transaction volumes and efficiency gains. If efficiency benchmarks could be established and monitored, these could be used by the regulator to monitor the effectiveness and net benefit of LCPs.

Notes:

a. The reader is referred to "Angola: A Legacy for Supply Chain and Local Content Development", downloadable from http://www.cdcdevelopmentsolutions.org/cds-supplier-training-initiative.

*b. A detailed list of achievements is listed in CAE Apoio Empresarial Angola, Results at a Glance, available at http://www.*cdcdevelopmentsolutions.org/sites/default/files/CAE%20Angola%20Results%20at%20a%20Glance.pdf.

Promoting Competition and the Emergence of an Efficient Domestic Economy

The components of the petroleum sector value chain have different degrees of technological complexity, risk profile, and rent size, ranging from high to relatively low when moving from exploration and production to petroleum products distribution. Most activities in the value chain are capital intensive and rely on economies of scale to generate profits. In the upper part of the value chain, backward and forward links are especially impacted by market dynamics (that is, commodity prices; level of demand; maturity, size, and location of the resource base; access to cheap and reliable sources of energy; and so on) and technology. Both are relevant considerations in the design of LCP policies aimed at developing productive links, particularly given the long lead time necessary to build a sustainable service and industrial capacity.

The technological intensity of the value chain limits the extent to which local suppliers are able to participate as efficient suppliers and beneficiaries of its spillovers and/or output. Recognizing this limitation, some countries have designed their LCP targets for subsectors with limited technological and investment barriers, focusing on products and services that the country is already producing or can produce profitably with the aim to develop comparative advantages over time by delivering goods and services "in time, in spec, and in budget."[2]

Many countries have a weak and narrow industrial base that would likely not develop without some form of government intervention. It is therefore not surprising that LCPs commonly contain some measures that allow for the preferential treatment of domestic, private, and/or state-owned companies. These policies have the potential to effectively address information and capacity asymmetries. Sheltering domestic companies from competition allows them to focus on developing the necessary competence and economies of scale. On the other hand, special privileges tend to become engrained and politically difficult to remove even in cases where sustainability is in doubt. Furthermore, if domestic companies believe that they can rely on positive discrimination indefinitely, their incentive to invest in improving efficiency and competency is greatly diminished. Thus for special privileges to local companies to create an incentive for efficiency and long-term competitiveness, they should be temporary. In reality, as the experience of many petroleum-producing countries shows, this is often not the case. Table 5.3, which compares LCPs in six petroleum-producing countries, shows that five countries make use of margins of domestic preference in the procurement of goods, works, and services, and none of them has imposed time limits on their application.

It is worth noting that some level of protection—whether in terms of explicit price margin or through taxes, duties, incentives, and other mechanisms—is often granted to domestic companies even in countries with a well-established industrial base. All forms of domestic preference entail distortionary effects and inefficiency, which should be carefully assessed by policy makers and weighted against alternative approaches prior to the introduction of LCPs. Price margins of preference are possibly one of the simplest tools to promote the development of a local supply base. But particularly when competition and transparency are weak, local companies may be able to use the price preference to charge higher than normal prices.

Even when price preferencing is mandated by contract or regulation, local companies may not be able to benefit from it because contracts are too large for them to bid. Indeed companies have an incentive to combine procurement into larger and fewer contracts so as to benefit from economies of scale and lower administration costs. On the other hand, unbundling contracts into smaller packages that are within the capability of local suppliers allows them to participate in complex supply chains and build their capacity and skills. In addition, unbundling can encourage local competition, leading to increased

Table 5.3 Domestic Preferencing in Case Study Countries

	Angola	Brazil	Indonesia	Kazakhstan	Malaysia	Trinidad and Tobago
Preference Local Goods and Services only if Competitive (no margins of domestic preference)	No	No	No	No	No	Yes Except for seismic processing services that shall be undertaken in-country.
Margin of Domestic Preference (advantage given to domestic suppliers or domestic goods and services)	Yes Restricted list of goods and services for Angolan owned suppliers (Order 127/03); Foreign companies to tender in association with Angolan owned company (Order 127/03); Preference to Angolan company if less then 10% foreign owner ship	No	Yes Tender price normalisation based on percentage of Local Content proposed in bids, in conjunction with status of company, equipment owner ship and share of contract execution (BP Migas PTK 007 r2)	Yes Preference to "Kazakhstani Producer" if within 20% of foreign bid price - non-PCA companies only (Sub Soil/ Soil User Law 2010)	Yes Petronas requires private sector companies to domestically source all goods and services incidental to upstream activities - procurement from foreign countries requires Petronas' approval.	No

Source: World Bank data.

efficiency and lower prices, which may partly offset additional costs arising from the need to administer and coordinate the implementation of a larger number of contracts. Unbundling or other structuring of procurement may be imposed by the regulator—for example through the reservation of specific activities to domestic suppliers as in Angola, or the classification of enterprises as in Indonesia, or the terms of new production sharing contracts in Trinidad and Tobago[3]—or carried out on the initiative of the contractor (directly or by passing the obligation to subcontractors). It is worth noting that, as for other measures related to LCPs, the host government always bears a share of any additional cost (and risk) associated with unbundling through the fiscal regime and production sharing terms. Therefore regulators should attempt to assess the cost of unbundling against its potential benefits in order to opine on the opportunity to mandate it.

Fostering Technology and Knowledge Spillovers

There is a large body of literature on the importance of technology and knowledge transfers between countries, and their impact on economic development and productivity of domestic firms. Technology flows across countries' boundaries through various channels, including through trade in product and services, licensing of technology, or through foreign direct investment. Studies on the effect of foreign trade partners' research and development (R&D) on domestic total factor productivity seems to indicate that countries that impose lower trade barriers are more likely to benefit from knowledge and technology spillovers. Coe, Helpman, and Hoffmaister (2008) find evidence that countries where the ease of doing business and the quality of tertiary education systems are relatively high tend to benefit more from their own R&D efforts, from international R&D spillovers, and from human capital formation. Earlier research had shown that positive spillovers occur when the technology gap between foreign and domestic firms is not too wide, and there exists a minimum level of human capital (Kokko 1994; Borensztein, de Gregorio, and Lee 1998; Xu 2000). But issues like the size of investment, access to market, and intellectual property rights often limit the flow of technology and knowledge across country boundaries and firms. Foreign direct investment can reduce some of the difficulties that arise with knowledge and technology transfers.[4] Furthermore, existing literature on the interaction between firms' ownership and efficiency generally suggests that the ownership structure affects the degree of knowledge and technological spillovers. Although evidence is mixed, it would seem that a certain level of domestic ownership would facilitate spillovers. But policies that mandate extreme forms of ownership do not necessarily generate positive spillovers.[5]

Because of the technological complexity of the petroleum sector and its use of specialized input, technology and knowledge spillovers are critical to the successful development of value-adding forward and backward links into the local economy. For this reason, almost all petroleum-producing countries have adopted policies to foster—and in some cases to force—the transfer of technology and knowledge. It is important to note that not all backward and forward links: (1) require the same technological complexity; (2) have the same potential to generate spillovers effects; (3) generate the same level of employment; (4) have the same growth potential; or (5) entail the same level of local value addition, which calls for a targeted approach whenever government intervention is considered necessary to correct for market inefficiency or failures. Box 5.6 summarizes examples of policies to foster R&D and technology transfers in support of the development of a local supply sector.

Box 5.6

Policies that Foster the Generation and Transfer of Knowledge and Technology

In **Malaysia**, in addition to the provision of training programs, every production sharing contractor is subject to an annual research contribution equivalent to 0.5 percent of the sum of cost oil and the contractor's share of profit oil. The research contribution goes toward funding of local research and development. R&D investment is supported through tax incentives. But in order to qualify for incentives, companies must spend at least 1 percent of their gross sales on domestic research and development and at least 15 percent of the company's workforce should have scientific and technical background with a minimum five years of experience. **Brazil** has adopted a similar approach requiring that operators invest 1 percent of each field's gross revenues on oil and gas related research and development. Up to half of this investment is allowed to occur in the operator's research facilities in Brazil. The rest funds research to be carried out by local universities or research institutes accredited by the regulator. The use of funds and the accreditation of institutions are governed by regulation. In addition, a percentage of government revenue is earmarked to the Ministry of Science and Technology to finance programs to support scientific research and technological development applied in the oil industry.

In 2001 BP **Trinidad and Tobago** (BP TT) undertook to construct the first offshore platform to be designed and built in Trinidad and Tobago. At the time local content was already a major priority of the Trinidad and Tobago government, which aimed to maximize the level of participation of its national people, enterprises, technology, and capital through the development and increasing use of locally owned businesses and human capabilities in the conduct of all activities connected with the energy sector. The Cannonball Project pioneered the way for a new engineering and fabrication industry in the country. This was a challenging decision since insufficient skills and capacity in engineering, design and fabrication were available locally, and investing in developing such skills and capacity would necessarily delay project completion and involve higher costs. Nonetheless the decision was made to move forward. Two joint ventures were created: TOFCO—a joint venture

(box continues on next page)

Box 5.6 Policies that Foster the Generation and Transfer of Knowledge and Technology
(continued)

between Welfab of Trinidad and Tobago and Chet Morrison of the United States—to build the platform and manage the construction site; and Fluor Summit—a joint venture (JV) between Fluor Corporation of the United States and local company Summit Engineering— responsible for the design. Both joint ventures provided the means to develop local capacities through both technical training and mentoring. The project was completed in March 2006. Prior to the Cannonball Project, platform projects had been managed, engineered, and constructed outside of Trinidad, and shipped to Trinidad for installation. This project made it possible to define and establish local infrastructure necessary to design and build platforms locally. An innovative platform design made it possible to standardize construction for future use, thus reducing costs and paving the way for the development of a local competitive industry. The TOFCO and the summit JVs won subsequent contracts to construct the Mango and Cashima platforms through a competitive tendering process. TOFCO has also secured further platform construction contracts with BHP Billiton and EOG Resources. Furthermore, local fabrication activities encouraged the development of nearby small- and medium-sized enterprises (SMEs), increased local employment in a previously deprived area of Trinidad, and paved the way for wider export opportunities in oil and gas fabrication (IPIECA 2011).

Norway is known for its approach to the development of strong local service and construction sectors related to oil exploration and development. Local participation ranged from favoring the national oil company, Statoil, in licensing rounds—on the premises that this would increase the chances of developing local suppliers—to encouraging the use of locally produced goods and services and leveraging the country's expertise in shipbuilding and marine services. In 1972 local content polices (LCPs) were formalized in legislation, and the Goods and Services Office was established to (1) support the local supply industry through JVs and encourage research and development and transfer of technology; (2) review tendering procedures to ensure that local companies were given a fair chance to participate; and (3) establish minimum local content requirements and monitor their implementation. Indeed LCPs in Norway have been driven mainly by a national focus on research and development and the transfer of technology. Foreign operators entering the Norwegian industry in the late 1970s were strongly encouraged to form R&D partnerships and joint development programs with Norwegian companies and research institutions. The operators' commitment and strategies for technology transfers were made a crucial and determining factor in the licensing processes (Accenture 2008). In addition, and crucially tax exemptions were granted for R&D expenditure. Norway's entry into the European Economic Area in the 1990s and WTO guidelines restricting protection of local industries have diminished the national focus of its policies. Nonetheless, the Petroleum Act (sections 8, 23, and 54) lays down requirements regarding oil companies' purchasing policy: (1) competitive Norwegian suppliers shall be given genuine opportunities to secure orders; (2) operating companies are required to inform the Norwegian supply and contractor industry in advance of the bidding

(box continues on next page)

Box 5.6 Policies that Foster the Generation and Transfer of Knowledge and Technology
(continued)

process; and (3) the operators have a duty to perform in Norway at least 50 percent of all R&D required by field development. But Norway's local industry had grown significantly even before its entry into the European Economic Community, leveraging an already available industrial capacity in shipping, ship building, and mining. Today Norwegian oil and gas and supply companies have developed leading-class, state-of-the-art technologies, and many international companies have located part of their R&D chain in Norway (Nordås, Vatne, and Heum 2003).

By contrast, the **United Kingdom**, which started its petroleum sector history at a more advanced level than Norway, opted for a market-based approach. Although a local content policy was in place in the 1970s and 1980s, local content was not a requirement and no sanctions were applied to companies that did not invest in developing the local supply sector. Moreover, the United Kingdom's speedy development of its North Sea resources attracted American service companies and expertise, thus limiting incentives to investment in local R&D and technology transfers (Hallwood 1990). Norway, instead, decided to develop its hydrocarbons more slowly than the United Kingdom, with the explicit objective of allowing a Norwegian service sector to develop.

Supporting the Development of Adequate Local Skills

Skill shortages across the industry value chain are pervasive in almost all petroleum-producing countries, although their level and distribution across countries and subsectors varies greatly. Shortages have been felt most acutely in Australia and South America due the sharp increase in the number and complexity of petroleum projects. North America and Europe are following closely, due to the resurgence of activity. The problem is made more acute by countries' policies aimed at increasing local employment. Besides the rise in demand for workers arising from the increased number of oil and gas projects around the world, skills shortages have been attributed to the structure of the industry job market where the average age of professionals is among the highest of any industry, and many people will be retiring in the next few years. Furthermore, student enrollment in petro-technical courses has been on the decline for many years, and remains well below that of the early 1980s (CRES 2008). In general, common gaps across countries and subsectors appear to exist at highly technical and senior levels, in professional disciplines such as geosciences and various forms of engineering, as well as mid-level technical and managerial positions.

Especially in the early stages of development of the petroleum sector, the capacity to meet the industry professional requirement is likely to be low, particularly in countries that lack an industrial base. Many factors may contribute to the skills gap, including the following: (1) the quality of the national education system, which may not be adequate to generate a local supply of workers with the necessary knowledge and skills; (2) the size of petroleum reserves, which may not be sufficient to support the development of sustainable backward links; and (3) the pace of exploitation or government depletion, which may be too fast to permit the development of local skills. This explains why gaps tend to be filled with expatriate workers, especially in technical or management positions. Existing literature confirms that a better-educated work-force and the increased supply of skills have a major impact on economic growth through increased productivity and adaptability to new routines and technological change (Barro 1999; Hanushek and Woessmann 2007; Morris, Kaplinsky, and Kaplan 2011). As countries develop and the industrial sector expands, more and more sophisticated skills become necessary. Therefore investing in local human resource development is essential to the success and sustainability of the local industrial and service capacity, and needs to be care-fully paced.

In our case study countries, local employment policies vary from "command and control" type of intervention (as in Angola, Indonesia, and Kazakhstan) to more market-oriented approaches (as in Brazil, Malaysia, and Trinidad and Tobago). The choice of policy and implementation tools is necessarily linked to the nature and level of the gap to be addressed. In some countries (for example, Indonesia, Malaysia, and Trinidad and Tobago) employment and educational policies aim to foster the creation of local capabilities that can be transferred to other sectors. This includes the development of skills that are common to all sectors, as well as the creation and support of cluster developments with other industries that have a natural synergy with the petroleum sector. A recent survey on skills shortage in the oil and gas industry suggests that the most effective solution to close the skills gap involves the close collaboration between industry and governments (CRES 2008). The survey further found that training pro-grams in low-income countries are among the most important elements of an effective strategy to reduce the skills gap. But often the lack of an adequate infrastructure, scarce teaching personnel, and little funding hinder the success of these initiatives. Nonetheless, a number of initiatives have been developed to establish learning institutions and training centers, including in our case study countries, often in close collaboration with leading foreign universities and/or industry. Box 5.7 discusses the impact of educational policies on local content requirements in Brazil and Malaysia.

Minimizing Compliance and Administrative Costs

Complex LCPs may make it difficult for policy makers to monitor their imple-mentation, assess their impact, and enforce their application. Target groups may have difficulty in applying LCPs, which may result in misapplication or lack of application, and intended beneficiaries may lack the capacity to take full advantage of implementation. Especially for small businesses, assimilating and

Box 5.7

Local Employment and Educational Policies: The Experience of Brazil and Malaysia

Despite a long history of higher education reforms, **Malaysia** still faces a number of challenges mainly related to the mismatch between supply and demand, and the national brain
drain, which have created a persistent shortage of skilled labor. Firm-level evidence suggests
that skill shortages and mismatches pose significant barriers to growth: roughly one-fifth of
those surveyed identified skill and educational shortages among major obstacles for successful operation and growth of their businesses. Approximately 90 percent of Malaysia's
workforce is under 30 years of age. Literacy levels are high (over 90 percent of the adult
population), and unemployment is low, except for holders of higher education degrees. The
Economic Transformation Program (ETP) anticipates the creation of 3.3 million jobs by 2020,
of which over 52,000 are in the oil, gas, and energy sector, with an estimated 40 percent in
technical disciplines such as geology and engineering. The human capital development portion of the ETP relies on public-private partnerships to improve the skills of existing workers.
Malaysia's policy with regard to local employment in the oil sector has traditionally been of
the encouraging type. Although production sharing agreements (PSAs) refer to the maximi-
zation of employment of nationals, no minimum targets (whether general- or position based)
have been established. Oil companies are free to determine the employment strategy that
best suits their projects' needs. But the recruitment of foreign personnel requires the specific
approval of the national oil company (NOC), Petronas. PSAs also include training obligations
aimed at ensuring the replacement of expatriate workers with national workers, and provide
for training-on-the job to be offered to Petronas' employees upon request. Companies are
also subject to a research contribution calculated on production. Training expenses are cost
recoverable for the purpose of calculating the production shares, and the research contribution is tax deductible, which means that part of the cost is financed by the government
through the fiscal regime. Many petroleum companies and international contractors have
established training courses, either in-house or in collaboration with local training institutions. But Petronas has been leading the effort to develop a skilled and competitive local
workforce. In addition to providing sponsorship to Malaysian students wishing to pursue tertiary education in country or overseas, the NOC has established four educational and training
institutions, and an e-learning platform. The Universiti Teknologi of Petronas (UTP), founded
in 1996, hosts over 5,000 students and offers engineering and technology-related academic
programs. The university has established several industry and academic partnerships. The
Maritime Academy of Malaysia (ALAM), established in 1983, is a one-stop training center for
maritime activities. The academy is owned and operated by Petronas and is a branch campus
of the World Maritime University and partners with leading maritime educational bodies
around the world. The Institut Teknologi Petroleum of Petronas (INSTEP), created in 1983,
offers training programs to technicians, engineers, and technical executives of Petronas and
other NOCs. To strengthen managerial capacity Petronas established a Leadership Centre in
1992. Furthermore, Petronas' online training courses are open to the private sector and

(box continues on next page)

Box 5.7 Local Employment and Educational Policies: The Experience of Brazil and Malaysia
(continued)

government agencies. So far this approach had served Malaysia well, balancing the requirement to strengthen local skills with the imperative to maintain production levels, and accelerate the search for new finds to supplement maturing fields. But in order to achieve the objectives of its 2010 Economic Transformation Program, new local skills development strategies have been adopted. The Talent Corporation was established at the beginning of 2011 under the prime minister to formulate and facilitate initiatives to address the availability of talent in line with the needs of the country's economic transformation. The company works in collaboration with the relevant government agencies and employers in priority economic sectors to develop demand-driven initiatives. A gap analysis was carried out by the MPRC to assess the distribution and shortage in skills that would need to be addressed for the successful establishment of Malaysia as a regional provider of oil field and equipment services. As a result, two pilot programs have been launched: the Pilot Internship Program for Engineering Consultancy Services, and the National Talent Enhancement Program. Both programs represent innovative training solutions that provide tax incentives for participating companies while ensuring that trainees receive on-the-job practical skills.

In **Brazil** education policy has been receiving great attention at both federal and local government levels since 1995. But Brazil's education lags behind that of the other BRICs. Unequal resources for public and private schools and poor infrastructure are among the factors hindering improvement in the quality of education, despite efforts to improve finance equalization, and the introduction of conditional cash transfers and results measurement. The quality of tertiary education is particularly concerning: out of the 183 universities, only 6 show up in the world's top 500. There is a vast shortage in skilled labor. Approximately, 22 percent of the population is not sufficiently qualified to enter the labor market, which has driven some companies to take matters in their own hands (CSIS 2010). There are no LCPs on local employment. In fact domestic employment only comes into play in the calculation of local content in services, based on the cost of local manpower relative to the total cost of manpower. But the Program for the Mobilization of the Oil and Gas Industry (PROMINP), launched in 2003 by the federal government, carried out an assessment of the demand and supply for labor by professional category and by state. The study identified a major need for specialized labor in some 175 professional categories considered as critical for the sector (30 on the basic; 56 on the middle; 13 on the technical; 45 on the college; and 27 on inspector levels) (Petrobras 2008). As a result, the National Professional Qualification Plan was created in 2006. The plan relies on technical schools and universities located in the states where oil and gas projects are planned and demand for upgraded skills is pressing. Overall the program involved 71 educational institutions offering 953 courses targeting over 100,000 professionals across 17 states between 2006 and 2010. In addition, in 2007 PROMINP helped to establish centers and networks of excellence in universities, aimed to enhance the quality of education in areas of special interest to the oil and gas industry, leveraging Petrobras' experience. Between 2008 and 2010 the skills gap was estimated at 112,625 professionals in construction and assembly, civil construction, operation maintenance, and engineering. Approximately 53,000 professionals reached

(box continues on next page)

Box 5.7 Local Employment and Educational Policies: The Experience of Brazil and Malaysia
(continued)

qualification through the program, and 25,000 were selected to implement projects envisaged by Petrobras' business plan in 2008–12. An additional 200,000 professionals were required to implement Petrobras' business plan 2009–13. (PROMINP 2010). A human resources program was a precursor of the national professional qualification plan and was carried out by the Agencia Nacional do Petroleo in 1999 to encourage training courses for specialized labor in the oil and gas industry. The program sees to the inclusion in learning institutions' curricula of subjects specific to the oil and gas industry, and focuses on both graduate and postgraduate courses, as well as technical and professional education. Funding for the program is provided by the ANP and the CI-PETRO Industry Fund—National Science and Technology Plan. Despite all these programs, companies and government entities heavily rely on Petrobras to generate the specialized and experienced human resources that are necessary to fulfill the strategic and operational objectives of the government sector and LCPs. Petrobras is being assigned significant and comprehensive responsibilities that could ultimately impair the company's competitiveness and operational efficiency (BNDES 2009).

In both **Malaysia** and **Brazil** the quality of education and the shortage of skilled labor have received policy makers' attention owing to their detrimental effect on economic growth and diversification. The countries have adopted similar education strategies with the aim to improve the overall quality of education in the long term, and to upgrade the existing labor force to address short-term gaps. In both countries, the NOC plays a central role in promoting technical and higher education in areas that are relevant to oil and gas operations. There are, however, important structural differences between the two countries, including the following:

- Approximately 90 percent of the 12,000-strong labor force in Malaysia is below 30 years of age, unemployment rates are low, and compared to Brazil, a larger percentage of the workforce is employed in knowledge-intensive services and manufacturing sectors. Brazil's labor force is approximately 9 times larger than Malaysia's, unemployment rates are more than double Malaysia's, and the country is facing an aging workforce. According to Eurostat figures, approximately 42 percent of Brazil's scientists and engineers are aged 45–64 and approaching retirement.
- Both countries rely heavily on their NOCs to lead the training and educational efforts in the oil and gas sector. But Petrobras and Petronas face rather different operational challenges, including the following: (1) the complexity of Petrobras' portfolio of assets and level of activity has increased exponentially following the pre-salt discoveries and the recent institutional reform; (2) the skill shortage that Petrobras is facing pales the estimates for the Malaysia's OFSE strategy; and (3) the Brazilian's government focus on Petrobras as the key player in developing the pre-salt discoveries—coupled with stepped-up local content requirements in goods, works, and services and the limited role allowed to international oil companies—place an unprecedented constraint on Petrobras' capacity. On the other hand, Petronas' portfolio of assets is much less complex, international oil

(box continues on next page)

Box 5.7 Local Employment and Educational Policies: The Experience of Brazil and Malaysia (*continued*)

companies (who have easier access to an international pool of HR resources) are still playing a considerable role in the sector, and BPMigas' estimate of the skill gaps that would need to be filled by 2020 in order to build a regional OFSE capacity is quite modest in comparison with Brazil, amounting to approximately 50,000 professionals across different categories of employment.

It would seem that a stronger role of the regulator in carrying out the educational policy, more reliance on international education institutions, and some relaxation of local manufacturing targets could be considered in order to better align Brazil's local content and sector development targets with country-specific constraints. Given that it takes a long lead time to gather the right type and spectrum of experience and expertise to become a petroleum industry professional, the quality of the education systems is essential. This is a matter for the government, although Petrobras' and Petronas' cases prove that corporate-led initiatives can effectively address short-term skills shortages. Deliberate public sector action and well-planned investments are necessary further down the education pipeline at higher education levels.[a]

a. The International Gas Union's 2012 report on Nurturing Future Generations for Oil and Gas Industry identifies five major issues that affect the availability, interest, and attraction of talents to the oil and gas industry, namely the quality of education systems, the mobility of highly skilled labor, changing demographic patterns, government-industry relationships, and perceptions and misconceptions, especially relating to environmental concerns and work-life balance. The report, which contains a discussion of how these factors affect the search for skilled labor in Malaysia and Brazil, can be downloaded at http://www.igu.org/wgc-2012/publications-from-wgc-2012/Nurturing-The-Future-Generations-Short1.pdf.

complying with complex administrative and/or technical rules can create an unreasonable burden. Complexity may translate into additional administrative costs for all parties involved, and inefficient or harmful outcomes. Therefore, in designing LCPs, regulators should be mindful of introducing measures for which the cost of compliance exceeds the social benefit.

As the experience of our case study countries show, the use of standardized definitions of local content and standard reporting templates improve the transparency and the comparability of information provided by different companies. These measures can also help to reduce the regulator's administrative costs. Standard reporting procedures—especially if electronic procedures are used for the preparation, submission, and assessment of reports, to track bidding and contracts award, and to provide information on expected demand and supply of relevant goods and services—are likely to:

- Reduce the regulator's monitoring cost
- Reduce or remove obstacles to the participation of local SMEs in procurement processes by lowering the cost of access to information

- Allow local suppliers to make investment or process adjustments in order to be able to meet future demand
- Eliminate duplication of requests that may arise when government entities involved in the regulation of LCPs lack coordination.

Compliance with local content regulations would necessarily involve additional costs for investors, especially when the regulatory requirements are complex, the measurement and reporting procedures are unclear, and modifications to the investors' procurement and/or reporting systems are necessary. Additional costs should be carefully considered since they may put small and medium investors at a disadvantage. Since these costs are normally recoverable for the purpose of calculation of petroleum sharing and/or corporate tax, regulators should have an incentive to design regulatory requirements that minimize compliance costs. Box 5.8 outlines examples of LCP processes aimed at reducing monitoring and administration costs.

Box 5.8

Standardization of LCP Reporting to Reduce Monitoring and Administration Costs

Kazakhstan's local content policies (LCPs) first appeared in the Petroleum Law of 1995. The law included only high-level provisions requiring that subcontractors in the oil sector be "largely" Kazakh-owned. This was followed by the 1996 Law on Subsurface and Subsurface Use, which required that companies propose, at tender stage, their own local content commitments. But local content requirements were vaguely expressed, which gave ample discretion to companies on their implementation. This resulted in uneven interpretation of requirements, uneven quality of reporting, difficulty in monitoring local content levels, and ultimately did not yield the local content levels that the regulator were hoping to achieve. This prompted the regulator to adopt a more prescriptive approach. Local content requirements were further detailed in the 2007 rules for procurement of goods, works, and services. The rules detailed the procurement process of all subsurface operations, outlined a monitoring and measurement procedure, and developed a clear definition of local content, as follows:

- Localization of the labor force—"the percentage of Kazakhstan personnel engaged in the implementation of a contract, broken down by category of personnel, indicating separately the percentage for each individual category in relation to foreign personnel, whose quantity must be reduced over years as mandatory training and qualification improvement programs are implemented for Kazakhstan personnel"
- Goods—"equipment, final product and other material and technical values, purchased for direct use in subsoil operations and for the activity, which is specified as auxiliary in the contract"

(box continues on next page)

Box 5.8 Standardization of LCP Reporting to Reduce Monitoring and Administration Costs
(continued)

- Works—"carrying out activities on a paid basis on creating (producing) goods, equipment assembly, construction of facilities and other sites, required for direct use in subsoil operations and for the activity which is specified as auxiliary in the contract"
- Services—"carrying out activities on a paid basis, required for direct use in subsoil operations and for the activity, which is specified as auxiliary in the contract, not aimed to create (produce) goods or other material objects." (MENAS 2009)

During 2010 new regulations on local content were introduced. The main concepts and objectives of previous regulations were preserved. In addition clear reporting procedures (Decree No. 965 and Decree No. 1018 of 2010) and measurement criteria (Decree No. 367 and Decree No. 964 of 2010) were introduced.

Prior to the publication of the unified methodology and the introduction of the certification process, each company reported local content levels using its own formulas. Some reported committed expenditure while others used actual spending, leading to inconsistency and difficulty in accounting for the impact of LCPs. Although statistics are not publicly available, the standardization of local content definition, and the introduction of the unified calculation methodology, together with the online procurement platform described in box 5.3, are likely to have resulted in lower monitoring costs, as well as improved coordination among government entities involved in the monitoring of LCPs, and have been cited by the regulator among the reasons for increased local content levels.

On the other hand, medium and small-sized investors have raised concerns over the cost of compliance associated with the implementation of the unified methodology and the certification process which is disproportionate vis-à-vis large companies and put them at disadvantage (Ospanova 2010).

Lowering the cost of local enterprises' participation in tender processes may also require companies to voluntarily amend their tender procedures and procurement policies to better align them with the requirements and objective of LCPs. This approach was used by British Petroleum as part of its strategy to develop local construction and engineering capability in Trinidad and Tobago (box 5.6). Following are some examples:

- Where no common platform has been created by the regulator to facilitate the sharing of information on upcoming and future bids, companies could consider adapting their systems for announcing tenders to local circumstances, by using local press or suppliers associations, or other facilitating bodies.
- Tender documentation could be published in local languages, particularly where language is a barrier to the participation of local enterprises.
- Longer deadlines for submission of offers, and simplified bid packages could be used to lower participation costs for small local enterprises.

- In the absence of formal suppliers' qualification programs, simplified supplier prequalification processes, or postqualification when appropriate, could be designed that would lower both suppliers' participation costs and the company's administrative costs by ensuring that only tenders from qualified suppliers would need to be assessed.

Developing Clusters and Regional Trade Synergies

Clusters can be defined as geographical and sectoral concentrations of enterprises that produce and sell a range of related or complementary products. Evidence from the study of clusters shows that these agglomerations can increase productivity and operational efficiency through links, spillovers, and synergies across firms and associated institutions. Clusters can contribute to the foundation of knowledge and help stimulate technological innovation through the efficient access to public goods, better coordination, the diffusion of best practices, and the ability to share workers among companies (Shakya 2009).[6] The oil and gas industry is generally known for the presence of large players, with substantial investment in R&D to reduce costs, improve productivity, and secure technological advantages. Therefore, the collaboration among, and interaction between, oil and gas companies, integrated service providers, the national oil company, and small specialized (often localized) suppliers and service providers are critical to the sustainable development of a local industrial capacity. Consequently, geographical and sectoral clusters have been used by some governments as a means to accelerate the development of local enterprises, as well as to strengthen the national system of innovation. Furthermore, some countries have taken the concept of clusters beyond the domestic market, by supporting the development of regional trade synergies through regional hubs and/or the integration of LCPs at the regional level with the objective to help provide the economies of scale necessary to sustain local comparative advantages. Box 5.9 provides examples of oil and gas clusters and regional hub developments.

Box 5.9

Oil and Gas Clusters and Regional Hubs

Since the early days of sector development Norway had to face the issue of how to build local capabilities in the context of an already well-established global industry. Although Norway had an industrial base, it had virtually no capability in the oil and gas sector. With good macroeconomic conditions and almost full employment, the government was concerned that, if left to the market, the development of oil resources would overheat the economy. Controlling the pace of development and build domestic capability became policy priorities. This resulted in direct intervention through the national oil company,

(box continues on next page)

Box 5.9 Oil and Gas Clusters and Regional Hubs *(continued)*

Statoil, and the establishment of licensing conditions that required technology transfer from foreign to domestic companies and supported the development of local suppliers. Through this strategy Norway has developed a significant domestic cluster of suppliers to oil and gas operators, employing approximately 114,000 people locally in 2010 with sales of $32 billion locally and $20 billion to customers outside of Norway (Sasson and Blomgren 2011; Skjellevik 2011). The cluster is positioned as a technology-driven innovator. Local companies are positioned in all parts of the oil and gas value chain, particularly in the upstream segment—given the small size of the products market in Norway. Their size ranges from multinational corporations to start-ups. The most successful suppliers are those that have been able to internationalize. According to recent research, the subclusters with the highest profit margins—geology, seismic, and drilling—have the highest percentage of international sales (Leskinen and others 2012). These capabilities developed as a result of collaboration and coordination, driven and supported by the national and local governments (Hatakenaka and others 2006). Furthermore, the government put in place effective policies that boosted preexisting competences in related industries (shipping, shipbuilding, and mining). Firms were forced to innovate given the harsh environment in which oil and gas extraction occurs, and tax deduction was offered to support the development cost. Meanwhile, Statoil's dominance in the local market afforded the company a unique position to develop suppliers and encourage innovation. Statoil has been actively pursuing cluster developments in various petroleum provinces, including Angola, the Gulf of Mexico, Brazil, and the Russian Federation.

According to the BP statistical review at the end of 2011 **Malaysia**'s oil and gas reserves were 5.9 billion barrels and 86 trillion cubic feed, respectively. Most of the shallow water fields have reached maturity, and at current levels of production existing reserves are expected to be depleted in 34 years. The undiscovered hydrocarbon resources, estimated to be around 10 billion barrels of oil equivalent, are located in deep and ultra-deep waters, and will be challenging to exploit with existing methods and technology. The availability of domestic hydrocarbon resources has been a natural driver to develop the oil and gas sector. The national oil company, Petronas, played and continues to play a major role in driving the industry's growth through its exploration and production activities as well as the creation of opportunities for local companies to build up their capacity and capability across the value chain. The oil field services and equipment (OFSE) industry supports primarily upstream activities. OFSE include land drilling services, offshore drilling services, geophysical services, engineering and contracting, equipment assembly and manufacturing, offshore structure fabrication and installation, and operations and maintenance. With the support of Petronas, local companies have developed alongside some of the largest international players that have established their operations in Malaysia. But given the declining conventional oil and gas resource base, future growth is expected to come from initiatives such as enhanced oil recovery, innovative approaches to the development of small fields, and the acceleration of exploration activities. To prepare for this, the government intends to strengthen other value creating activities in the oil and gas value chain, and support the development of a sustainable energy

(box continues on next page)

Box 5.9 Oil and Gas Clusters and Regional Hubs *(continued)*

platform for the future. Under the 2010 Economic Transformation Program (ETP) the government of Malaysia has laid out a comprehensive package of measures to increase the competitiveness of its domestic OFSE industry with the objective to transform the country into a leading oil and gas services hub in Asia, as well as grow Malaysia's role in oil storage, logistics, and trading and import LNG to serve latent gas demand and attract new gas-based industries. Most OFSE players in the region have set up their operations in Malaysia, Singapore, and Thailand. As a result, the market is fragmented, unlike Europe and the United States, where OFSE operators concentrate their activities in a few centers (that is, Aberdeen, Stavanger, and Houston). This creates an opportunity for Malaysia, which has a competitive domestic workforce, technically challenging domestic reserves driving a growing demand for OFSE, and geographical proximity to resource-rich countries in Asia and the Middle East. To capitalize on these advantages the government has set out a strategy to (1) further attract OFSE multinationals to set out the center of their operations in the country; (2) build regional champions out of domestic companies by incentivizing the rationalization of local fabricators; and (3) establish joint ventures with OFSE multinationals in critical value-adding activities. To this end the Malaysia Petroleum Resources Corporation (MPRC), set up in 2011, was tasked with the responsibility to oversee the domestic industry and ensure coordination between all existing, planned, and potential clusters of OFSE activity, and to create an attractive business environment for multinationals by simplifying administrative procedures and provide recommendations on reforms to the fiscal regime that are necessary to ensure its attractiveness. Following the introduction of fiscal incentives, several companies, including Vitol Trading, YTL Power International Bhd, and BB Energy & Rotterdam Group, have already moved part of their operations to Malaysia, and the consolidation of fabricators has started.[a]

a. A detailed description of the rationale, objectives, and institutional measures for the realization of Malaysia's OFSE regional hub can be found in Powering the Malaysian Economy with Oil, Gas, and Energy, chapter 6, Economic Transformation Program, http://etp.pemandu.gov.my/upload/etp_handbook_chapter_6_oil_gas_and_energy.pdf.

Key Policy Questions

Assertive or Encouraging Policies?

Existing literature on local content requirements in various industries around the world would seem to indicate that there is value to the use of modest levels of local content requirements aimed at incentivizing or pushing companies toward making investment decisions beyond what they would normally do. At the same time LCPs appear to have a clear maximum benefit, and command and control–type intervention runs the risk of having harmful effects on the economy.

Indeed setting a single policy that is equal for all investors in all subsectors is likely to carry unintended consequences, especially when differences exist in scale and learning curves. This might explain why countries that do opt for setting minimum local content targets often end up breaking those down by subsector or activity. Table 5.4 contains a summary of the local content minimum targets for the countries in our case study sample.

Table 5.4 Aggregate or Overall Targets?

	Angola	Brazil	Indonesia	Kazakhstan	Malaysia	Trinidad and Tobago
Policy classification						
Recruitment and Training of Nationals in Direct Workforce						
Targets for Nationals (Targets mandated for total workforce)	Yes — At least 70% of the workforce of employers with more than 5 workers must be Angolan nationals (Decree 5/95)	No — No specific targets, but individual targets for itemized services, which drives an increase in national workforce	No	Yes	No	No
Targets for Different Positions (different targets for different categories of positions)	Yes — Angolanization targets by job grade set by the Ministry of Petroleum	No	Yes — Targets are set by skill level and phase of development of the project	Yes — Medium and large companies to have minimum 70% Kazakh executives and 90% techical personnel (Decree 45/112)	No	No
Sourcing of Local Goods and Services						
Mandated Targets for Procurement of Local Goods and Services (sanctions if non-compliant)	No — Aggregate and item-specific targets. Targets differ by bid round and are modified by the offer of the concessionaire. Fines linked to percentage of non-compliance with targets	Yes — Minimum percentage of local content to be eligible to tender (the percentage is variable) (BP Migas PTK 007 r2)	Yes — In private companies minimum 82.5 percent for services and 11 percent for goods	Yes	No	No

Source: World Bank data.

As argued in chapter 2, "command and control"–type interventions have a greater risk of missing the socially optimum level of local content, and should be used with great caution by policy makers. But when policy makers opt for establishing minimum targets, these should be clear, reasonable (that is, within the reach and capability of the country), and objectively measurable to avoid creating unrealistic expectations, introducing distortions and inefficiency, or creating conditions that may favor one investor over the other. To this end the first step would logically be to carry out an assessment of existing capacity and current and future demand, which in turn would provide the regulator with a better understanding of the nature and magnitude of the gaps, and serve as basis for deciding the need for and kind of regulatory intervention. Box 5.10 contains examples of alternative approaches for the countries in our case study sample.

Box 5.10

Needs Assessment to Determine the Need for and Type of Policy Intervention

Angola and **Brazil** carried out an assessment of existing capacity gaps with the objective to ensure coherence between local content requirements and the pace and scheduling of petroleum sector's activities. The idea was to tailor policy intervention to the ability of the rest of the economy to develop service capacity through backward links and to the speed at which such capacity could be created as well as to foster local employment. This way—at least in theory—local content requirements could be fine-tuned, and targets if necessary could be set at a level that would avoid exacerbating supply bottlenecks and inefficiency (which is the case when minimum targets far exceed existing capabilities).

Notwithstanding the good intentions, industry observers have noted that minimum local content targets recently established at the subsector level in **Brazil** may be too ambitious, affecting the timing and implementation cost of Petrobras' field development plans related to the pre-salt discoveries. Nonetheless, and setting aside economic efficiency consider-ations, significant progress has been made through a series of infrastructure, capacity building, and financing initiatives designed to address skills and technological gaps, taking into consideration the relative competitiveness of each subsector.

In **Angola** a capacity assessment led to a modification of the local content regulatory framework in 2010. Among others, generic sectorwide Angolanization targets that were introduced in 1982 were eliminated. Under the current legal regime, companies operating in the oil sector may only hire expatriates if they can demonstrate that no Angolan personnel duly qualified to perform the job are available on the local market, and with prior authoriza-tion from the Ministry of Petroleum. The change aims to bolster companies' training and requalification investments, but its effectiveness may be at odds with the lack of a wide-ranging reform of the national education system.

Incentives as opposed or in addition to minimum targets may be used to close capacity gaps. For example, to close technological gaps in strategic manufacturing sectors both **Brazil**

(box continues on next page)

Box 5.10 Needs Assessment to Determine the Need for and Type of Policy Intervention
(continued)

and **Trinidad and Tobago** opted to incentivize inward investment and joint ventures between local and foreign companies, especially in subsectors where domestic competitiveness was limited. A similar approach has been recently followed by **Malaysia** for the implementation of its 2010 Economic Transformation Plan. Meanwhile, very few countries in our sample have adopted local content policies to develop forward links. Indeed forward links are more complex to develop and require scale and technology that is often not within the reach of a country. Recognizing this limitation Trinidad and Tobago's policy has been to incentivize foreign investment and joint-venture projects (as opposed to imposing minimum targets and sector restrictions) so as to spread investment risk and fast-track development by providing access to technical, managerial, and marketing skills, as well as access to markets that are required for large investments to be economically feasible.

Whether or not policy makers opt for assertive LCPs, metrics to measure local content performance should be carefully chosen as they are as critical to a policy's success as are objectives and targets. This is because it is often the metrics that end up driving companies' and regulators' behavior. Furthermore, as Brazil and Kazakhstan show, metrics should be specific and uniformly applied, with widely disclosed methodologies for calculating them. This allows policy makers to (1) more precisely target public policy and monitor its effect on the economy, (2) monitor and benchmark policy implementation by companies, and (3) limit the arbitrary use or abuse of incentives and penalties.

Preliminary observations from our review of LCPs in petroleum countries suggest that, in general terms, more formal regulatory frameworks and mandatory local content targets (that is, assertive LCPs) may be easier to define in countries that: (1) have an established hydrocarbon sector, (2) have a clear understanding of future demand for services, and (3) have basic capacity and skills. Frontier or exploration countries where (1) industry players tend to be small and dynamic exploration companies, (2) future demand for services is difficult to predict, and (3) capacity and skills gaps are considerable, may be better off adopting encouraging LCPs, including incentives when appropriate. Particularly in these countries the government should consider focusing on improving local skills, business know-how, technology, capital market development, wealth capture, and wealth distribution to create the conditions for domestic companies to emerge.

National or Domestic Content?

As discussed in previous chapters, a local content requirement is a regulation that requires a specified fraction of a final good, work, or service to be sourced domestically. The requirement may be specified in value terms (for example by setting some minimum share of total value-added of a good to represent domestic valued-added), or it may be set in physical units (for example by specifying a minimum share of domestic employment). Some countries add a further parameter to the definition of local content, by requiring some minimum share of national ownership in the manufacturing of goods or the provision of services. Indeed the terms "local" and "content" do not have the same meaning across all countries in our sample. For some, local goods are those that are mostly produced in the country (for example, Brazil), and local services are those that are rendered by companies that mostly employ citizens (for example, Kazakhstan). In others the ownership of the company producing the goods or supplying the services determines the extent to which they can be considered as "local" (for example, Indonesia). For some countries "local content" means the immediate and direct contribution of the oil and gas companies to the local economy (for example, Angola), while others include both the direct and indirect contributions (for example, Malaysia, Indonesia, and Kazakhstan). Furthermore, for some, local content relates to the geographical location of the provider of goods and services regardless of value-added (for example, Angola), while others take into account the share of value that is added locally (for example, Brazil and Kazakhstan). Table 5.5 summarizes the definition of local content across our sample countries.

There is no right or wrong definition. What should be considered local content depends on the policy objectives that a government wants to achieve. For example, the classification system used in Indonesia—although rather complex—constrains the ability of companies of certain sizes to bid for contracts of certain values, for certain types of goods and services that are prioritized by the government to support the development of local capabilities considered to be sustainable and competitive in the long term. The lack of ownership requirements in Brazil and Kazakhstan is consistent with these countries' objectives to fast-track the transfer of knowledge and capacity by leveraging foreign investment. Given Malaysia's policy objective to become a regional oil field services and equipment hub, it is not surprising that the requirement that the foreign ownership of locally incorporated suppliers of oil field services and equipment be limited to 30 percent has been relaxed under the 2010 Economic Transformation Program to incentivize inward investment and the transfer of technology in a sector where high-end technical solutions are the realm of a limited number of global oil service companies.

In general terms, although governments pursue a variety of objectives through LCPs, often these are used as tools to support economic diversification, increase domestic income levels, and widen the tax base. This being the case, from a strictly economic standpoint, national ownership is not a prerequisite to achieving these objectives. In addition, existing research shows that foreign investors may be reluctant to transfer proprietary technology or invest in a local company when their ownership share is limited to minority. Therefore, when the development of a local industry rests on the access to complex and evolving proprietary technology, or requires large capital investments at high risk, ownership requirements that more closely reflect foreign and national investors'

Table 5.5 What Is Domestic Content?

Geographical base Ownership	In-country Domestic	Partially domestic	Totally foreign	Abroad Domestic	Comments
Angola	X	X			A company is extended preferential rights in procurement if at least 51% of the capital is owned by Angolan citizens
Brazil	X	X	X		There is no discrimination between foreign and Brazilian owned locally registered companies. For goods, the local content (LC) level is linked to the value of imports relative to total cost. For services, LC level is based on the cost of local manpower relative to total cost of manpower
Indonesia Goods	X	X	X		A price preference is given based on the LC level, regardless of ownership status. An additional price preference is given in case more than 50% of the company's shares are owned by Indonesian(s)
Services	X	X			Prequalification and price preference rules require the inclusion of companies for which more than 50% of the share capital is owned by Indonesian(s)
Kazakhstan	X	X	X		There are no ownership requirements for companies engaged in the supply of goods and services. But suppliers of goods must be locally registered, and carry out manufacturing processes in Kazakhstan according to the rules applicable for obtaining a CT-KZ certificate, and suppliers of services are considered local if at least 95% of their staff is made up of Kazakh citizens
Malaysia	X	X		X	Locally established manufacturing companies with at least 50% Malaysian ownership may obtain fiscal incentives. The local ownership threshold may be as high as 70% depending on the type of incentive. All companies—domestic or foreign—providing oil field services and equipment must be approved by Petronas Foreign suppliers can obtain such approval if they partner with local suppliers or act as contractors. If incorporated locally, foreign suppliers are restricted to a 30% equity share (except priority sectors under the 2010 Economic Transformation Program)
Trinidad & Tobago	X	X		X	Local content and participation is defined in terms of ownership, control and financing by citizens. But minimum ownership thresholds or other criteria have not been established by the authorities

Source: World Bank data.

contributions are likely to be more effective. It is also worth noting that, if not carefully designed, LCPs predicated on minimum levels of national ownership may lead to the creation of front companies that import goods manufactured abroad or sell services provided by foreign companies with little domestic value addition and capacity building, thus defying the very purpose of LCPs.

Does the National Oil Company Have a Special Role?

Approximately 90 percent of the world's oil reserves and 75 percent of production are controlled by national oil companies (NOCs), which also control many of the major oil and gas infrastructure systems.[7] In addition, an estimated 60 percent of the world's undiscovered reserves lie in countries where NOCs have privileged access to reserves. Furthermore, many NOCs have a global reach and influence operating on an international scale, competing with international oil companies, and more and more investing in the development of new technology (Tordo 2011).

Given their influential role in their home markets, governments often give their NOCs a primary role in promoting local content policies. NOCs can be a channel for capital, technology, and know-how, including by supporting the development of local suppliers for their oil field service needs. Some NOCs—such as Petrobras (Brazil), Petronas (Malaysia), and Statoil (Norway)—have led the way by pursuing a strategy of localization to build capacity and provide the scale that allows the sustainable and competitive development of local suppliers. Specific examples of these NOC roles were presented in boxes 5.6, 5.7, and 5.9.

But the mere existence of an NOC does not imply that it should or could be the main tool for implementing LCPs. Indeed, although NOCs are usually given a special role in promoting their countries' economic development, governments should be mindful of the need to avoid overburdening the NOC with objectives that may be at odds with its capacity and commercial objectives. In other words, only those NOCs that are technically and managerially capable can be effective catalysts of economic development.

Incentives, Penalties, or Both?

All LCP incentive programs have potential costs and benefits. The former are associated with losses from business choices that would have been made even without the incentives, economic distortions, and administrative costs induced by the program. The latter include social benefits such as jobs and positive externalities, and higher tax bases from the development of a domestic supply sector. Estimating the likely costs and potential benefits of an incentive program is the first step toward its efficient and effective design. There is an ample body of literature on the effectiveness of tax and on tax incentives to affect investment decisions—although not specifically focused on LCPs. Most researches focus on developed countries, while evidence from developing countries has largely been anecdotal. Nonetheless it would seem that incentives work best for certain kinds of investments, in specific situations, and for specific sectors, such as export-oriented investments, and are far less effective in weaker investment climates than in stronger ones (Morisset and Pirnia 2001; James 2009).

Furthermore, economic theory shows that a firm's incentive to comply with regulations is a function of the cost of both compliance and noncompliance. Compliance costs include the expense of applying the regulations, while noncompliance costs are related to the probability that the regulator will detect the lack of compliance, and the size of the penalty that will be imposed. Other considerations, such as market pressure, the firm's size, and the extent to which compliance costs can be passed on to consumers, also affect a firm's behavior. In a study on regulatory effectiveness in various economic sectors, the authors conclude that if firms lack sufficient incentives to comply voluntarily with regulations, a cooperative enforcement approach is not likely to induce compliance (Shapiro and Rabinowitz 1997). On the contrary, the regulator's failure to punish the firm results in its continued noncompliance, unless the firm's incentives are shifted by the imposition of penalties.

Whether a country chooses to impose general local content requirements (for example, Brazil prior to the 7th licensing round, and Malaysia) or detailed mandatory minimum local content targets (for example, Angola, Brazil, Indonesia, Kazakhstan), or to simply encourage companies to further its local content objectives (for example, Trinidad and Tobago), implementation is likely to be ineffective if companies think that promised incentives, subsidies, or privileges may be voided, or no penalty or a discretionary or negotiable penalty is associated with lack of compliance. Credibility problems are common to all areas of public policy. Though a government may establish a policy to encourage the allocation of resources in a particular direction, companies may be reluctant to commit resources if they believe that the policy is not credible. This is likely one of the factors that explain the relatively slow progress of LCP implementation in Trinidad and Tobago compared to other countries in our sample, as well as the relatively low outcome of LCP implementation in Kazakhstan prior to the 2010 regulatory reform.

A review of existing literature and our analysis of the case study countries would seem to indicate that, particularly in less-developed economies where market opportunities are often beyond the capability and reach of local suppliers and contractors, a mix of incentives and mandatory requirements is necessary to support LCP implementation.

Conclusion: What Really Matters

"Success is to be measured not so much by the position that one has reached in life as by the obstacles which he has overcome."

—Booker T. Washington

Sustainable economic development from the oil and gas sector is a long-term proposition. To achieve it, policy makers should focus on the design of policies that promote inclusive employment, maximize synergies among economic sectors, and adapt to the global and evolving nature of the oil and gas industry. Starting on the "right foot" is therefore particularly important. The following considerations might help to guide the process.

Establish Realistic and Clear Objectives

Countries that have made use of LCPs to foster economic diversification have not always been successful. Reasons may include high political risk, poor legal and regulatory framework, weak governance, lack of contextualization, and poor planning. LCPs cannot correct for some of these issues. But their design should certainly take such issues into consideration to better ensure cost-efficient and effective implementation.

A review of the case studies suggests that LCPs should be designed taking into account long-term opportunities to pursue a broad-based economic diversification strategy. To this end:

- Policy makers should carefully analyze which subsectors or clusters should be promoted (for example, oil field services, equipment and tools, petroleum products, petrochemicals, fertilizers, and so on), and how these may enable the development of other subsectors and clusters that make use of the same input or output (electronics, engineering services, construction, and so on).
- There should be a clear understanding of (1) the factors that a given sector might require at each stage of development, (2) the ability of the local market to support such sector and possibilities to expand internationally, and (3) each sector's contribution to the country's economy, so that clusters and subsectors can be prioritized.
- A skill and capacity gaps assessment should be carried out so as to ensure that the proper corrective measures are deployed, the policy targets are realistic, and appropriate metrics are designed to monitor the effect of policy implementation.

Furthermore, the perspective of investors, regional and local authorities, and affected populations should be sought in the early phase of LCP conception, as this would help to ensure the sustainability of outcomes.

Assess the Costs and Benefits of Alternative Policies

There is no "blueprint" solution to the design of LCPs to enhance industrial development from the exploration and extraction of oil and gas. The choice of policy and implementation tools depends on the specific country context. But lessons learned from countries' experience with LCPs and industrial policy in general show the importance of a clear understanding of the trade-offs and pitfalls that the development of such policies may entail. Indeed local content for the sake of it would only lead to the waste of scarce development resources. The assessment of cost and benefits of alternative policies should not be done as an afterthought to justify policies already undertaken, and policy effectiveness should be periodically assessed to ensure that appropriate corrective measures are taken where necessary.

In determining the cost of LCPs, policy makers should not forget to consider the short- and long-term effects of changes in procurement and investment policies on government fiscal revenue and export earnings, including the increase in cost of material and equipment, and possible delays in project/production start that may be induced by stringent local content requirements that do not fit local capacity. In fact, depending on the structure of the fiscal regime, the cost of LCPs and any induced inefficiencies may be borne in majority by the government. This loss of revenue may be offset by the increase in tax base arising from economic diversification and additional employment.

Ensure Interagency Coordination

While duplication and overlap of responsibility among level of government and government agencies is common to most policy areas, LCPs aimed at promoting economic diversification and growth from the oil and gas sector are inherently cross-cutting, and thus require the balancing and careful arbitrage among different, sometimes conflicting, priorities. Lack of coordination among different government entities and level of governments may result in conflicting regulation, increased administrative costs, delays in project execution, and in some cases may create an incentive to rent-seeking behavior and corrupt practices.

While country specific context determines the choice of institutional arrangements, countries experience suggests the creation of a dedicated government entity tasked with policy conception, intergovernmental coordination, and monitoring of results enhances policy coherence and interagency coordination. Where appropriate, the oversight and enforcement of LCPs—a role that belongs to the state—should be clearly separated from the facilitation and implementation of the policy—a role that is often played by both NOCs and international oil companies.

Notes

1. The reader is referred to chapter 1 for some general observations derived from the analysis of forward and backward links in a wide sample of countries, including the case study countries.

2. An example of this policy is discussed in the case study on Angola, Local Content Policies in the Oil and Gas Sector, downloadable from http://issuu.com/world.bank.publications/docs/local_content_policies_in_the_oil_and_gas_sector.

3. A new batch of production sharing contracts in Trinidad and Tobago includes provisions that relate to the unbundling of contracts to match the capability of local suppliers in terms of timing, finance, and manpower (see http://business.fiu.edu/InterAmericanSCF2012/presentations/ZKhan.pptx).

4. Glass and Saggi (2008) focus on the role of foreign investment and argue that in order to realize the full benefits of technology transfers, the technologies introduced from abroad need to spread locally.

5. Blomstrom and Sjoholm (1999) find that domestic firms benefit from spillovers in terms of productivity levels, but the degree of foreign ownership does not affect the extent, while Dimelis and Louri (2001) argue that productivity spillovers are stronger when the foreign investors' share of ownership in the local firm is the minority.

Similar conclusions are reached by Muller and Schitzer (2003), who find that positive spillovers increase with the domestic ownership share of a joint venture, but the incentive to transfer technology decreases.

6. There is an ample literature on industrial clusters and their effect on competitiveness (Porter 1990, 1998), innovation processes (Freeman 1987; Lundvall 1992; Nelson 1993), and knowledge spillovers (Jaffee, Trachtenberg, and Henderson 1993; Audretsch and Feldman 1996).

7. Similar numbers apply to natural gas.

References

Audretsch, D. B., and M. P. Feldman. 1996. "R&D Spillovers and Geography of Innovation and Production." *American Economic Review* 86 (3): 630–40.

Barro, R. J. 1999. "Human Capital and Growth in Cross-country Regressions." *Swedish Economic Policy Review* 6 (2): 237–77.

Blomstrom, M., and F. Sjoholm. 1999. "Technology Transfer and Spillovers: Does Local Participation with Multinational Matter?" *European Economic Review* 43: 915–23.

BNDES (Brazilian National Development Bank). 2009. *Studies of Regulatory, Corporate and Financial Alternatives for the Exploration and Production of Oil and Gas and the Industrial Development of the Oil and Gas Production Chain in Brazil*. Sao Paulo: BNDES, http://www.bain.com/bainweb/images/LocalOffices/BNDES_Consolidated_Report_BNDES_eng.pdf.

Borensztein, E., K. de Gregorio, and J. W. Lee. 1998. "How Does Forewing Direct Investment Affect Economic Growth?" *Journal of International Economics* 45 (1): 115–35.

Coe, D. T., E. Helpman, and A. W. Hoffmaister. 2008. "International R&D Spillovers and Institutions." IMF Working Paper No. WP/08/104, International Monetary Fund, Washington, DC.

CRES (Centre des Recherches Entreprises et Sociétés). 2008. "Skills Shortages in the Global Oil and Gas Industry: How to Close the Gap." CRES and the United Nations Institute for Training and Research. http://www.cres.ch/Documents/SKILLS%20SHORTAGE%20PART%20I%20pdf.pdf.

CSIS (Center for Strategic International Studies). 2010. "Brazil's Education System Falls Behind." Center for Strategic International Studies, Washington, DC. http://csis.org/blog/brazil%E2%80%99s-education-system-falls-behind.

Dimelis, S., and H. Louri. 2001. "Foreign Direct Investment and Efficiency Benefits: A Conditional Quantile Analysis." CEPR Discussion Paper n. 2868, Centre for Economic Policy Research, London.

EEPC (Engineering Export Promotion Council). 2002. "Report on Oil and Gas Field Equipment and Services Market in Indonesia." Prepared by the Engineering Export Promotion Council's (EEPC) Singapore office, January 2002.

Freeman, C. 1987. *Technology Policy and Economic Performance: Lessons from Japan*. London: Pinter.

Glass, A. J., and K. Saggi. 2008. "The Role of Foreign Direct Investment in International Technology Transfer." In *International Handbook of Development Economics*, edited by A. Dutt and J. Ros. Cheltenham, UK, and Northampton, MA: Edward Elgar Publishing.

Hallwood, C. P. 1990. *Transactions Costs and Trade between Multinational Corporations: A Study of Offshore Oil Production*. Boston, MA: Unwin Hyman.

Hanushek, E. A., and L. Woessmann. 2007. "Education Quality and Economic Growth." Working Paper No. 4122, World Bank Policy Research, Washington, DC.

Hatakenaka, S., P. Westnes, M. Gjelsvik, and R. K. Lester. 2006. "The Regional Dynamics of Innovation: A Comparative Case Study of Oil and Gas Industry Development in Stavanger and Aberdeen." Working Paper MIT-IPC–06–008, Massachusetts Institute of Technology, Cambridge, MA.

IPIECA (International Petroleum Industry Environmental and Conservation Association). 2011. "Local Content Strategy: A Guidance Document for the Oil and Gas Industry." Prepared by the International Petroleum Industry Environmental and Conservation Association. http://www.ipieca.org/sites/default/files/publications/Local_Content.pdf.

Jaffee, A., M. Trachtenberg, and R. Henderson. 1993. "Geographic Localization of Knowledge Spillovers as Evidenced by Patent Citations." *Quarterly Journal of Economics* 63: 577–98.

James, S. 2009. "Incentives and Investments: Evidence and Policy Implications." World Bank Group. https://www.wbginvestmentclimate.org/uploads/Incentivesand Investments.pdf.

Kokko, A. 1994. "Technology, Market Characteristics, and Spillovers." *Journal of Development Economics* 43 (2): 279–93.

Leskinen, O., P. K. Bekken, H. Razafinjatovo, and M. García. 2012. "Oil and Gas Cluster: A Story of Achieving Success through Supplier Development." Harvard Business School. http://www.isc.hbs.edu/pdf/Student_Projects/2012%20MOC%20 Papers/120503%20MOC%20Norway%20final.pdf.

Levett, M., and A. E. Chandler. 2012. *Maximizing Development of Local Content across Industry Sectors in Emerging Markets*. Washington, DC: Center for Strategic and International Studies.

Lundvall, B. -Å. 1992. *National Innovation Systems: Toward a Theory of Innovation and Interactive Learning*. London: Pinter.

MENAS. 2009. *Local Content Online*. London: MENAS. http://www.menas.co.uk/ localcontent/home.aspx?country=6&tab=law.

Morisset, J., and N. Pirnia. 2001. "How Tax Policy and Incentives Affect Foreign Direct Investment: A Review". In *Using Tax Incentives to Compete for Foreign Investment*, edited by L. T. Wells, N. J. Allen, J. Morisset, and N. Pirnia. Washington, DC: World Bank Group, Foreign Investment Advisory Service.

Morris, M., R. Kaplinsky, and D. Kaplan. 2011. "Commodities and Links: Industrialisation in Sub Saharan Africa." MMCP Discussion Paper No. 13, Centre for Social Science Research. http://www.cssr.uct.ac.za/sites/cssr.uct.ac.za/files/pubs/MMCP%20Paper% 2013_0.pdf.

Muller, T., and M. Schitzer. 2003. "Technology Transfer and Spillovers in International Joint Ventures." Munich Discussion Paper No. 2003–22, Department of Economics, University of Munich, Munich, Germany.

Nelson, R. R. 1993. *National Innovation System: A Comparative Analysis*. Oxford: Oxford University Press.

Nordås, H., E. Vatne, and P. Heum. 2003. "The Upstream Petroleum Industry and Local Industrial Development: A Comparative Study." SNF Report No. 08/03, Institute for Research in Economics and Business Administration (SNF), Bergen, Norway.

Olcott, M. B. 2007. "Kazmunaigaz: Kazakhstan's National Oil and Gas Company. Carnegie Endowment for International Peace." Prepared in conjunction with an energy study sponsored by the James A. Baker III Institute for Public Policy, Rice University and Japan Petroleum Energy Center, March. http://www.bakerinstitute. org/programs/energy-forum/publications/energy-studies/docs/NOCs/Papers/NOC_ Kaz_Olcott.pdf.

Ospanova, S. 2010. "Local Content Policy: Kazakhstan Review." International Institute for Environment and Development. http://pubs.iied.org/pdfs/G02761.pdf.

PEMANDU (Performance Management and Delivery Unit). 2010. *Powering the Malaysian Economy with Oil, Gas and Energy.* Kuala Lumpur: PEMANDU.

Petrobras. 2008. "The National Oil & Natural Gas Industry Mobilization Program." Petrobras News Agency. http://www.agenciapetrobras.com.br/en_materia.asp?id_ editoria=11&id_noticia=5502.

Porter, M. 1990. *The Competitive Advantage of Nations.* New York: Basic Books.

———. 1998. "Clusters and the New Economics of Competition." *Harvard Business Review* 76 (6): 77–90.

PROMINP (Programa de Mobilização da Indústria Nacional de Petróleo e Gás Natural). 2010. "Oil and Gas Brazilian Industry Mobilization Program." http://www.mdic.gov. br/sistemas_web/renai/public/arquivo/arq1274106807.pdf.

———. 2011. *Local Content Content Framework Framework: Challenges and Opportunities for E&P Sector.* Rio de Janeiro: PROMINP.

Sasson, A., and A. Blomgren. 2011. "Knowledge Based Oil and Gas Industry." BI Norwegian Business School. http://web.bi.no/forskning/papers.nsf/0/f025a647fbc57 59dc1257871004ae50e/$FILE/2011-03-Sasson&Blomgren.pdf.

Shakya, M. 2009. "Clusters for Competitiveness: A Practical Guide and Policy Implications for Developing Cluster Initiatives." International Trade Department, World Bank, Washington, DC. http://siteresources.worldbank.org/INTRANETTRADE/ Resources/cluster_initiative_pub_web_ver.pdf.

Shapiro, S. A., and R. S. Rabinowitz. 1997. "Punishment versus Cooperation in Regulatory Enforcement: A Case Study of OSHA." *HeinOnline*, 49 *Administrative Law Review* 713 (97). http://www.wcl.american.edu/journal/alr/49/shapiro49-4.pdf.

Skjellevik, T. I. 2011. "The Norwegian Oilfield Service Analysis 2011." Ernst & Young. http://www.ey.com/Publication/vwLUAssets/Oljeserviceanalysen_2011/$FILE/ oljeserviceanalysen-2011_ny_web.pdf.

Teka, Z. 2011. "Backward Linkages in the Manufacturing Sector in the Oil and Gas Value Chain in Angola." Making the Most of Commodity Program Discussion Paper No. 11, The Open University. http://www.prism.uct.ac.za/Papers/MMCP%20 Paper%2011_0.pdf

Tordo, S., B. S. Tracy, and N. Arfaa. 2011. "National Oil Companies and Value Creation." World Bank Working Paper No. 218, Washington, DC. http://go.worldbank.org/ UOQSWUQ6P0.

Xu, B. 2000. "Multinational Enterprises, Technology Diffusion, and Host Country Productivity Growth." *Journal of Development Economics* 62 (2): 477–93.

CHAPTER 6

What Remains Unanswered

Our review of local content policies (LCPs) in various petroleum-producing countries shows that there is no standard package of LCPs and tools that work for every country in every circumstance. Indeed countries use LCPs to achieve specific economic and social objectives and choose policy tools that address specific shortcomings (that is, externalities or market failures). Determining the right level of government intervention is complicated: different activities require different kinds of intervention, and there may be no clear price signals to guide government choices. Perhaps owing to this difficulty, some argue that LCPs create distortions, inefficiency, and, in some cases, even corruption. But existing research is mainly qualitative, with few attempts to measure the economic impact of LCPs and their sustainability over time. This may be due to the paucity of publicly available information on LCPs.[1]

Intuitively, limited or primitive economies would face considerable challenges with LCPs that hinge on quickly establishing a domestic supply service capability, and would very likely struggle with the creation of more complex forward links. The magnitude of the challenge is likely compounded by the pace at which oil and gas resources are developed, which in turn is affected by, among others, the government's depletion policy. For example, Norway decided to develop its petroleum resources more slowly than the United Kingdom, with the explicit objective of allowing a Norwegian service sector to develop. By contrast, the United Kingdom opted for a faster development of its North Sea resources, relying on foreign service companies and the expertise and spillover effects of their participation in the market (Hallwood 1990). Today both countries have developed internationally competitive oil and oil service sectors as well as strong forward links. But which strategy was the most efficient? Contrary to Norway and the United Kingdom, most resource-rich developing countries have a weak and narrow industrial base. Would Norway's or the United Kingdom's experience be of any relevance to them? If so, which aspect? Given the global nature and technological intensity of the petroleum industry, which services and products are more likely to be efficiently and competitively localized? In other words, what are the factors that affect the design and economic impact of LCPs and drive policy efficiency? Finally, although trade agreements do not appear to have been policy makers' principal concern in the design of LCPs, is this likely to change in light of recent trade proposals that promote the further liberalization of energy (and oil and gas) services?

Note

1. Many countries have instituted formal reporting procedures whereby local and foreign companies are required to periodically report on their local content performance. Most have developed specific reporting criteria (for example, Brazil, Kazakhstan, Indonesia, and Malaysia), and in some cases past local content performance is a factor in the award of future contracts (for example, Kazakhstan, Indonesia). But companies' reports are not publicly available, and regulators often do not publicly share their analysis of local content levels and policy effectiveness (for example, Angola and Malaysia). There is also no publicly available evidence that countries systematically compare companies' performance to establish benchmarks and targets and to identify opportunities for transferring best practices.

Activities at Each Stage
of the Oil and Gas Value Chain

Goods	Exploration	Development	Production	Oil & Gas Treatment & LNG	Transport & Storage	Refining	Petrochem.	Primary Distribution
Subsea Equipment		Wellheads, Sub-surface Safety Valves, Compressors, Meters, Separators, Risers, Umbilicals						
Downhole Equipment		Casing Hardware, Completion Equipment, Drilling tools, Wireline Logging Tools, Perforating Systems						
Tubular Goods		Drill Pipe, Casing, Tubing, Manifolds						
Rigs, Platforms & FPSOs		Land Rigs, Offshore Fabrication, Vessel Conversions, Rig Equipment, Unit Manufacturing		Steel Structures, Production Topsides			Steel Structures	
Rotating Equipment					Compressors, Blowers, Turbines & Pumps			
Static Equipment			Surface Equipment, Columns & Exchangers		Transport Pipes, Tanks		Columns & Exchanges (e.g. Reactors, Vessels)	
Pipes, Valves & Fittings					Pipes, Valves & Fittings			
Electrical Equipment					Transformers & Switchboards, Drive Motors, Cables			
Instrumentation & Control		Sub-surface Sensors, Surface Production Monitoring (e.g., Separators, Multi-phase Flowmeters)				Control Systems & Valves, Instruments & Analysers		
Fluids & Chemicals		Drilling & Completion Fluids, Upstream Specialty Chemicals				Catalysts & Additives		
Other Materials				Corrosion protection, Insulation, Coating & Painting				

Source: World Bank data.

Services

Services	Exploration	Development	Production	Oil & Gas Treatment & LNG	Transport & Storage	Refining	Petrochem.	Primary Distribution
Geophysical Services	Acquisition of Seismic Data, Data Processing, Imaging of Reservoirs, Management of Data							
Drilling Services	Land Contract Drilling, Offshore Contract Drilling, Directional Services, Mud Logging							
Reservoir Services	Logging While-Drilling (LWD), Wireline Logging, Production Testing Services							
Well Services	Coil Tubing Services, Well Servicing, Rental & Fishing Services							
Downhole Pumping	Downhole Pumping Services							
Completion Services	Casing & Tubing Services, Coating and Piping, Completion Services							
Engineering & EPC		Engineering, Procurement, Construction and Construction Management				Technology Licensors		
Erection & Trade Works		Upstream Erection & Civil Works	Erection & Civil Works (Pipelines, Depots, Jetties &Terminals)		Erection & Civil Works (Refineries and Processing Plants)			
O&M Services		Facilities O&M, Maintenance, Ship & Rig Maintenance, Dry-Docking						
Logistics		Aviation, Land Transportation Services, Operations Support Vessels, Heavy Goods Transport, Catering						
Utilities		Fuel, Steam, Power, Water Supply and Treatment, Industrial Gases						
Other Services		Auditing and Certification, inspection, Surveying, Hot-Tapping & Freezing, HSE Services, Consulting	Inspection, Vetting, Pigging					

Source: World Bank data.

Input-Output Tables, Forward and Backward Links

The standard input-output model of an economy links the gross output of a sector to the final demand for that sector and to the intermediate demands made by other sectors for its output. This can be expressed as

$$X = AX + F \qquad (1)$$

where X is a vector of gross outputs of the N sectors of the economy, F is a vector of final demands for these sectors, and A is the $N \times N$ matrix of technical coefficients that indicate how much output from sector i is directly required to produce one unit in sector j.

The gross output is then related to final demand by equation 2 where the coefficient matrix L (Leontief inverse) measures the total amount of sector i that is required to be produced in order to satisfy the direct and indirect demands produced by one unit increase in the final demand for sector j:

$$X = (I-A)-1 \ F \equiv LF \qquad (2)$$

The direct backward link of sector j to all other sectors (Chenery-Watanabe 1958) measuring the total of inputs from all sectors required to produce one unit of sector j is defined as:

$$BL(CW)j = \sum_{i=1}^{N} a_{ij} \qquad (3)$$

This measure ignores the fact that extra outputs of all these supply sectors themselves require inputs from other sectors and so on. Rasmussen (1956) suggested a measure taking into account all links, both direct and indirect, based on the Leontief inverse:

$$BL(R)j = \sum_{i=1}^{N} l_{ij} \qquad (4)$$

The forward Rasmussen link is then defined analogously:

$$FL(R)j = \sum_{j=1}^{N} l_{ij} \qquad (5)$$

The interpretation of the forward link index is that it indicates that the amount of output of sector j that would be demanded if every sector increased its final demand by one unit. A more general approach weights the increases in final demand by their relative shares in total output.

These indices can be used to compare a given sector's link with the average for all sectors. For example, the normalized backward link index is given by:

$$NBLj = N \times BLj / \sum_{i=1}^{N} BL_i \qquad (6)$$

Where NBL is greater than unity the sector uses more inputs (directly and indirectly) than the average of all sectors in the economy.

These concepts can be generalized to calculate the amount of employment (direct and indirect) or value-added required to produce one unit of output of the given sector (Scottish Government 2011).

APPENDIX C

Building Blocks of GTAP Social Accounting Matrices

Sectors		
Wheat	Beverages and tobacco products	Water
Cereal grains nec	Textiles	Construction
Vegetables, fruit, nuts	Wearing apparel	Trade
Oil seeds	Leather products	Transport nec
Plant-based fibers	Wood products	Water transport
Crops nec	Paper products, publishing	Air transport
Bovine cattle, sheep and goats, horses	Chemical, rubber, plastic products	Communication
Animal products nec	Mineral products nec	Financial services nec
Forestry	Ferrous metals	Insurance
Fishing	Metals nec	Business services nec
Petroleum and coal products	Metal products	Recreational and other services
Minerals nec	Motor vehicles and parts	Public Administration, Defense, Education, Health
Bovine meat products	Transport equipment nec	Coal
Vegetable oils and fats	Electronic equipment	Electricity
Dairy products	Machinery and equipment nec	Oil and Gas
Sugar	Manufactures nec	Imports of Intermediate goods and services
Food products nec	Gas manufacture, distribution	—

Final demand				
Consumption	Government	Investment	Transport in trade	Exports

value added block			
Labor	Capital	Resources	Taxes

Source: World Bank data.

Selected Countries' Backward and Forward Links for the Oil and Gas Sector

Region	Country	Code	Sectors	Oil & gas sector facts ($ Bn)				Oil and gas sector links							
				Total output	Imports	Domestic inputs	Value added	NBL$_{cw}$	Rank	NFL$_{cw}$	Rank	NBL$_R$	Rank	NFL$_R$	Rank
Americas	Argentina	ARG	53	16.75	0.79	4.66	11.31	0.63	12	2.70	48	0.81	10	2.97	53
	Bolivia	BOL	54	2.36	0.22	0.58	1.56	0.50	7	1.74	48	0.75	6	3.18	52
	Brazil	BRA	54	37.42	3.49	16.23	17.70	0.90	23	1.60	46	0.93	20	1.71	49
	Canada	CAN	53	93.57	4.95	21.91	66.70	0.55	4	1.80	46	0.78	3	1.91	50
	Chile	CHL	53	0.51	0.18	0.29	0.04	1.27	43	0.13	11	0.94	21	0.66	20
	Colombia	COL	54	11.49	0.50	3.12	7.88	0.70	18	2.13	47	0.86	17	1.79	50
	Ecuador	ECU	54	10.54	0.27	0.53	9.73	0.10	2	3.30	53	0.56	2	2.78	53
	Mexico	MEX	54	55.98	1.65	7.49	46.84	0.36	3	1.83	48	0.76	2	1.89	52
	Peru	PER	54	2.10	0.05	0.41	1.64	0.45	4	1.01	38	0.76	6	1.14	42
	United States	USA	54	152.50	4.74	34.40	113.35	0.45	1	0.64	29	0.72	1	1.08	42
	Venezuela	VEN	52	51.07	1.08	5.65	44.34	0.24	1	2.26	46	0.66	1	1.99	49
East, South Asia and Pacific	Australia	AUS	54	19.32	0.33	2.86	16.13	0.29	1	1.19	43	0.65	1	1.25	47
	Bangladesh	BGD	51	2.41	0.16	0.16	2.08	0.14	2	1.47	44	0.63	2	1.83	49
	China	CHN	53	78.62	5.05	27.21	46.36	0.64	12	0.55	21	0.82	13	1.00	35
	India	IND	54	16.73	0.81	4.06	11.87	0.53	10	0.36	20	0.79	11	0.90	35
	Indonesia	IDN	53	32.78	0.00	2.56	30.22	0.18	3	1.59	42	0.66	3	2.04	50
	Malaysia	MYS	52	25.60	0.81	3.39	21.40	0.27	3	1.33	42	0.65	3	1.62	45
	New Zealand	NZL	53	1.54	0.03	0.43	1.08	0.56	3	0.78	30	0.80	4	0.96	36
	Pakistan	PAK	54	2.00	0.08	0.44	1.47	0.50	6	0.63	36	0.80	7	1.07	45
	Philippines	PHL	53	0.32	0.03	0.28	0.01	2.40	52	2.34	47	3.69	53	3.59	53
	Thailand	THA	53	6.03	0.01	1.64	4.39	0.64	10	0.78	32	0.87	10	1.19	40
	Vietnam	VNM	52	7.69	1.26	0.65	5.79	0.29	7	0.72	29	0.80	7	0.87	28

Region	Country	Code	Sectors	Oil & gas sector facts ($ Bn)								Oil and gas sector links			
				Total output	Imports	Domestic inputs	Value added	NBL$_{CW}$	Rank	NFL$_{CW}$	Rank	NBL$_R$	Rank	NFL$_R$	Rank
Europe & Central Asia	Azerbaijan	AZE	52	21.01	0.78	1.44	18.79	0.18	2	1.96	46	0.64	2	3.32	50
	France	FRA	52	2.86	0.11	0.80	1.94	0.64	8	0.08	8	0.84	8	0.61	11
	Kazakhstan	KAZ	54	31.99	2.85	14.90	14.24	1.04	33	2.10	50	0.99	26	1.93	50
	Netherlands	NLD	51	13.43	0.17	1.18	12.08	0.25	2	0.57	29	0.73	2	0.88	30
	Norway	NOR	52	80.32	2.11	11.20	67.00	0.33	2	1.70	43	0.70	2	1.39	45
	Russia	RUS	53	234.59	6.51	78.47	149.61	0.67	11	2.15	49	0.81	11	2.88	52
	Turkey	TUR	54	1.07	0.01	0.17	0.89	0.48	8	0.17	9	0.82	8	0.76	19
	United Kingdom	GBR	53	44.48	1.23	6.15	37.11	0.34	3	0.83	35	0.74	3	1.06	40
Middle East & North Africa	Bahrain	BHR	49	5.24	0.26	0.34	4.64	0.23	5	7.45	49	0.72	3	3.91	48
	Egypt, Arab Rep.	EGY	52	20.94	0.43	1.62	18.89	0.24	5	6.34	52	0.76	4	4.11	52
	Iran, Islamic Rep.	IRN	54	104.57	1.00	1.87	101.70	0.04	1	1.90	46	0.56	1	4.71	53
	Kuwait	KWT	42	64.22	0.72	1.49	62.01	0.08	1	7.74	42	0.72	1	3.50	42
	Oman	OMN	50	23.27	0.21	0.66	22.40	0.10	2	9.12	50	0.71	2	4.95	50
	Qatar	QAT	50	32.86	8.09	6.49	18.27	0.70	25	8.67	50	0.82	23	3.14	49
	Saudi Arabia	SAU	47	239.17	24.01	9.67	205.49	0.14	2	5.02	46	0.72	2	4.84	47
	Tunisia	TUN	51	2.31	0.12	0.25	1.94	0.28	5	1.30	42	0.72	5	1.35	45
	UAE	ARE	51	66.72	18.55	6.18	42.00	0.40	12	4.06	49	0.84	12	1.74	50
SubSaharan Africa	Cameroon	CMR	51	2.16	0.18	0.44	1.54	0.39	3	1.14	42	0.70	4	1.54	47
	Côte d'Ivoire	CIV	52	1.15	0.13	0.42	0.59	0.71	12	0.66	31	0.81	11	1.18	43
	Madagascar	MDG	48	0.80	0.09	0.20	0.51	0.68	22	2.36	43	0.91	24	1.39	42
	Malawi	MWI	53	0.39	0.04	0.06	0.29	0.43	7	2.56	49	0.80	7	1.63	50
	Mauritius	MUS	50	0.82	0.24	0.15	0.43	0.74	26	3.40	47	0.94	25	1.63	47
	Mozambique	MOZ	52	0.54	0.10	0.06	0.38	0.33	7	0.03	9	0.81	7	0.72	9
	Nigeria	NGA	53	60.85	6.38	1.71	52.76	0.10	5	4.62	50	0.77	5	2.21	52
	South Africa	ZAF	54	0.98	0.06	0.42	0.50	0.78	13	0.11	11	0.85	12	0.57	19
	Uganda	UGA	54	1.28	0.24	0.28	0.76	0.61	18	1.50	41	0.84	20	1.30	43

Source: World Bank data.

Note: NBL = Normalized Backward Link; NFL = Normalized Forward Link; CW = Chenery-Watanabe Basis; R = Rasmussen Basis. A rank of one indicates that the sector has the lowest value of that link across all sectors, while the maximum rank that could be attained (equal to the number of sectors) indicates that the oil and gas sector has the highest link on that particular measure. All data refer to 2007.

APPENDIX E

Typology of LCPs for Selected Countries

	Angola	Australia	Brazil	Ghana
Policy Classification				
Assertive; Encouraging; Neutral	Assertive	Encouraging	Assertive	Assertive
Recruitment and Training of Nationals in Direct Workforce				
Maximise Nationals (maximise nationals in workforce, but no targets)	No	Yes	No	Yes Policy Framework 2010
Targets for Nationals (Targets mandated for total workforce)	Yes At least 70% of the work-force of employers with more than 5 workers must be Angolan nationals (Decree 5/ 95)	No	No no specific targets, but indiviual targets for itemised 'services', which drives an increase in national workforce	No
Targets for Different Positions (different targets for difference categories of positions)	Yes Angolanization targets by job grade set by the Ministry of Petroleum.	No	No	Yes Management -50% rising to 80% in year 5 Technical: 30% rising to 80% in yr 5 and 90% yr 10 Other staff: 100% Ghanaians (Policy Framework, 2010)
Positions Retricted to Nationals (some form of restrictive practice)	Yes May only hire foreign workers if no qualified Angolan is available (Decree 17/ 09)	Yes May only hire foreign workers if no qualified Australians available	No	
Sourcing of Local Goods and Services				
Preference Local Goods and Services only if Competitive (no margins of domestic preference)	No	Yes Framework 2001; Guide 201 0	No	No

Indonesia	Kazakhstan	Malaysia	Nigeria	Trinidad and Tobago
Policy Classification				
Assertive	Assertive	Encouraging	Assertive	Encouraging
Recruitment and Training of Nationals in Direct Workforce				
No	No	Yes	Yes Nigerian Oil and Gas National Content Development Act, 2010	Yes
No	Yes	No	Yes Minimum targets set for Nigerian labour in identified services, by manhours (2010 Act) Requirement for Succession Plan for nationals (210 Act)	No
Yes Targets are set by skill level and phase of development of the project	Yes Medium and large companies to have minimum 70% Kazakh executives and 90% techical personnel (Decree 45/ 112)	No	Yes Maximum 5 percent management positions for expatriates; 100 percent Nigerian labor in junior and intermediate positions (2010 Act) Projects > US$100 Million to include a "Labor Clause" identifying minimum percentage Nigerian labor in different positions (20 10 Act)	No
Yes Expatriates for certain positions and expertise that cannot be fulfilled by nationals. Positions controlled by the regulator, and require Indonisation plan.	No	No	Yes Minimum targets set for Nigerian labour in identified services, by manhours (2010 Act)	Yes Work permits issued by the Minister of National Security to expatriates if their employment does not preclude the employment of nationals
Sourcing of Local Goods and Services				
No	No	No	No	Yes Except for seismic processing services that shall be undertaken in-country.

	Angola	Australia	Brazil	Ghana
Margin of Domestic Preference (advantage given to domestic suppliers or domestic goods and services)	Yes Restricted list of goods and services for Angolan owned suppliers (Order 127/ 03); Foreign companies to tender in association with Angolan owned company (Order 127/ 03); Preference to Angolan company if less then 10% foreign ownership	No	No	Yes Foreign suppliers required to be incor porated in Ghana (Policy Framewor k, 2010) Foreign suppliers required to be incorporated in Ghana (Policy Framewor k, 2010)
Guideline Targets for Procurement of Local Goods and Services (no sanctions for non-compliance)	No	No No targets, but official guidance on local sourcing, tendering etc (Guide 2010)	No	No
Mandated Targets for Procurement of Local Goods and Services (sanctions if non-compliant)	No		Yes Aggregate and item-specific targets. Targets differ by Bid Round and modified by 'offer' of concessionaire. Fines linked to percentage of noncompliance with targets	Yes 90 percent local par ticipation by 2020 (Policy Framework, 2010) In opera-tions: minimum 10 percent Ghanaians in provision of goods and services in year 1; 20% year 2, 10% rise each yea thereafter (Policy Framewor k, 2010)
Local Content Leveraged during Tendering Process	Yes	Yes Guide 2010	Yes No weighting of local content within tender evaluation but Local Content targets required for contractors in sub-contracts	-
Development of Domestic Supply Chains				
Regulatory Requirement to Develop Domestic Suppliers (eg alliances, partnerships, consortia, technology transfer)	Yes For specific goods and services, foreign companies only permit-ted to tender through association with Angolan owned company	No	No But targets drive alliances and inward investment by international contrac-tors. Various finacing, subsidies and develop-ment programs available to local companies.	Yes Foreign suppliers required to partner with Ghanaian owned and reg-istered company (Policy Framework, 2010)
Clients Incentivise Development of Domestic Suppliers	-	Yes Tariff reduction on selected imports, in part for supplier development (Framework, 2001; Guide, 2010)	-	No

Source: World Bank data.

Indonesia	Kazakhstan	Malaysia	Nigeria	Trinidad and Tobago
Yes	**Yes**	**Yes**	**Yes**	**No**
Tender price normalisation based on percentage of Local Content proposed in bids, in conjunction with status of company, equipment ownership and share of contract execution (BP Migas PTK 007 r2)	Preference to "Kazakhstani Producer" if within 20% of foreign bid price - non-PCA companies only (Sub Soil/ Soil User Law 201 0)	Petronas requires private sector companies to domestically source all goods and services incidental to upstream activities - procurement from foreign countries requires Petronas' approval	Service contracts "on land and swamp" reserved exclusively for Nigerian Indigenous service companies (2010 Act)	
No	**No**	**No**		**Yes**
				National Policy Guidelines for the Utilization of Local Good and Services for Government and Government Related Projects.
Yes	**Yes**	**No**	**Yes**	**No**
Minimum percentage of Local Content to be eligible to tender (the percentage is variable) (BP Migas PTK 007 r2)	In private companies minimum 82.5 percent for services and 11 percent for goods.		Operators and contractors to comply with minimum Nigerian content targets. Waiver option for up to 3 yrs (itemized targets in Schedule to 2010 Act) Minimum 50 percent Nigerian ownership of equipment deployed for execution of work (2010 Act)	
Yes	**No**	**No**	**Yes**	**Yes**
For Goods: additional Local Content scored in tender if investment in small enterprise through partnerships			Bid with highest LC percentage selected if within 1 percent on price (2010 Act) Plan required on how operator and	Tender evaluation process shall discriminate in favor of local value added.
		Development of Domestic Supply Chains		
No	**No**	**No**	**Yes**	**No**
Companies may benefit from increase in contract local content levels by up to 15 % if they invest in developing the local supply industry.	But local suppliers benefit from interst-free loans, advance payments for equipment and personnel mobilization, and technology transfer	But fiscal incentives packages and infrastructure developments to make Malaysia a hub for OFSE by 2017	Where Nigerians not employed because of lack of training, Operator to supply training locally (2010 Act)	
-	-	-	-	-